# Oracle DBA
## Test 3 and Test 4

# The Cram Sheet

This Cram Sheet contains the distilled, key facts about Oracle7.3 in the areas of tuning and backup and recovery. Review this information last thing before you enter the test room, paying special attention to those areas you feel you need the most review. You can transfer any of these facts from your head onto a blank piece of paper before beginning the exam.

## TUNING OVERVIEW

1. Tuning goals should be specific and quantifiable. Tune in the following order: design, application, memory, I/O, and contention. (DAMIOC)

2. UTLBSTAT and UTLESTAT report performance statistics. If the instance is shut down between UTLBSTAT and ULTESTAT, the report.txt statistics are not reliable and both scripts must be resubmitted.

3. A OLTP system is a high-activity system with a large number of concurrent users. Indexing is important in an OLTP system. Have lots of small rollback segments in an OLTP system. A DSS stores large volumes of data and uses full table scans. Use the Parallel Query option in a DSS system. **DB_BLOCK_SIZE** should be set to the maximum value allowed by the OS in a DSS system. Use fewer, large rollback segments in a DSS system.

## TUNING APPLICATIONS

4. The biggest tuning return is from tuning SQL statements. You can use autotrace, SQL Trace, Explain Plan, and TKPROF to identify which and how SQL statements need to be tuned. Use **DBMS_APPLICATION_INFO** to register applications in the database to get data on performance and resource usage. Adding indexes improves the performance of SQL statements.

5. There are two optimizers: cost-based (CBO) and rule-based (RBO). The default for the init.ora parameter **OPTIMIZER_MODE** is **CHOOSE**, using RBO unless statistics are available. To generate statistics, use the **ANALYZE** command or **DBMS_UTILITY.ANALYZE_SCHEMA**. Hints override the optimizer mode for a specific SQL statement.

## DATABASE CONFIGURATION

6. File placement (control, log, archive, and datafiles) is critical to performance. Distribute I/O evenly. Use OS tools to check for contention between Oracle and non-Oracle activities. Place data and indexes on separate drives. Tables are stripped more easily using the OS than by hand.

7. Have a minimum of six tablespaces: **SYSTEM, RBS, TEMPORARY, USERS, DATA**, and **INDEX**. Place SYS and SYSTEM objects in the **SYSTEM** tablespace.

**TEMPORARY** tablespace for temporary extents only.

8. Avoid chaining: Create your database with a **DB_BLOCK_SIZE** that fits your largest row. To change block size, you re-create the database. The **CHAIN_CNT** column in **USER_TABLES** contains the number of migrated rows for the table. Object storage parameters control space usage within blocks. Set **PCTFREE** to have space for updates to avoid row migration. **PCTUSED** determines when blocks are placed on the **FREELISTS**.

9. The MTS is used for shared connections. The maximum number of dispatchers and shared servers are set in the initialization parameter file (**MTS_MAX_DISPATCHERS** and **MTS_MAX_SERVERS**).

**TUNING THE SGA**

10. The SGA contains: database buffer cache, redo log buffer, shared pool. The shared pool consists of the library and data dictionary caches. Use of the MTS causes the shared pool to house the UGA. The UGA stores user session information, including private SQL areas, cursor state information, and sort areas.

11. The virtual table **X$KCBRBH** shows statistics on the impact of increasing (or raising) the number of buffers in the buffer cache. The virtual table **X$KCBCBH** shows statistics on the impact of reducing (or canceling) the buffers in the buffer cache. The buffer cache hit ratio is determined by placing statistics from the **V$SYSSTAT** table or the report.txt file into the hit ratio formula.

12. **V$LIBRARYCAHCE** view is used to determine the library cache hit ratio. The **V$DB_OBJECT_CACHE** view shows objects cached in the library cache. The **V$ROWCACHE** view is used to find the hit ratio of the dictionary cache.

**TUNING ROLLBACK SEGMENTS**

13. Rollback segments store "undo" information. Rollback segments allow for read consistent images by keeping the before image of blocks taking part in data changing transactions.

14. Rollback segments are stored in their own tablespace, not with other objects.

15. Size rollback segments with **INITIAL=NEXT** and a **PCTINCREASE** of zero. The **INITIAL** size is your average transaction size. The **OPTIMAL** storage parameter is set for the odd larger transaction processed during normal processing. Set **OPTIMAL** to **MINEXTENTS*INITIAL** or some multiple of this value.

16. For systems with large batch transactions, create an offline large rollback segment.

17. Rollback segments should have enough extents to allow each expected concurrent DML transaction to have its own extent:
    - # of users/**MINEXTENTS** = Number of private rollback segments
    - **TRANSACTIONS/TRANSACTIONS_ PER_ROLLBACK_SEGMENT** for public

18. Determine if you have the proper size of rollback segment extents by monitoring the **DBA_ROLLBACK_SEGS** for **SHRINKS** and **WRAPS**.

19. Monitor the **V$ROLLSTAT** and **V$WAITSTAT** virtual performance tables for rollback (listed as **UNDO**) related statistics.

20. If **V$ROLLSTAT** shows **WAITS** you need more rollback extents allocated.

**TUNING REDO LOGS**

21. Redo logs record all data manipulation commands. During recovery, redo log entries are applied in a roll forward operation and then rollback entries are applied to perform a rollback of uncommitted transactions. Redo logs are written by the LGWR process.

22. You must have two groups of one redo log per instance. Most experts suggest a minimum of three groups of two logs (located on separate disks or file systems) especially if you are using archive logging.

23. If a database is in **ARCHIVELOG** mode the ARCH process is started. The ARCH process copies filled redo logs to the location specified by the **LOG_ARCHIVE_DEST** initialization parameter. If the archive log destination fills, processing stops until space is available.

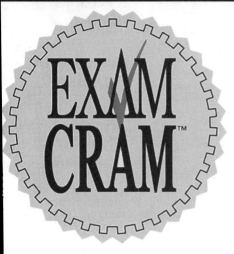

# EXAM CRAM™

# Oracle DBA
## Test 3 and Test 4
### Backup and Recovery • Performance Tuning

## Oracle
## Certified
## Professional

Michael R. Ault, Paul Collins,
Barbara Ann Pascavage, Michelle Berard

**Oracle DBA Exam Cram: Test 3 And Test 4**

**Limits of Liability and Disclaimer of Warranty**

The author and publisher of this book have used their best efforts in preparing the book and the programs contained in it. These efforts include the development, research, and testing of the theories and programs to determine their effectiveness. The author and publisher make no warranty of any kind, expressed or implied, with regard to these programs or the documentation contained in this book.

The author and publisher shall not be liable in the event of incidental or consequential damages in connection with, or arising out of, the furnishing, performance, or use of the programs, associated instructions, and/or claims of productivity gains.

**Trademarks**

Trademarked names appear throughout this book. Rather than list the names and entities that own the trademarks or insert a trademark symbol with each mention of the trademarked name, the publisher states that it is using the names for editorial purposes only and to the benefit of the trademark owner, with no intention of infringing upon that trademark.

The Coriolis Group, Inc.
An International Thomson Publishing Company
14455 N. Hayden Road, Suite 220
Scottsdale, Arizona 85260

602/483-0192
FAX 602/483-0193
http://www.coriolis.com

Library of Congress Cataloging-in-Publication Data
Ault, Michael R.
    Oracle DBA exam cram : test 3 and test 4 / by Michael R. Ault... (et al.)
      p.  cm.
    Includes index.
    ISBN 1-57610-331-5
    1.  Relational databases.   2.  Oracle (computer file) I.  Ault, Michael R.
QA76.9.D30714   1998
005.75'65--dc21                   98-29351
                                   CIP

Printed in the United States of America
10 9 8 7 6 5 4 3 2 1

**Publisher**
Keith Weiskamp

**Acquisitions**
Shari Jo Hehr

**Marketing Specialist**
Cynthia Caldwell

**Project Editor**
Jeff Kellum

**Production Coordinator**
Kim Eoff

**Cover Design**
Anthony Stock

**Layout Design**
April Nielsen

*an International Thomson Publishing company*

Albany, NY • Belmont, CA • Bonn • Boston • Cincinnati • Detroit • Johannesburg • London • Madrid
Melbourne • Mexico City • New York • Paris • Singapore • Tokyo • Toronto • Washington

# Are You Certifiable?

That's the question that's probably on your mind. The answer is: You bet! But if you've tried and failed or you've been frustrated by the complexity of the OCP program and the maze of study materials available, you've come to the right place. We've created our new publishing and training program, *Certification Insider Press*, to help you accomplish one important goal: to ace an OCP exam without having to spend the rest of your life studying for it.

The book you have in your hands is part of our *Exam Cram* series. Each book is especially designed not only to help you study for an exam but also to help you understand what the exam is all about. Inside these covers you'll find hundreds of test-taking tips, insights, and strategies that simply cannot be found anyplace else. In creating our guides, we've assembled the very best team of certified trainers, OCP professionals, and networking course developers.

Our commitment is to ensure that the *Exam Cram* guides offer proven training and active-learning techniques not found in other study guides. We provide unique study tips and techniques, memory joggers, custom quizzes, insights about trick questions, sample tests, and much more. In a nutshell, each OCP *Exam Cram* guide is closely organized like the exams it is tied to.

To help us continue to provide the very best certification study materials, we'd like to hear from you. Write or email us (craminfo@coriolis.com) and let us know how our *Exam Cram* guides have helped you study, or tell us about new features you'd like us to add. If you send us a story about how an *Exam Cram* guide has helped you ace an exam and we use it in one of our guides, we'll send you an official *Exam Cram* shirt for your efforts.

Good luck with your certification exam, and thanks for allowing us to help you achieve your goals.

Keith Weiskamp
Keith Weiskamp
Publisher, Certification Insider Press

*As with all my other books, I want to dedicate this to my loving family: Susan, my wife; Marie, my eldest daughter; and Michelle, my youngest. I also want to dedicate this book to my Mother and Father who were the pillars upon which I stood to reach adulthood. My love and thanks go out to all of them.*
—Michael R. Ault

*To my wife Terri and my children, Justin and Jordan. Without the support of my wife and the understanding of my children, none of my accomplishments would be possible.*
—Paul Collins

*To my parents Stan and Betty Pascavage, my big brother Stanley, and my kid sister Judy.*
—Barbara Ann Pascavage

*To the memory of Clayton Montgomery, better known as Archie, for his wit, support, and encouragement throughout the majority of this project.*
—Michelle Berard

# About The Authors

## Michael R. Ault

Michael R. Ault has been working in the data processing field since 1974 and with Oracle since 1990. Mike has attended numerous Oracle and university classes dealing with all areas of Oracle database administration and development and holds five Oracle masters' certificates. Mike began his certification history with the Oracle Corporation test-based Oracle6 certification, continued it as one of the developers and recipients of the Chauncey Oracle7 certification exam, and is currently an Oracle7.3 Oracle Certified Professional. Mike has written several books, including *Oracle 7.0 Administration and Management* (John Wiley & Sons), *Oracle8 Administration & Management* (John Wiley & Sons), and *Oracle8 Black Book* (Coriolis Group Books). Mike has written numerous articles for *Oracle* magazine, *DBMS Magazine*, and *OREVIEW* magazine and is a frequent presenter at ECO, IOUG-A, and Oracle Open World conferences. Mike also SYSOPS for the CompuServe ORAUSER forum and the RevealNet, Inc., Web page's DBA Pipeline at http://www.revealnet.com/. Mike is also the primary author for the Oracle Administrator Knowledge Base product from RevealNet, Inc.

## Paul Collins

Paul Collins is a senior Oracle consultant for Skyler-Marks Consulting, where he specializes in Oracle database design and administration. He has been a speaker at both Oracle Open World and IOUG-A Live conferences. Paul was one of the database administrators who worked with Oracle and the Chauncey Group in developing the Oracle7 Database Administrator Certification test and is certified under the new OCP program.

## Barbara Ann Pascavage

Barbara Ann Pascavage is a Senior Oracle DBA at *The Washington Post*. She has been working with Oracle since 1987 and has been an Oracle DBA since 1991. She is both Chauncey Oracle7 and Oracle7.3 OCP certified. She has taught several Oracle SQL and relational database classes and is responsible for creating standards for Oracle databases at the *Post*.

## *Michelle Berard*

Michelle Berard is a Senior Database Administrator at *The Washington Post*. She is an Oracle Certified Professional and also holds a Chauncey certification in Oracle Database Administration. Michelle has been a guest speaker and substitute instructor for the Oracle Advanced Relational Databases classes at the University of Maryland. She is an active member of Oracle Users Groups and has been an Oracle DBA since 1993.

# Acknowledgments

## Michael R. Ault

As an author, I sometimes fail to see all the hands that the manuscript passes through on its way to becoming a real book. I would be remiss if I cannot thank these folks personally, not to thank them here in the acknowledgements. To that end I would like to thank: Kim Eoff, Production Coordinator; Mark Gokman, Technical Editor; Bruce Owens, Copyeditor; Shelly Crossen, Proofreader; and last but not least, Shari Jo Hehr, Acquisitions Editor. Of course, Jeff Kellum deserves thanks for all of his hard work herding us cats together to make the book come out somewhere near on time. My deepest gratitude to you all.

## Paul Collins

I would like to acknowledge the team at The Coriolis Group: Jeff Kellum, Kim Eoff, Mark Gokman, Bruce Owens, Shelly Crossen, and Shari Jo Hehr for using their talents to help get this book published.

## Barbara Ann Pascavage

I would like to thank Michael Ault for giving me the opportunity of working with him on this book. I would like to extend a very enthusiastic thank you to the people at Coriolis who guided me through the process: Jeff Kellum, Mark Gokman, Bruce Owens, Kim Eoff, Shelly Crossen, and Shari Jo Hehr. I would like to thank my neighbors for performing "Callie duty": Diana Wodder, Elizabeth O'Brien, and Grace Marie Schmitt. I would also like to thank Thomas Zinn and Michael Chin for everything they taught me about Oracle and Unix.

## Michelle Berard

I want to express my gratitude to my best friend John Montgomery, my son Michael, and my Aunt Joan for their support and enthusiasm during this project. I'd also like to thank my mentors, Adrian Brown and Professor Mary Hofferek, for their wisdom, vision, and encouragement. I am especially grateful to the fine folks at The Washington Post for providing an exceptional work environment and challenging Oracle opportunities. Thanks to the unsung heroes at The Coriolis Group: Jeff Kellum, Mark Gokman, Bruce Owens, Kim

# Acknowledgments

Eoff, Shelly Crossen, and Shari Jo Hehr. They united this project and made it a success with their diligent work, guidance, and patience. Last, but certainly not least, I'd like to thank my friend, Mike Ault, for being as kind as he is knowledgeable and providing me with the wonderful opportunity to participate in this project.

# Table Of Contents

# Introduction

Welcome to *Oracle DBA Exam Cram: Test 3 and Test 4!* This book aims to help you get ready to take—and pass—the last two of the four-part Oracle Certified Professional Database Administrator (OCP-DBA) track series of exams (the first two tests are covered in *Oracle DBA Exam Cram: Test 1 and Test 2*). In this introduction, we introduce Oracle's certification programs in general and talk about how the *Exam Cram* series can help you prepare for Oracle's certification exams.

*Exam Cram* books help you understand and appreciate the subjects and materials you need to pass Oracle DBA certification exams. The books are aimed strictly at test preparation and review. They do not teach you everything you need to know about a topic. Instead, we (the authors) present and dissect the questions and problems that you're likely to encounter on a test. We've worked from Oracle's own training materials, preparation guides, and tests, as well as from third-party test preparation tools. Our aim is to bring together as much information as possible about Oracle certification exams.

Nevertheless, to completely prepare yourself for any Oracle test, we recommend that you begin your studies with some classroom training or that you pick up and read one of the many DBA guides available from Oracle and third-party vendors. We also strongly recommend that you install, configure, and fool around with the software or environment that you'll be tested on, because nothing beats hands-on experience and familiarity when it comes to understanding the questions you're likely to encounter on a certification test. Book learning is essential, but hands-on experience is the best teacher of all!

# The Oracle Certified Professional (OCP) Program

The OCP program for DBA certification currently includes four separate tests. A brief description of each follows:

➤ **Test 1: Introduction to Oracle: SQL and PL/SQL** This test is the base test for the series. Knowledge tested in this test will also be used in all

other tests in the DBA series. Test 1 tests knowledge of SQL and PL/
SQL language constructs, syntax, and usage. Test 1 covers Data Definition Language (DDL), Data Manipulation Language (DML), and Data
Control Language (DCL). Also covered in Test 1 are basic data modeling and database design and basic Oracle Procedure Builder usage.

➤ **Test 2: Oracle7.3: Database Administration** Test 2 deals with all levels
of database administration in Oracle7.3. Topics include architecture,
startup and shutdown, database creation, managing database internal
and external constructs (such as redo logs, rollback segments,
tablespaces), and all other Oracle structures. Database auditing, use of
National Language Support (NLS) features, and use of SQL*Loader
and other utilities are also covered.

➤ **Test 3: Oracle7.3: Backup and Recovery Workshop** Test 3 covers one
of the most important parts of the Oracle DBA's job: database backup
and recovery operations. Test 3 tests knowledge in backup and recovery
motives, architecture as it relates to backup and recovery, backup
methods, failure scenarios, recovery methodologies, archive logging,
supporting 24×7 shops, troubleshooting, and use of Oracle7.3's standby
database features.

➤ **Test 4: Oracle7.3: Performance Tuning Workshop** Test 4 covers all
aspects of tuning an Oracle7.3 database. Topics in both application and
database tuning are covered. Test 4 tests knowledge in diagnosis of
tuning problems, database optimal configuration, shared pool tuning,
buffer cache tuning, Oracle block usage, tuning rollback segments and
redo mechanisms, monitoring and detecting lock contention, tuning
sorts, tuning in OLTP, DSS, and mixed environments, and load
optimization.

*Note: Oracle seldom uses the actual test numbers and usually refers to the
tests by their names. In fact, this book covers the last two tests out of order.
Test 4, "Oracle7.3: Performance Tuning Workshop," is discussed first
followed by Test 3, "Oracle7.3: Backup and Recovery Workshop." We feel
that it is a more logical progression. When you sign up for an exam,
specify the test by name instead of the number.*

To obtain an OCP certificate in Database Administration, an individual must
pass all four exams. The core exams require individuals to demonstrate compe-
tence with all phases of Oracle7.3 database lifetime activities. This book covers
Tests 3 and 4.

However you mix the tests, individuals must pass all four tests to meet the OCP-DBA requirements. It's not uncommon for the entire process to take a year or so, and many individuals find that they must take a test more than once to pass. Our primary goal with the *Exam Cram* series is to make it possible, given proper study and preparation, to pass all of the OCP-DBA tests on the first try.

Finally, certification is an ongoing activity. Once an Oracle product becomes obsolete, OCP-DBAs (and other OCPs) typically have a six-month time frame in which they can become recertified on current product versions. (If individuals do not get recertified within the specified time period, their certification becomes invalid.) Because technology keeps changing and new products continually supplant old ones, this should come as no surprise.

The best place to keep tabs on the OCP program and its various certifications is on the Oracle Web site. The current root URL for the OCP program is at http://education.oracle.com/certification. Oracle's Web site changes frequently, so if this URL doesn't work, try using the Search tool on Oracle's site (www.oracle.com) with either "OCP" or the quoted phrase "Oracle Certified Professional Program" as the search string. This will help you find the latest and most accurate information about the company's certification programs.

# Taking A Certification Exam

Alas, testing is not free. You'll be charged $125 for each test you take, whether you pass or fail. In the United States and Canada, tests are administered by Sylvan Prometric. Sylvan Prometric can be reached at 800-755-EXAM (3926), any time from 7:00 A.M. to 6:00 P.M., Central Time, Monday through Friday. If you can't get through on this number, try 612-896-7000 or 612-820-5707.

To schedule an exam, call at least one day in advance. To cancel or reschedule an exam, you must call at least one day before the scheduled test time (or you may be charged). When calling Sylvan Prometric, please have the following information ready for the telesales staffer who handles your call:

➤ Your name, organization, and mailing address.

➤ The name of the exam you wish to take.

➤ A method of payment must be arranged. (The most convenient approach is to supply a valid credit card number with sufficient available credit. Otherwise, payments by check, money order, or purchase order must be received before a test can be scheduled. If the latter methods are required, ask your order-taker for more details.)

An appointment confirmation will be sent to you by mail if you register more than five days before an exam, or will send the confirmation by fax if less than five days. A Candidate Agreement letter, which you must sign to take the examination, will also be provided.

On the day of the test, try to arrive at least 15 minutes before the scheduled time slot. You must bring and supply two forms of identification, one of which must be a photo ID.

All exams are completely closed book. In fact, you will not be permitted to take anything with you into the testing area; you will be furnished with a blank sheet of paper and a pen. We suggest that you immediately write down the most critical information about the test you're taking on the sheet of paper. *Exam Cram* books provide a brief reference—The Cram Sheet, located inside the front cover—that lists the essential information from the book in distilled form. You will have some time to compose yourself, to record this information, and even to take a sample orientation exam before you must begin the real thing. We suggest you take the orientation test before taking your first exam; they're all more or less identical in layout, behavior, and controls, so you probably won't need to do this more than once.

When you complete an Oracle certification exam, the software will tell you whether you've passed or failed. All tests are scored on a basis of 800 points, and results are broken into several topical areas. Whether you pass or fail, we suggest you ask for—and keep—the detailed report that the test administrator should print out for you. You can use the report to help you prepare for another go-round, if necessary, and even if you pass, the report shows areas you may need to review to keep your edge. If you need to retake an exam, you'll have to call Sylvan Prometric, schedule a new test date, and pay another $125.

# Tracking OCP Status

Oracle generates transcripts that indicate the exams you have passed and your corresponding test scores.

Once you pass the necessary set of four exams, you'll be certified as a DBA. Official certification normally takes anywhere from four to six weeks (generally within 30 days), so don't expect to get your credentials overnight. When the package arrives, it will include a Welcome Kit that contains a number of elements, including:

➤ An OCP-DBA certificate, suitable for framing, along with an OCP Professional Program membership card and lapel pin.

➤ A license to use the OCP logo, thereby allowing you to use the logo in advertisements, promotions, documents, on letterhead, business cards, and so on. An OCP logo sheet, which includes camera-ready artwork, comes with the license. (Note: Before using any of the artwork, individuals must sign and return a licensing agreement that indicates they'll abide by its terms and conditions.)

Many people believe that the benefits of OCP certification go well beyond the perks that Oracle provides to newly anointed members of this elite group. We are starting to see more job listings that request or require applicants to have an OCP-DBA certification, and many individuals who complete the program can qualify for increases in pay and/or responsibility. As an official recognition of hard work and broad knowledge, OCP certification is a badge of honor in many IT organizations.

# How To Prepare For An Exam

At a minimum, preparing for the OCP-DBA exams requires that you obtain and study the following materials:

➤ The Oracle7 Server version 7.3 Documentation Set on CD-ROM.

➤ The exam prep materials, practice tests, and self-assessment exams on the Oracle certification page (education.oracle.com/certification). Find the materials, download them, and use them!

➤ Both Oracle *Exam Cram* books! They are the first and last thing you should read before taking the exams.

In addition, you'll probably find any or all of the following materials useful in your quest for Oracle7.3 DBA expertise:

➤ **OCP Resource Kits** Oracle Corporation has a CD-ROM with example questions and materials to help with the exam. Generally, these are provided free.

➤ **Classroom Training** Oracle, TUSC, LearningTree, and many others offer classroom and computer-based training-type material that you will find useful to help you prepare for the exam. But a word of warning: These classes tend to be fairly expensive (in the range of $300 per day of training). However, they do offer a condensed form of learning to help you "brush up" on your Oracle knowledge. The tests are closely tied to the Oracle-provided classroom training, so we would suggest at least taking the introductory classes to get the Oracle-specific (and classroom-specific) terminology under your belt.

➤ **Other Publications** You'll find direct references to other publications and resources in this book, but there's no shortage of materials available about Oracle7.3 DBA topics. To help you sift through some of the publications out there, we end each chapter with a "Need To Know More?" section with pointers to more complete and exhaustive resources covering the chapter's subject matter. This tells you where we suggest you look for further details.

➤ **The Oracle Support CD-ROM** Oracle provides a Support CD-ROM on a quarterly basis. This CD-ROM contains useful white papers, bug reports, technical bulletins and information about release-specific bugs, fixes, and new features. Contact your Oracle representative for a copy.

➤ **The Oracle Administrator and PL/SQL Developer** These are online references from RevealNet, Inc. They provide instant lookup on thousands of database and developmental topics and are an invaluable resource for study and learning about Oracle. Demo copies can be downloaded from www.revealnet.com. Also available at the RevealNet Web site are the DBA and PL/SQL Pipelines, online discussion groups where you can get expert information from Oracle DBAs worldwide. The costs of these applications run about $400 each (current pricing is available on the Web site) and are worth every cent.

This set of required and recommended materials represents a nonpareil collection of sources and resources for Oracle DBA topics and software. In the section that follows, we explain how this book works, and give you some good reasons why this book should also be in your required and recommended materials list.

# About This Book

Each topical *Exam Cram* chapter follows a regular structure, along with graphical cues about especially important or useful material. Here's the structure of a typical chapter:

➤ **Opening Hotlists** Each chapter begins with lists of the terms, tools, and techniques that you must learn and understand before you can be fully conversant with the chapter's subject matter. We follow the hotlists with one or two introductory paragraphs to set the stage for the rest of the chapter.

➤ **Topical Coverage** After the opening hotlists, each chapter covers a series of topics related to the chapter's subject. Throughout this section, we highlight material most likely to appear on a test using a special Study Alert layout, like this:

This is what a Study Alert looks like. Normally, a Study Alert stresses concepts, terms, software, or activities that will most likely appear in one or more certification test questions. For that reason, we think any information found offset in Study Alert format is worthy of unusual attentiveness on your part. Indeed, most of the facts appearing in The Cram Sheet (inside the front of this book) appear as Study Alerts within the text.

Even if material isn't flagged as a Study Alert, *all* the contents of this book are associated, at least tangentially, to something test-related. This book is lean to focus on quick test preparation; you'll find that what appears in the meat of each chapter is critical knowledge.

We have also provided tips that will help build a better foundation of networking knowledge. Although the information may not be on the exam, it is highly relevant and will help you become a better test-taker.

This is how tips are formatted. Keep your eyes open for these, and you'll become a test guru in no time!

➤ **Practice Questions**  This section presents a series of mock test questions and explanations of both correct and incorrect answers. We also try to point out especially tricky questions by using a special icon, like this:

Ordinarily, this icon flags the presence of an especially devious question, if not an outright trick question. Trick questions are calculated to "trap" you if you don't read them carefully and more than once, at that. Although they're not ubiquitous, such questions make regular appearances in the Oracle exams. That's why we say exam questions are as much about reading comprehension as they are about knowing DBA material inside out and backwards.

➤ **Details And Resources**  Every chapter ends with a section entitled "Need To Know More?". This section provides direct pointers to Oracle and third-party resources that offer further details on the chapter's subject matter. In addition, this section tries to rate the quality and thoroughness of each topic's coverage. If you find a resource you like in this collection, use it, but don't feel compelled to use all these resources. On the other hand, we recommend only resources we use on a regular basis, so none of our recommendations will be a waste of your time or money.

The bulk of the book follows this chapter structure slavishly, but there are a few other elements that we'd like to point out. There is one appendix: a reasonably exhaustive glossary of DBA-specific and general Oracle terminology. Finally, look for The Cram Sheet, which appears inside the front of this *Exam Cram* book. It is a valuable tool that represents a condensed and compiled collection of facts, figures, and tips that we think you should memorize before taking the test. Because you can dump this information out of your head onto a piece of paper before answering any exam questions, you can master this information by brute force—you need to remember it only long enough to write it down when you walk into the test room. You might even want to look at it in the car or in the lobby of the testing center just before you walk in to take the test.

# How To Use This Book

If you're prepping for a first-time test, we've structured the topics in this book to build on one another. Therefore, some topics in later chapters make more sense after you've read earlier chapters. That's why we suggest you read this book from front to back for your initial test preparation. If you need to brush up on a topic or you have to bone up for a second try, use the index or table of contents to go straight to the topics and questions that you need to study.

> *Note: This book covers two tests. Chapters 1 through 10 deal with the performance tuning test and Chapters 11 through 15 focus on backup and recovery. Although these are two separate topics, we suggest you read the entire book to get a general feel for the series of OCP-DBA tests.*

Beyond the tests, we think you'll find this book useful as a tightly focused reference to some of the most important aspects of topics associated with being a DBA, as implemented under Oracle7.3.

Given all the book's elements and its specialized focus, we've tried to create a tool that you can use to prepare for—and pass—the Oracle OCP-DBA set of examinations. Please share your feedback on the book with us, especially if you have ideas about how we can improve it for future test-takers. We'll consider everything you say carefully, and we try respond to all suggestions. You can reach us easiest through Michael R. Ault's email at mikerault@compuserve.com. Please remember to include the title of the book in your message; otherwise, we'll be forced to guess which book of ours you're making a suggestion about.

For up-to-date information on certification, online discussion forums, sample tests, content updates, and more, visit the Certification Insider Press Web site at www.certification.com.

Thanks, and enjoy the book!

# Oracle OCP Certification Tests

**Terms you'll need to understand:**

√ Radio button

√ Checkbox

√ Exhibit

√ Multiple-choice question formats

√ Careful reading

√ Process of elimination

**Techniques you'll need to master:**

√ Preparing to take a certification exam

√ Practicing (to make perfect)

√ Making the best use of the testing software

√ Budgeting your time

√ Saving the hardest questions until last

√ Guessing (as a last resort)

As experiences go, test-taking is not something that most people anticipate eagerly, no matter how well they're prepared. In most cases, familiarity helps ameliorate test anxiety. In plain English, this means you probably won't be as nervous when you take your third or fourth Oracle certification exam as you will be when you take your first one.

But no matter whether it's your first test or your tenth, understanding the exam-taking particulars (how much time to spend on questions, the setting you'll be in, and so on) and the testing software will help you concentrate on the material rather than on the environment. Likewise, mastering a few basic test-taking skills should help you recognize—and perhaps even outfox—some of the tricks and gotchas you're bound to find in some of the Oracle test questions.

In this chapter, we'll explain the testing environment and software, as well as describe some proven test-taking strategies you should be able to use to your advantage. We've compiled this information based on the Oracle certification exams we have taken and helped develop, and have also drawn on the advice of our friends and colleagues, some of whom have also taken more tests than they care to remember!

# The Testing Situation

When you arrive at the Sylvan Prometric Testing Center where you scheduled your test, you'll need to sign in with a test coordinator. He or she will ask you to produce two forms of identification, one of which must be a photo ID. Once you've signed in and your time slot arrives, you'll be asked to deposit any books, bags, or other items you brought with you, and you'll be escorted into a closed room. Typically, that room will be furnished with anywhere from one to half a dozen computers, and each workstation is separated from the others by dividers designed to keep you from seeing what's happening on someone else's computer.

You'll be furnished with a pen or pencil and a blank sheet of paper, or in some cases, an erasable plastic sheet and an erasable felt-tip pen. You're allowed to write down any information you want on this sheet, and you can write stuff on both sides of the page. We suggest that you memorize as much as possible of the material that appears on The Cram Sheet (inside the front this book), and then write that information down on the blank sheet as soon as you sit down in front of the test machine. You can refer to it any time you like during the test, but you'll have to surrender the sheet when you leave the room.

Most test rooms feature a wall with a large picture window. This is to permit the test coordinator to monitor the room, to prevent test-takers from talking to one another, and to observe anything out of the ordinary that might go on. The test coordinator will have preloaded the Oracle certification test you've signed up for—for this book, that's either Test 3, "Oracle7.3: Backup and

Recovery Workshop" or Test 4, "Oracle7.3: Performance Tuning Workshop"—
and you'll be permitted to start as soon as you're seated in front of the machine.

All Oracle certification exams permit you to take up to a certain maximum
amount of time (usually 90 minutes) to complete the test (the test itself will
tell you, and it maintains an on-screen counter/clock so that you can check the
time remaining any time you like). Each exam consists of between 60 and 70
questions, randomly selected from a pool of questions. You're permitted to take
up to 90 minutes to complete the exam.

All Oracle certification exams are computer generated and use a multiple-
choice format. Although this might sound easy, the questions are constructed
not just to check your mastery of basic facts and figures about Oracle7.3 DBA
topics, but also require you to evaluate one or more sets of circumstances or
requirements. Often, you'll be asked to give more than one answer to a question; likewise, you may be asked to select the best or most effective solution to
a problem from a range of choices, all of which technically are correct. It's quite
an adventure, and it involves real thinking. This book will show you what to
expect and how to deal with the problems, puzzles, and predicaments you're
likely to find on the test.

# Test Layout And Design

A typical test question is depicted in Question 1. It's a multiple-choice question
that requires you to select a single correct answer. Following the question is a
brief summary of each potential answer and why it was either right or wrong.

## Question 1

You issue this import command:

```
$ exp system/manager ignore=y file=tables.dmp
```

What is the purpose of the **IGNORE=Y** clause?

- ○ a. The command is not really run, it is ignored.
- ○ b. If the database is shutdown, ignore this and continue.
- ○ c. Ignore any object creation errors caused by the import.
- ○ d. No task was accomplished because ignore is not an
  Import option clause.

The correct answer is c. If the **IGNORE=Y** clause is added to an import command, it tells Import to ignore object creation errors that otherwise might
interfere with its operation. Therefore, answers a, b, and d are incorrect.

This sample question corresponds closely to those you'll see on Oracle certification tests. To select the correct answer during the test, you would position the cursor over the radio button next to answer c and click the mouse to select that particular choice. The only difference between the certification test and this question is that the real questions are not immediately followed by the answers.

Next, we'll examine a question that requires choosing multiple answers. This type of question provides checkboxes, rather than the radio buttons, for marking all appropriate selections.

## Question 2

What are two characteristics of the Oracle hot backup? [Check all correct answers]

❐ a. A hot backup is performed with the database shutdown.

❐ b. A hot backup is performed with the database running.

❐ c. A hot backup can be performed with the database in **NOARCHIVELOG** mode.

❐ d. A hot backup can only operate on one tablespace at a time.

❐ e. A hot backup allows 7X24 operations.

❐ f. No users can be using the database during a hot backup.

The correct answers for this question are b and e. Hot backups are performed with the database operating and were primarily designed for allowing 7×24 operations. In hot backup, the tablespaces are placed in backup mode forcing block type writes to the redo logs. The database must be in **ARCHIVELOG** mode in order to use hot backups. You have the choice of performing a hot backup linearly or one tablespace at a time, or in parallel by placing all the tablespaces in backup mode and using multiple operating system backup commands to do several tablespace backups at the same time.

For this type of question, one or more answers must be selected to answer the question correctly. As far as we can tell (and Oracle won't comment), such questions are scored as wrong unless all the required selections are chosen. In other words, a partially correct answer does not result in partial credit when the test is scored. For Question 2, you would have to position the cursor over the checkboxes next to items b and e to obtain credit for a correct answer.

Although there are many forms in which these two basic types of questions can appear, they constitute the foundation upon which all the Oracle certification exam questions rest. More complex questions may include so-called "exhibits," which are usually table or data content layouts of one form or another. You'll be expected to use the information displayed therein to guide your answer to the question.

Other questions involving exhibits may use charts or diagrams to help document a workplace scenario that you'll be asked to troubleshoot or configure. Paying careful attention to such exhibits is the key to success—be prepared to toggle between the picture and the question as you work. Often, both are complex enough that you might not be able to remember all of either one!

# Using Oracle's Test Software Effectively

A well-known test-taking principle is to read over the entire test from start to finish first, but to answer only those questions that you feel absolutely sure of on the first pass. On subsequent passes, you can dive into more complex questions, knowing how many such questions you have to deal with.

Fortunately, Oracle test software makes this approach easy to implement. At the bottom of each question, you'll find a checkbox that permits you to mark that question for a later visit. (Note: Marking questions makes review easier, but you can return to any question by clicking the Forward and Back buttons repeatedly until you get to the question.) As you read each question, if you answer only those you're sure of and mark for review those that you're not, you can keep going through a decreasing list of open questions as you knock the trickier ones off in order.

 There's at least one potential benefit to reading the test over completely before answering the trickier questions: Sometimes, you find information in later questions that sheds more light on earlier ones. Other times, information you read in later questions might jog your memory about facts, figures, or behavior that also will help with earlier questions. Either way, you'll come out ahead if you defer those questions about which you're not absolutely sure of the answer(s).

Keep working on the questions until you are absolutely sure of all your answers or until you know you'll run out of time. If there are still unanswered questions, you'll want to zip through them and guess. No answer guarantees no credit for a question, and a guess has at least a chance of being correct. This strategy only works because Oracle grades blank answers and incorrect answers as equally wrong.

At the very end of your test period, you're better off guessing than leaving questions blank or unanswered.

# Taking Testing Seriously

The most important advice we can give you about taking any Oracle test is this: Read each question carefully! Some questions are deliberately ambiguous; some use double negatives; others use terminology in incredibly precise ways. We've taken numerous practice tests and real tests, and in nearly every test, we've missed at least one question because we didn't read it closely or carefully enough.

Here are some suggestions on how to deal with the tendency to jump to an answer too quickly:

➤ Make sure you read every word in the question. If you find yourself jumping ahead impatiently, go back and start over.

➤ As you read, try to restate the question in your own terms. If you can do this, you should be able to pick the correct answer(s) much more easily.

➤ When returning to a question after your initial read-through, reread every word again—otherwise, the mind falls quickly into a rut. Sometimes seeing a question afresh after turning your attention elsewhere lets you see something you missed before, but the strong tendency is to see what you've seen before. Try to avoid that tendency at all costs.

➤ If you return to a question more than twice, try to articulate to yourself what you don't understand about the question, why the answers don't appear to make sense, or what appears to be missing. If you chew on the subject for a while, your subconscious might provide the details that are lacking, or you may notice a "trick" that will point to the right answer.

Above all, try to deal with each question by thinking through what you know about being an Oracle7.3 DBA: utilities, characteristics, behaviors, facts, and figures involved. By reviewing what you know (and what you've written down on your information sheet), you'll often recall or understand things sufficiently to determine the answer to the question.

# Question-Handling Strategies

Based on the tests we've taken, a couple of interesting trends in the answers have become apparent. For those questions that take only a single answer, usually two or three of the answers will be obviously incorrect, and two of the answers will be plausible. But, of course, they cannot all be correct. Unless the answer leaps out at you (and if it does, reread the question to look for a trick; sometimes those are the ones you're most likely to get wrong), begin the process of answering by eliminating those answers that are obviously wrong.

Things to look for in the "obviously wrong" category include spurious command choices or table or view names, nonexistent software or command options, and terminology you've never seen before. If you've done your homework for a test, no valid information should be completely new to you. In that case, unfamiliar or bizarre terminology probably indicates a totally bogus answer. As long as you're sure what's right, it's easy to eliminate what's wrong.

Numerous questions assume that the default behavior of a particular Oracle utility (such as SQL*Plus or Export) is in effect. It's essential, therefore, to know and understand the default settings for Import, Export, SQL*Plus, SQL*Loader, and Server Manager. If you know the defaults and understand what they mean, this knowledge will help you cut through many Gordian knots.

Likewise, when dealing with questions that require multiple answers, you must know and select all of the correct options to get credit. This, too, qualifies as an example of why "careful reading" is so important.

As you work your way through the test, another counter that Oracle thankfully provides will come in handy—the number of questions completed and questions outstanding. Budget your time by making sure that you've completed one-fourth of the questions one-quarter of the way through the test period (or between 13 and 17 questions in the first 22 or 23 minutes). Check again three-quarters of the way through (between 39 and 51 questions in the first 66 to 69 minutes).

If you're not through after 85 minutes, use the last 5 minutes to guess your way through the remaining questions. Remember, guesses are potentially more valuable than blank answers, because blanks are always wrong, but a guess might turn out to be right. If you haven't a clue with any of the remaining questions, pick answers at random, or choose all a's, b's, and so on. The important thing is to submit a test for scoring that has some answer for every question.

# Mastering The Inner Game

In the final analysis, knowledge breeds confidence, and confidence breeds success. If you study the materials in this book carefully and review all of the practice questions at the end of each chapter, you should be aware of those areas where additional studying is required.

Next, follow up by reading some or all of the materials recommended in the "Need To Know More?" section at the end of each chapter. The idea is to become familiar enough with the concepts and situations that you find in the sample questions to be able to reason your way through similar situations on a real test. If you know the material, you have every right to be confident that you can pass the test.

Once you've worked your way through the book, take the practice tests in Chapters 9 and 15. This will provide a reality check and will help you identify areas you need to study further. Make sure you follow up and review materials related to the questions you miss before scheduling a real test. Only when you've covered all the ground and feel comfortable with the whole scope of the practice tests should you take a real test.

 If you take our practice tests (Chapter 9 and Chapter 15) and don't score at least 75 percent correct, you'll want to practice further. At a minimum, download the practice tests and the self-assessment tests from the Oracle training and certification Web site's download page (its location appears in the next section). If you're more ambitious or better funded, you might want to purchase a practice test from one of the third-party vendors that offers them. We've had good luck with tests from Self Test Software (the vendor who supplies the practice tests). See the next section in this chapter for contact information.

Armed with the information in this book, and with the determination to augment your knowledge, you should be able to pass the certification exams. But if you don't work at it, you'll spend the test fee more than once before you finally do pass. If you prepare seriously, the execution should go flawlessly. Good luck!

# Additional Resources

By far, the best source of information about Oracle certification tests comes from Oracle itself. Because its products and technologies—and the tests that go with them—change frequently, the best place to go for exam-related information is online.

If you haven't already visited the Oracle training and certification pages, do so right now. As we're writing this chapter, the certification home page resides at http://education.oracle.com/certification/ (see Figure 1.1).

*Note: The home page might not be there by the time you read this, or it may have been replaced by something new and different, because things change regularly on the Oracle site. Should this happen, please read the sidebar titled "Coping With Change On The Web" later in this chapter.*

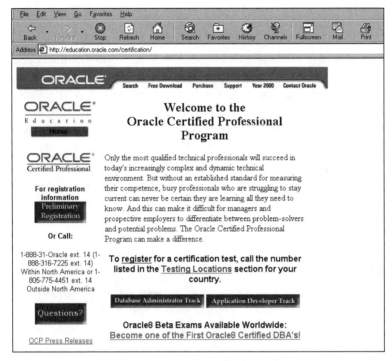

**Figure 1.1** The Oracle certification home page should be your starting point for further investigation of the most current exam and preparation information.

The menu options in the left column of the home page point to the most important sources of information in the training and certification pages. Here's what to check out:

➤ **Step-by-Step** Use this to jump to a step-by-step guide on how to prepare for and take the OCP tests.

➤ **Managers and Candidates** These sections provide facts that managers should know about why their employees should be OCP certified and facts that candidates should know about the exams.

➤ **Program Guide** Here is a detailed section that provides many jump points to test-related topics; everything you need know but didn't know to ask.

➤ **Assessment Tests** This section provides a download of the latest copy of the assessment test after you fill out an online application.

Of course, these are just the high points of what's available in the Oracle training and certification pages. As you browse through them—and we strongly recommend that you do—you'll probably find other things we didn't mention here that are every bit as interesting and compelling.

## Coping With Change On The Web

Sooner or later, all the specifics we've shared with you about the Oracle training and certification pages, and all the other Web-based resources we mention throughout the rest of this book, will go stale or be replaced by newer information. In some cases, the URLs you find here might lead you to their replacements; in other cases, the URLs will go nowhere, leaving you with the dread "404 File Not Found" error message.

When that happens, please don't give up! There's always a way to find what you want on the Web—if you're willing to invest some time and energy. To begin with, most large or complex Web sites—and Oracle's qualifies on both counts—offer a search engine. As long as you can get to Oracle's site itself (and we're pretty sure that it will stay at www.oracle.com for a long while yet), you can use the Search tool to help you find what you need.

The more particular or focused you can make a search request, the more likely it is that the results will include information you can use. For instance, you can search the string

```
"training and certification"
```

to produce a lot of data about the subject in general. But if you're looking for the Preparation Guide for the Oracle DBA tests, you'll be more likely to get there quickly if you use a search string such as this:

```
"DBA" AND "preparation guide"
```

Likewise, if you want to find the training and certification downloads, try a search string such as this one:

```
"training and certification" AND "download page"
```

Finally, don't be afraid to use general search tools such as www.search.com, www.altavista.com, or www.excite.com to search for related information. Even though Oracle offers the best information about its certification exams online, there are plenty of third-party sources of information, training, and assistance in this area that do not have to follow a party line like Oracle does. The bottom line is this: If you can't find something where the book says it lives, start looking around. If worse comes to worse, you can always email us!

# Third-Party Test Providers

There are third-party companies that provide example assessment tests. We suggest obtaining and taking as many of these as you can so that you become completely familiar and confident with test taking. Among these third-party providers are:

➤ **RevealNet, Inc.** In the Oracle Administrator program, there is a complete review section for the DBA examination with example test questions. A fully functional 15-day demo can be downloaded from the Web site free of charge. The company is reached through its Web site at http://www.revealnet.com/. You can also call RevealNet at 800-738-3254 or 202-234-8557. RevealNet's address is RevealNet, Inc., 3016 Cortland Place NW, Washington DC, 20008.

➤ **Self Test Software** Self Test also offers sample Oracle tests for all four of the OCP-DBA tests. Self Test is located at 4651 Woodstock Road, Suite 203-384, Roswell, GA, 30075. The company can be reached by phone at 800-200-6446 or 770-641-9719, and by fax at 770-641-1489. Visit Self Test's Web site at http://www.stsware.com; you can even order the software online.

# Tuning
# Overview

. . . . . . . . . . . . . . . . . . . . . . . . .

### Terms you'll need to understand:

√   Performance Pack

√   V$ views

√   UTLBSTAT, UTLESTAT, and report.txt

√   Timed statistics

√   OLTP, DSS, and hybrid systems

### Techniques you'll need to master:

√   Taking a structured approach to tuning analysis

√   Understanding the variety of diagnostic tools available
for database tuning and using them effectively

√   Understanding how to use the V$ views and report.txt
for pinpointing performance problems

√   Customizing tuning for different application
environments

The Oracle server is a complex, highly tunable software system. Because performance is a key issue at most sites, one of the many responsibilities of the database administrator (DBA) is to address performance issues at each phase of the system's life cycle. Performance tuning should be viewed as an iterative process that never ends.

In most organizations, the DBA is often regarded as the individual responsible for tuning an Oracle system. In an Oracle environment, as in most complicated systems, tuning is not the sole responsibility of any single individual. Designers, analysts, application developers, administrators, and DBAs all play an important role at one time or another in tuning an Oracle system. However, the DBA should assume an active role in all phases.

This chapter provides an overview of the tuning process and reviews some of the Oracle tools that assist in identifying and addressing performance issues. This chapter also provides a tuning checklist that uses a structured methodology and details the use of UTLBSTAT and UTLESTAT. Finally, this chapter explains how to customize your tuning approach for different application environments.

# Tuning Toolbox

Oracle offers many tools to assist in the tuning process. Table 2.1 lists some tools provided by Oracle for tuning diagnostics. Each tool is discussed in detail in the following sections.

## Performance Pack

In addition to the standard set of applications, Oracle offers an optional Performance Pack that consists of integrated monitoring and performance tuning tools. Performance Pack is a set of tuning diagnostics within Enterprise Manager that provides realtime graphical performance information. The components of Performance Pack include the following:

➤ **Oracle Expert** Helps the DBA optimize database performance. It assists with initial database configuration and with the collection and evaluation of performance statistics in existing databases. It also provides recommendations for performance improvements on the basis of current database activity and scenarios provided by the DBA.

➤ **Oracle Tablespace Manager** Allows the DBA to monitor and manage database storage at the tablespace level. It also provides the ability to drill down to the segment and extent level.

| Table 2.1 Tools for tuning. | |
|---|---|
| **Diagnostic Tool** | **Description** |
| Performance Pack | An optional Oracle diagnostic tool for integrated monitoring and tuning of the database |
| V$ views | Dynamic performance views used for tuning diagnostics |
| ANALYZE command | Provides detailed storage statistics on tables, indexes, and clusters |
| UTLBSTAT/UTLESTAT | SQL scripts that take a beginning snapshot (UTLBSTAT) and an ending snapshot (UTLESTAT) of database performance statistics and produce a report (report.txt) on system performance |
| SQL Trace/TKPROF | Gathers performance information for a SQL statement, including the optimizer access method, CPU utilization, and percentage of logical and physical reads |
| Explain Plan | Passes a SQL statement through the Oracle optimizer to give an execution plan on how that statement will be executed in the database |
| Trace files | Provides debugging information for the background processes (for example, LGWR and DBWR); the alert logfile records all significant instance events and errors |

➤ **Oracle Trace** Monitors system performance by collecting data about events that occur in an application. The application must contain calls to Oracle Trace routines in order to gather performance statistics.

➤ **Oracle Performance Manager** Allows the DBA to monitor database performance in realtime. Provides database statistics regarding throughput, users, tablespaces, redo logs, buffers, caches, and I/O.

➤ **Oracle Top Sessions** Monitors how connected sessions use instance and database resources in realtime. It identifies and isolates the most resource-intensive sessions and displays the SQL being executed for those sessions.

➤ **Oracle Lock Manager** Provides lock monitoring for users holding locks or waiting for locks within the database.

## V$ Views

To tune and troubleshoot the Oracle database, you must familiarize yourself with V$ dynamic performance views that are commonly used for diagnostics.

The **V$** views are created by running the catalog.sql script and are based on **X$** tables, which are memory structures that hold information about the instance. The database user SYS owns the **V$** views, and the DBA can grant **SELECT** on the views to any database user. The **V$** views and the **X$** tables are populated at instance startup and are reinitialized each time the instance is restarted. Table 2.2 lists **V$** views that can be used for performance tuning grouped by the following categories:

➤ Instance/database

➤ Memory

➤ Disk

➤ User/session

➤ Contention

**Table 2.2   V$ views for performance tuning.**

| View | Description |
|---|---|
| **Instance/database** | |
| V$DATABASE | Database information from the control file |
| V$INSTANCE | State of the current instance |
| V$OPTION | Options that are installed with the Oracle7 server |
| V$PARAMETER | Information about current parameter values |
| V$PQ_SYSSTAT | Session statistics for all parallel queries |
| V$PROCESS | Information about processes currently active |
| V$SESSTAT | User session statistics |
| V$WAITSTAT | Block contention statistics (updated only when timed statistics is enabled) |
| V$SYSTEM_EVENT | Information on total waits for an event |
| **Memory** | |
| V$DB_OBJECT_CACHE | Database objects that are cached in the library cache (for example, tables, clusters, indexes, synonym definitions, PL/SQL packages, procedures, and triggers) |
| V$LIBRARY_CACHE | Statistics about library cache performance and activity |
| V$SYSSTAT | System statistics |
| V$SGASTAT | Detailed information on the system global area (SGA) |
| V$ROWCACHE | Statistics on data dictionary activity |

*(continued)*

**Table 2.2    V$ views for performance tuning (continued).**

| View | Description |
|---|---|
| **Disk** | |
| V$DATAFILE | Datafile information from the control file |
| V$FILESTAT | Information about file read-write statistics |
| V$LOG | Log file information from the control file |
| V$LOG_HISTORY | Archived log names for all logs in the log history |
| **User/session** | |
| V$LOCK | Information about locks and resources |
| V$OPEN_CURSOR | Information about cursors that each session currently has opened and parsed |
| V$PROCESS | Information about currently active processes |
| V$SESSION | Session information for each current session |
| V$SESSTAT | User session statistics |
| V$TRANSACTION | Active transactions in the system |
| V$SYSTEM_EVENT | Information of total waits for an event |
| V$SESSION_EVENT | All waits for an event by a session |
| **Contention** | |
| V$LOCK | Locks that are being held and requests for a lock or a latch |
| V$ROLLNAME | Names of all online rollback segments |
| V$ROLLSTAT | Rollback segment statistics |
| V$LATCH | Statistics for nonparent latches and summary statistics for parent latches |
| V$WAITSTAT | Block contention statistics (updated only when timed statistics are enabled) |

Some of the columns in the **V$** views can store CPU timing information. To populate the views with timing statistics, you must set the **TIMED_STATISTICS** parameter to **TRUE**. The **TIMED_STATISTICS** parameter enables and disables the collection of CPU timing statistics for the **V$** views, UTLBSTAT/UTLESTAT, and SQL Trace.

You can enable **TIMED_STATISTICS** in the database initialization file by adding the following parameter (the instance must then be restarted in order for the change to take effect):

```
TIMED_STATISTICS = TRUE
```

The following database initialization file parameter disables **TIMED_ STATISTICS**:

```
TIMED_STATISTICS = FALSE
```

Version 7.3 contains several database initialization parameters that can be changed while the database is running. You can dynamically enable the **TIMED_STATISTICS** value for an instance with the following command:

```
ALTER SYSTEM SET timed_statistics = TRUE;
```

The following command will disable **TIMED_STATISTICS** for an instance:

```
ALTER SYSTEM SET timed_statistics = FALSE;
```

The default for the **TIMED_STATISTICS** parameter is **FALSE**.

 Enabling **TIMED_STATISTICS** has been known to degrade performance by about 10 percent, so it should be used sparingly.

## The ANALYZE Command

The **ANALYZE** command is used to gather statistical information or to validate the storage format of a table, index, or cluster. Many of the statistics gathered when the **ANALYZE** command is issued are used by the cost-based optimizer to obtain the optimal execution path for your SQL statements. The **ANALYZE** command also provides statistics on chained and migrated rows for a table or cluster. The DBA can use many of the statistics gathered by the **ANALYZE** command to obtain detailed storage information on a table, cluster, or index. This information helps determine whether the object needs to be rebuilt. You must have the **ANALYZE ANY** system privilege or own the object to analyze a table, cluster, or index. The syntax for the **ANALYZE** command is shown in Figure 2.1.

When you issue the **ANALYZE** command with the **STATISTICS** option, statistics are stored about the physical characteristics of the table, cluster, or index that you analyzed. You can estimate or compute statistics with the **ANALYZE** command. When you use **ESTIMATE STATISTICS**, Oracle collects a representation of information from a portion of the data in an object. When **COMPUTE STATISTICS** is used, Oracle performs a full table scan on the object to gather the exact statistics. If you are working with a large object, you

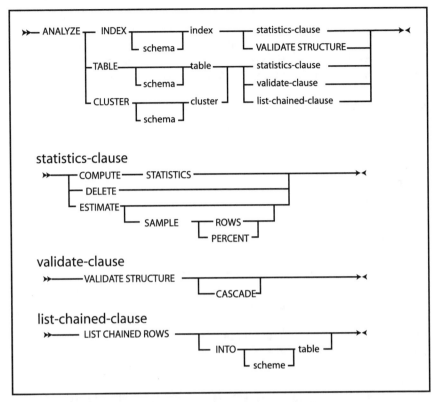

**Figure 2.1**    The syntax for the **ANALYZE** command.

might want to use **ESTIMATE STATISTICS** first on a specified number of rows or a percentage of the object. When statistics are analyzed on a table or cluster, the indexes for the object are analyzed as well.

The following query is from RevealNet's Oracle Administration product and is used with their permission. This query can be executed after tables have been analyzed to produce detailed storage statistics on the tables in the database.

```
rem  FUNCTION: Will show table statistics for a user's tables or
rem  all tables.
rem  File: tab_stat.sql
rem set pages 56 lines 130 newpage 0 verify off echo off feedback
rem off
rem
column owner           format a12          heading "Owner"
column table_name      format a20          heading "Table"
column tablespace_name format a20          heading "Tablespace"
column num_rows        format 999,999,999  heading "Rows"
```

```
column blocks           format 999,999      heading "Blocks"
column empty_blocks     format 999,999      heading "Empties"
column space_full       format 999.99       heading "% Full"
column chain_cnt        format 999,999      heading "Chains"
column avg_row_len      format 99,999,999,999 heading "Avg Len"
rem
start title132 "Table Statistics Report"
DEFINE OUTPUT = 'rep_out\&db\tab_stat.lis'
spool &output
rem
BREAK ON OWNER SKIP 2 ON TABLESPACE_NAME SKIP 1;
select owner,
        table_name,
        tablespace_name,
        num_rows,
        blocks,
        empty_blocks,
        100*((NUM_ROWS * AVG_ROW_LEN)/((GREATEST(blocks,1) +
        empty_blocks) * 4096)) space_full,
        chain_cnt, avg_row_len
from dba_tables
WHERE OWNER NOT IN ('SYS','SYSTEM')
order by owner, tablespace_name;
spool off
pause Press enter to continue
 set pages 22 lines 80 newpage 1 verify on echo on feedback on
clear columns
clear breaks
ttitle off
```

Table 2.3 shows a partial output of the RevealNet query.

The value in the **BLOCKS** column indicates the number of blocks *below* the high water mark. The high water mark indicates the highest level of blocks that has been used at any given time in the segment. The high water mark is reset when the table is truncated but not when rows are deleted from a table. The value in the **EMPTIES** column indicates the number of empty (never used) blocks. The **CHAINS** column indicates the number of chained or migrated rows in a table.

To remove statistics for a table, cluster, or index from the data dictionary, use **DELETE STATISTICS** with the **ANALYZE** command. When statistics are deleted for a table or cluster, the index statistics on the object are also deleted. The following command deletes statistics for the **DEPARTMENT** table:

```
ANALYZE TABLE department DELETE STATISTICS;
```

**Table 2.3    Table storage statistics.**

| OWNER | TABLE | TABLE-SPACE | ROWS | BLOCKS | EMPTIES | % FULL | CHAINS | AVG LEN |
|-------|-------|-------------|------|--------|---------|--------|--------|---------|
| SCOTT | CLASS | PDATA1 | 4,746 | 105 | 59 | 52.28 | 0 | 74 |
| | STDENTS | | 20,577 | 350 | 1,189 | 20.89 | 0 | 64 |
| | ACCTS | | 871 | 10 | 4 | 37.97 | 4 | 25 |
| | ZONE | PDATA2 | 494 | 3 | 141 | 1.59 | 0 | 19 |
| | MODELS | | 13 | 1 | 258 | .02 | 0 | 17 |
| APPL | CLASS2 | PDATA1 | 1,338 | 20 | 239 | 6.94 | 7 | 55 |
| | PRICES | | 754 | 10 | 154 | 3.37 | 0 | 30 |

Use caution when you delete statistics for tables or clusters. If you are using the cost-based optimizer and there are no statistics for an object, the cost-based optimizer will assume that the object has no rows. You need to understand how the cost-based optimizer will use the information provided by the **ANALYZE** command and you should keep your statistics current.

## UTLBSTAT And UTLESTAT

If your instance has been running for an extended period of time, the statistics in the V$ views might not help in your evaluation of the true performance of your system during busy times. If users tell you that the system runs smoothly in the morning but that performance is sluggish in the afternoon, you need to evaluate a time slice of the system performance. To accomplish this, Oracle provides the scripts UTLBSTAT.SQL and UTLESTAT.SQL, which are located in the $ORACLE_HOME/rdbms/admin directory in a Unix environment.

At the beginning of the time period you want to monitor, submit the UTLBSTAT.SQL script from Server Manager while connected as SYSDBA. The UTLBSTAT script creates tables owned by SYS that store cumulative beginning database statistics. The tables that are created contain the word *begin*, as in **STAT$BEGIN_FILE**. At the end of the monitoring time period, submit the UTLESTAT.SQL script from Server Manager while connected as SYSDBA. The UTLESTAT script creates additional tables and populates them with ending database statistics. The tables created contain the word *end*, as in **STAT$END_STATS**. In addition, UTLESTAT creates the report.txt file, which shows the differences in the statistics from the time that UTLBSTAT was submitted until the time that UTLESTAT was submitted. To obtain time-based statistics from UTLBSTAT and UTLESTAT, the **TIMED_ STATISTICS** parameter must be set to **TRUE**.

Before you submit UTLBSTAT, you should ensure that the database has been running for a period of time that is sufficient to populate the V$ tables with dynamic performance statistics. This time period is dependent on the level of activity in your database. Remember that Oracle initializes the dynamic performance tables at instance startup. Information gathered from a recently started database might not reflect true performance statistics. Additionally, if you shut down the database or have an instance crash *after* UTLBSTAT was submitted, but *before* UTLESTAT was submitted, the statistics will not provide a valid picture of the performance on your database. You will need to run both scripts again after the database has been restarted.

UTLESTAT always writes database statistics to the report.txt file in the current directory. If you want to run multiple sets of UTLBSTAT and UTLESTAT to compare statistics for several time slices, remember to rename the report.txt file after each submission of UTLESTAT. If you do not rename the report.txt file, it will be overwritten with the latest statistics gathered by UTLESTAT.

The report.txt file provides information on:

➤ System summary statistics

➤ Systemwide wait statistics

➤ Library cache statistics

➤ Dictionary cache statistics

➤ DBWR statistics

➤ File I/O statistics

➤ Latch statistics

➤ Database initialization parameters

➤ The date and time that UTLBSTAT and UTLESTAT scripts were run

Report.txt includes system statistics on virtually every aspect of database internals. Many of the statistics from report.txt contain truncated statistic names and lines that wrap on the report. Although Oracle's report.txt file provides valuable performance diagnostics, it is not a well-formatted report and some sections are difficult to read. As with all statistics in report.txt, the period of statistical gathering is from the time UTLBSTAT was submitted until the time UTLESTAT was submitted. Table 2.4 lists some of the system statistics provided in report.txt.

Library cache statistics are included in the report.txt file. The library cache is
the portion of the shared pool in the SGA that stores information regarding

| Table 2.4    System statistics report in report.txt. | | |
|---|---|---|
| **Statistic** | **Total** | **Per Transact** |
| CPU used by this session | 71,454 | 84.16 |
| CPU used when call started | 71,407 | 84.11 |
| DBWR buffers scanned | 95,686 | 112.7 |
| DBWR checkpoints | 64 | .08 |
| DBWR free buffers found | 30,774 | 36.25 |
| DBWR LRU scans | 274 | .32 |
| DBWR timeouts | 1,065 | 1.25 |
| SQL*Net roundtrips to/from | 76,394 | 89.98 |
| Background timeouts | 3,360 | 3.96 |
| Bytes received via SQL*Net | 14,022,597 | 16,516.6 |
| Bytes sent via SQL*Net to c | 10,948,276 | 12,895.5 |
| Calls to get snapshot SCN | 67,798 | 79.86 |
| Calls to kcmgas | 1,072 | 1.26 |
| Calls to kcmgcs | 130 | .15 |
| Calls to kcmgrs | 87,650 | 103.24 |
| Change write time | 606 | .71 |
| Cleanouts and rollbacks: c | 112 | .13 |
| Cleanouts only: consistent | 38 | .04 |
| Cluster key scan block gets | 20,885 | 24.6 |
| Cluster key scans | 2,191 | 2.58 |
| Commit cleanout failures: b | 8 | .01 |
| Commit cleanout number succ | 8,257 | 9.73 |
| Consistent changes | 1,779 | 2.1 |
| Consistent gets | 2,631,477 | 3,099.5 |
| Cursor authentications | 29,690 | 34.97 |
| Data blocks consistent read | 1,779 | 2.1 |
| Database block changes | 178,516 | 210.27 |

*(continued)*

**Table 2.4    System statistics report in report.txt** *(continued).*

| Statistic | Total | Per Transact |
|---|---|---|
| Database block gets | 182,024 | 214.4 |
| Deferred (CURRENT) block cl | 3,026 | 3.56 |
| Enqueue conversions | 724 | .85 |
| Enqueue releases | 5,927 | 6.98 |
| Enqueue requests | 5,961 | 7.02 |
| Enqueue timeouts | 40 | .05 |
| Enqueue waits | 3 | 0 |
| Execute count | 74,846 | 88.16 |
| Free buffer requested | 28,110 | 33.11 |
| Logons cumulative | 177 | .21 |
| Logons current | 10 | .01 |
| Messages received | 1,388 | 1.63 |
| Messages sent | 1,388 | 1.63 |
| Opened cursors cumulative | 24,804 | 29.22 |
| Opened cursors current | 242 | .29 |
| Parse count | 32,869 | 38.71 |
| Parse time CPU | 18,198 | 21.43 |
| Parse time elapsed | 19,088 | 22.48 |
| Physical reads | 17,181 | 20.24 |
| Physical writes | 6,292 | 7.41 |
| Recursive calls | 483,538 | 569.54 |
| Recursive CPU usage | 12,922 | 15.22 |
| Redo blocks written | 34,045 | 40.1 |
| Redo buffer allocation retr | 5 | .01 |
| Redo entries | 90,139 | 106.17 |
| Redo log space requests | 8 | .01 |
| Redo log space wait time | 418 | .49 |
| Redo size | 16,594,148 | 19,545.52 |
| Redo small copies | 4,668 | 5.5 |

*(continued)*

| Table 2.4 | System statistics report in report.txt *(continued)*. | |
|---|---|---|
| **Statistic** | **Total** | **Per Transact** |
| Redo synch time | 4,457 | 5.25 |
| Redo synch writes | 952 | 1.12 |
| Redo wastage | 271,372 | 319.64 |
| Redo write time | 6,221 | 7.33 |
| Redo writer latching time | 11 | .01 |
| Redo writes | 1,215 | 1.43 |
| Rollback changes: undo rec | 1,762 | 2.08 |
| Rollbacks only: consistent | 1,595 | 1.88 |
| Session logical reads | 2,797,112 | 3,294.6 |
| Session PGA memory | 73,996,476 | 87,157.22 |
| Session PGA memory maximum | 76,544,228 | 90,158.1 |
| Session UGA memory | 1,910,768 | 2,250.61 |
| Session UGA memory maximum | 35,363,760 | 41,653.43 |
| Sorts (disk) | 4 | 0 |
| Sorts (memory) | 10,468 | 12.33 |
| Sorts (rows) | 319,077 | 375.83 |
| Table fetch by ROWID | 956,150 | 1,126.21 |
| Table fetch continued row | 4,352 | 5.13 |
| Table scan blocks gotten | 221,624 | 261.04 |
| Table scan rows gotten | 1,485,858 | 1,750.13 |
| Table scans (long tables) | 8 | .01 |
| Table scans (short tables) | 9,285 | 10.94 |
| Total number commit cleanout | 8,300 | 9.78 |
| Transaction rollbacks | 3 | 0 |
| User calls | 72,708 | 85.64 |
| User commits | 849 | 1 |
| User rollbacks | 106 | .12 |
| Write requests | 1,189 | 1.4 |

shared SQL objects. The goal for the library cache is to achieve a high pin ratio and a low number of reloads. Table 2.5 shows library cache statistics in report.txt.

The report.txt file also reports statistics on the dictionary cache, which is the portion of the shared pool that holds information from the data dictionary. The **GET_MISS** and **SCAN_MIS(S)** statistics should be significantly lower than the requests. If the overall ratio of **GET_MISS** to **GET_REQS** is greater than 10 percent, you should consider increasing the **SHARED_POOL_SIZE** parameter in the database initialization file. Table 2.6 shows dictionary cache statistics in report.txt.

The buffer cache is the area in memory where data is stored from tables, indexes, rollback segments, clusters, and sequences. When you have a good buffer cache hit ratio, you can speed execution by reducing reads from disk to satisfy data requests. If the buffer cache hit ratio is less than 80 percent and the database has been operating with activity for some time, you might need to increase the **DB_BLOCK_BUFFERS** parameter or reevaluate your indexes and SQL in your applications. Table 2.7 shows report.txt statistics that can be used to determine the buffer cache hit ratio.

The formula used to determine the buffer cache hit ratio is

```
Logical reads = db block gets + consistent gets
```

then:

```
Buffer cache hit ratio (%) =
(( logical reads - physical reads)
/ logical reads) * 100
```

In this example, the buffer cache hit ratio is 99.39 percent.

> *Note: The **V$SYSSTAT** view also provides information to determine the buffer cache hit ratio, but the statistics reflected in **V$SYSSTAT** are from instance startup.*

Report.txt provides information on sorts in memory and on disk. Ideally, you want most of your sorting done in memory. This requires proper configuration of **SORT_AREA_SIZE** and **SORT_AREA_RETAINED_SIZE**. Sorts to disk indicate the number of sorts writing to the temporary tablespace on disk. Sorts to memory indicate the number of sorts performed in the SGA. The **sorts (rows)** statistic in report.txt indicates the number of rows sorted during the monitoring period. Oracle recommends that the ratio of **sorts(disk) / sorts(memory)** be less than 5 percent. Table 2.8 lists sort statistics from report.txt.

## Table 2.5    Library cache statistics in report.txt.

| LIBRARY | GETS | GET HIT RATIO | PINS | PIN HIT RATIO | RELOADS | INVALIDATIONS |
|---|---|---|---|---|---|---|
| BODY | 8 | 1 | 8 | 1 | 0 | 0 |
| CLUSTER | 7 | 1 | 11 | 1 | 0 | 0 |
| INDEX | 0 | 1 | 0 | 1 | 0 | 0 |
| OBJECT | 0 | 1 | 0 | 1 | 0 | 0 |
| PIPE | 0 | 1 | 0 | 1 | 0 | 0 |
| SQL AREA | 434 | .963 | 1432 | .977 | 0 | 9 |
| TABLE/PROCED | 42 | .905 | 104 | .942 | 0 | 0 |
| TRIGGER | 0 | 1 | 0 | 1 | 0 | 0 |

## Table 2.6    Dictionary cache statistics in report.txt.

| NAME | GET_ REQS | GET_ MISS | SCAN_ REQ | SCAN_ MIS | MOD_ REQS | COUNT | CUR_ USAGE |
|---|---|---|---|---|---|---|---|
| dc_tablespaces | 72 | 1 | 0 | 0 | 0 | 8 | 4 |
| dc_free_extents | 310 | 67 | 33 | 0 | 165 | 63 | 34 |
| dc_segments | 43 | 4 | 0 | 0 | 35 | 53 | 41 |
| dc_rollback_seg | 56 | 0 | 0 | 0 | 0 | 10 | 8 |
| dc_used_extents | 66 | 33 | 0 | 0 | 66 | 50 | 32 |
| dc_users | 31 | 0 | 0 | 0 | 0 | 21 | 14 |
| dc_user_grants | 20 | 0 | 0 | 0 | 0 | 21 | 14 |
| dc_objects | 33 | 3 | 0 | 0 | 0 | 222 | 214 |
| dc_usernames | 9 | 1 | 0 | 0 | 0 | 20 | 4 |
| dc_object_ids | 14 | 1 | 0 | 0 | 0 | 132 | 130 |
| dc_profiles | 3 | 0 | 0 | 0 | 0 | 3 | 1 |
| dc_histogram_de | 73 | 73 | 0 | 0 | 73 | 77 | 73 |

## Table 2.7    Buffer cache statistics from report.txt.

| Statistic | Total | Per Transaction | Per Logon | Per Second |
|---|---|---|---|---|
| consistent gets | 2,631,477 | 3,099.5 | 14,867.1 | 768.54 |
| db block gets | 182,024 | 214.4 | 1,028.38 | 53.16 |
| physical reads | 17,181 | 20.24 | 97.07 | 5.02 |

| Table 2.8 | Sort statistics in report.txt. | | | |
|---|---|---|---|---|
| **Statistic** | **Total** | **Per Transaction** | **Per Logon** | **Per Second** |
| sorts (disk) | 4 | 0 | .02 | 0 |
| sorts (memory) | 10,468 | 12.33 | 59.14 | 3.06 |
| sorts (rows) | 319,077 | 375.83 | 182.09 | 93.19 |

Another useful set of statistics provided by report.txt is file I/O statistics, which provides information about file read and write statistics. Use this information to determine how well the I/O load is distributed across disk devices on your system and to pinpoint disks where excessive I/O could be a problem. Ideally, the disk I/O should be as even as possible between disks. If you find that the disk I/O is too high on one or more disks, you should consider moving a datafile to a disk with lighter activity. Table 2.9 shows a partial listing of report.txt statistics that can be used to determine the file I/O distribution. The total I/O activity for a disk can be determined by summing the **BLKS READ** and **BLKS WRIT** columns.

Latches protect access to internal structures such as the shared cursors in the library cache or the LRU list for the buffer cache. A process must acquire a latch when making a change to these types of structures. You should aim for a latch hit ratio of at least 0.98. If your hit ratio is below 0.98, this could indicate latch contention problems. Table 2.10 shows a partial listing of latch contention statistics in report.txt.

Another statistic provided by report.txt is rollback segment statistics. The **TRANS_TBL_GETS** column indicates the number of rollback segment accesses. The **TRANS_TBL_WAITS** column indicates the number of times a user process waited on a rollback segment. The ratio of **TRANS_**

| Table 2.9 | Disk I/O statistics in report.txt. | | | | | |
|---|---|---|---|---|---|---|
| **Tablespace** | **File_ Name** | **Blks Read** | **Read Time** | **Blks Writ** | **Write Time** | **Mega- bytes** |
| ap_data | db01ce/oratst/ ad01.dbf | 402 | 163 | 125 | 1,248 | 524 |
| ap_indexes | db02nc/oratst/ apx01.dbf | 270 | 159 | 670 | 7,540 | 524 |
| system | db03ce/oratst/ system1.dbf | 4,421 | 454 | 253 | 3,290 | 524 |
| temp | db04ce/oratst/ temp1.dbf | 0 | 0 | 617 | 9,216 | 524 |

**Table 2.10    Latch contention statistics in report.txt.**

| LATCH_NAME | GETS | MISSES | HIT_RATIO | SLEEPS | SLEEPS/ MISSES |
|---|---|---|---|---|---|
| cache buffer handl | 180 | 0 | 1 | 0 | 0 |
| cache buffers chai | 5445625 | 98 | 1 | 13 | .133 |
| cache buffers lru | 20657 | 4 | 1 | 1 | .25 |

**TBL_WAITS** to **TRANS_TBL_GETS** should be less than 5 percent. If you have a high number of **TRANS_TBL_WAITS**, you should add additional rollback segments. Excessive shrinks indicate that the **OPTIMAL** size for the rollback segment may be too low. Oracle recommends that you set your **MINEXTENTS** to 20 for rollback segments. You should set **OPTIMAL** at a number that will ensure that rollback segments do not shrink below 20 extents. Rollback segments should be equal in size. The exception might be a large rollback segment that is used for lengthy transactions or batch jobs. Table 2.11 shows rollback statistics in report.txt.

Report.txt includes all database initialization file parameters that are not set to the default value. The date and time of the beginning and ending statistical period are also included in report.txt.

## SQL Trace

When SQL statements are performing poorly, you can use the SQL Trace utility to obtain performance statistics for the SQL statements being executed. SQL Trace writes a trace file that contains statistics on the parse, execute, and

**Table 2.11    Rollback segment statistics in report.txt.**

| UNDO SEGMENT | TRANS TBL GETS | TRANS TBL WAITS | UNDO BYTES WRITTEN | SEGMENT SIZE BYTES | XACTS | SHRINKS | WRAPS |
|---|---|---|---|---|---|---|---|
| 0 | 16 | 0 | 0 | 180,224 | 0 | 0 | 0 |
| 1 | 1,009 | 0 | 1,978,858 | 21,295,104 | 1 | 0 | 2 |
| 2 | 685 | 0 | 975,323 | 21,295,104 | 1 | 0 | 1 |
| 3 | 310 | 0 | 296,471 | 21,295,104 | 1 | 0 | 1 |
| 4 | 674 | 0 | 814,744 | 21,295,104 | 0 | 0 | 1 |
| 5 | 903 | 0 | 1,502,274 | 21,295,104 | 0 | 0 | 1 |
| 6 | 32 | 0 | 932,786 | 42,590,208 | 0 | 0 | 0 |

fetch stages of statement execution. It reports on the number of logical buffers retrieved (reads from memory) and the number of physical blocks retrieved from disk. On addition, SQL Trace provides its own rendition of Explain Plan to determine an execution plan, and also provides the optimizer hint, if one is used during statement execution. The trace file can be formatted using TKPROF. SQL Trace is detailed in Chapter 3.

# Explain Plan

The Explain Plan tool can be used to determine the access path used by the optimizer without running the actual SQL statement. When you run Explain Plan, you insert rows into a table called **PLAN_TABLE**. The rows in **PLAN_TABLE** can then be evaluated to check the efficiency of the access path and determine which indexes are being used during execution of the SQL statement. Chapter 3 covers Explain Plan concepts and usage in detail.

# Trace Files

Trace files assist in the troubleshooting process. When an Oracle instance is started, several background processes are started to support the Oracle database system. In Oracle7, you will have a minimum of four background processes on your system:

➤ **SMON**  Responsible for instance recovery

➤ **PMON**  Responsible for recovery from a user process

➤ **DBWR**  Writes from database buffers to database files

➤ **LGWR**  Writes from the redo log buffer to the online redo logs

When you encounter an error in a background process, Oracle will write information about the error to its trace file, which uses the .trc extension. For example, an error in the SMON process might create a trace file named ptw01-smon_3204.trc. The information in these files can assist the DBA in the troubleshooting process. Some of the information in trace files is used only by kernel experts at Oracle WorldWide Support for troubleshooting.

Oracle writes a chronological log of major database events and errors within an instance to an alert log. The alert logfile is a special kind of trace file that usually includes the instance name. For example, an instance named **TEST** might have the alert logfile name alert_TEST.log on a Unix system. The alert logfile includes:

➤ All internal errors, deadlock errors, and block corruption errors

➤ Administrative errors, such as **CREATE, ALTER,** or **DROP DATA-BASE, TABLESPACE,** or **ROLLBACK SEGMENT** SQL statements. (There is no **DROP DATABASE** command in Oracle).

➤ Startup, shutdown, and log switch information

➤ Optionally, all checkpoint start and stop times if **LOG_CHECKPOINTS_TO_ALERT** is set to **TRUE**

You should periodically check the alert logfile and trace files to see whether any errors have been encountered. The **BACKGROUND_DUMP_DEST** parameter in the database initialization file specifies the location of the alert logfile and all background trace files.

You can control the maximum size of all trace files (with the exception of the alert logfile) using the init.ora parameter **MAX_DUMP_FILE_SIZE.** This parameter specifies, in operating system blocks, the maximum size of each trace file.

All entries to the alert logfile are appended to the existing alert logfile. This file can easily grow to an unmanageable size if not monitored and maintained regularly. Keep the alert logfile to a reasonable size by renaming it periodically. You can do this while the database is closed or open. If Oracle cannot find the expected name for the alert logfile for a given instance, it will create a new alert logfile with the proper name.

# The Tuning Process

It is imperative to take a proactive approach to the Oracle tuning process. If a DBA waits until users complain about performance, it is usually too late to take advantage of some of the most effective tuning strategies. The later in the life cycle performance issues are identified and addressed, the more it costs in time and resources to resolve the problems. When unforeseen performance issues do arise, it is the responsibility of the DBA to pinpoint the cause of the problem as early—and to correct the situation as promptly—as possible.

Before you start any tuning process, you need to establish a set of quantifiable goals that directly relate to a reason for tuning. You should keep these goals in mind as you evaluate any modifications that you are considering for your system. Your tuning goals should be specific and measurable rather than generic. For example, a tuning goal for a catalog ordering system might be the ability to process 25,000 orders a day by the end of the month.

Before you attempt to tune the Oracle system, you should first ensure that the operating system is performing at its peak level. Work with your system administrator to take advantage of the operating system monitoring tools to check for paging and swapping. Paging occurs when a portion of a process is moved to secondary storage to accommodate large amounts of information that will not fit into real memory. Swapping occurs when the entire process must be moved to secondary storage due to real-memory constraints. Excessive paging or swapping at the operating system level can significantly degrade the performance of an Oracle system. You should also ensure that non-Oracle applications are not causing significant resource contention on your system.

It is best to approach tuning with a structured methodology. After ensuring that the operating system is performing at its peak and that sufficient operating system resources have been allocated to your Oracle system, Oracle recommends that you tune the following in this order:

1. Design

2. Application

3. Memory

4. I/O

5. Contention

## Tuning The Design

A properly designed system can dramatically reduce performance problems throughout the life cycle of an application. Spend enough time in the design phase to ensure that the application will operate at an acceptable (that is, optimal) level of performance.

The application designer should clearly understand the performance expectations of the system he or she is designing and must have a solid understanding of Oracle's query processing to design the database for optimal efficiency and minimal maintenance.

Careful consideration to tuning during the design phase gives you the maximum benefit at the lowest cost in the life cycle of the application. You need to avoid any possibility of needing to completely revamp the logical design of the database simply because performance is unacceptable and all other tuning options have been exhausted.

## Tuning The Application

Developers also play an important role in writing applications with effective SQL statements. They should utilize hints, indexes, and bind variables whenever necessary to obtain optimal performance. Do not underestimate the importance of application tuning. Many industry experts agree that as much as 80 percent of performance gains will be accomplished through application tuning.

The application developer should have a solid understanding of Oracle's SQL processing, including:

➤ DML (Data Manipulation Language)

➤ DDL (Data Definition Language)

➤ Transaction control

➤ Shared SQL and PL/SQL areas

➤ Optimizer modes

➤ Parallel query

It is important for developers to use as many PL/SQL packages as possible because PL/SQL packages are stored in parsed format. If necessary, the packages can be pinned in the shared pool to increase performance.

Database design and application design might not fall under the job description of the DBA in your organization. However, you need to understand the importance of proper initial design and, if necessary, be able to guide designers and developers to achieve this goal.

Proper education of Oracle designers, developers, and DBAs is the key to ensuring a solid foundation for a successful Oracle system. It is strongly recommended that all parties involved in the development and maintenance of an Oracle system have the proper training in the version of Oracle that is used for the application. Remember that, as a DBA, you can have a finely tuned instance that runs poorly if database design is improper or SQL statements are poorly written within the application.

## Tuning Memory

The DBA's primary tuning responsibility really begins once you have a well-designed model and a properly tuned application. The proper sizing of memory structures allows sufficient information to be stored in memory. Because memory access is significantly faster than disk access, it is always better to satisfy requests for information in memory rather than from disk. Tuning memory allocation involves proper memory distribution to each Oracle memory area while ensuring that paging and swapping is not occurring at the operating system level.

The system global area (SGA) is the memory area that holds the most commonly requested information about the database. When a database is started, the SGA is allocated, and the background processes are started. The combination of the SGA and the background processes is called an *instance*. The SGA is divided into three memory components:

➤ Buffer cache

➤ Shared pool

➤ Redo log buffers

By setting the database initialization file parameter **PRE_PAGE_SGA** to **YES**, Oracle will read the entire SGA into memory when you start the instance. Setting this parameter will most likely increase the amount of time required for instance startup, but it should decrease the amount of time required for Oracle to reach its full performance capacity after instance startup.

The buffer cache is the area of the SGA that stores copies of the data blocks that are read into memory from the physical database files. These data blocks include tables, clusters, rollback segments, and indexes. Each buffer holds a single Oracle data block. The size of the buffer cache, in bytes, is determined by multiplying the database initialization file parameter **DB_BLOCK_BUFFERS** by **DB_BLOCK_SIZE**. Once the database has been created, the size of the buffer cache can be altered only by changing the **DB_BLOCK_BUFFERS** parameter; the **DB_BLOCK_SIZE** parameter should never be modified unless the database is re-created. When the database buffer cache is properly sized, performance is optimized by satisfying the requests for data blocks from memory rather than disk.

The shared pool is an area of the SGA that contains two major memory areas: the library cache and the dictionary cache. The library cache consists of shared and private SQL areas, PL/SQL packages and procedures, and control structures. When there is insufficient memory in the library cache, no space will be available to cache new statements until old statements are removed to make room. Any statements that were removed but are needed again will need to be reparsed. Excessive reparsing is shown by large values for the **RELOADS** and **INVALIDATIONS** columns of the library cache statistics in the report.txt file. This reparsing procedure requires CPU and I/O resources. To avoid objects being unloaded and reloaded in the library cache, be sure that the value of **SHARED_POOL_SIZE** is large enough, and be sure to use functions, procedures, and packages whenever possible as they do not need to be parsed when they are loaded into the database. Objects can also be pinned in the library cache so they remain in memory until they are unpinned or the instance is shut down. In Oracle version 7.3 and later, database triggers do not need to be parsed because they are stored in compiled format. The library cache is sized only indirectly with the database initialization file parameter **SHARED_POOL_SIZE.**

The dictionary cache stores information about the database, its structures, and its users. Information in the dictionary cache includes segment names, users, privileges, and locations of extents. Before most operations can take place in the Oracle database, the data dictionary tables must be read; that data is then stored in the dictionary cache. As with the buffer cache and the library cache, the efficiency of the dictionary cache is determined by its hit ratio. The **V$ROWCACHE** view is useful in determining the hit ratio of the dictionary cache. The dictionary cache is sized only indirectly with the database initialization file parameter **SHARED_POOL_SIZE.**

If you are running in a multithreaded server (MTS) environment, user session information, such as private SQL and sort areas, is stored in the shared pool rather than in the memory of user processes. If you are using an MTS, you might need to make your shared pool larger to accommodate the extra memory requirements caused by moving some user session and sort information into the user global area (UGA). The size of the shared pool is determined by the database initialization file parameter **SHARED_POOL_SIZE.** The size of the library cache and dictionary cache is limited by the size of the shared pool.

The redo log buffer is an area of the SGA that records all changes made to the database. Information is periodically written from the redo log buffer to the online redo logfiles so that they can be applied in a roll-forward action if recovery is needed. The size of the redo log buffer, in bytes, is specified by the database initialization file parameter **LOG_BUFFER.**

# Tuning I/O

To obtain maximum performance on your system, I/O distribution is optimized by spreading the Oracle database files across multiple devices. Disk contention can occur when multiple processes try to access the same disk simultaneously. When the maximum number of accesses to a disk has been reached, other processes will need to wait for access to the disk.

The **V$FILESTAT** view provides information about datafile read and write statistics. **FILE#** can be used to join to the **V$DATAFILE** view to obtain the file name. Table 2.12 describes the columns in the **V$FILESTAT** view.

The sum of **PHYRDS** and **PHYWRTS** will give the total I/O for a given file. Excessive I/O on the **SYSTEM** tablespace might indicate that the shared pool is too small, causing excessive physical reads and writes to the data dictionary, which resides in the **SYSTEM** tablespace.

**Table 2.12    V$FILESTAT view.**

| Column | Description |
| --- | --- |
| FILE# | File number |
| PHYRDS | Number of physical reads performed |
| PHYWRTS | Number of physical writes performed |
| PHYBLKRD | Number of physical blocks read |
| PHYBLKWRT | Number of physical blocks written |
| READTIM | Time spent doing reads if the TIMED_STATISTICS parameter is TRUE; 0 if FALSE |
| WRITETIM | TIME spent doing writes if the TIMED_STATISTICS parameter is TRUE; 0 if FALSE |

Another cause of heavy I/O on the **SYSTEM** tablespace can result from a failure to specify a user's default tablespace. Make sure that the user's data segments are not written to the **SYSTEM** tablespace. If a user is created without a default tablespace assignment, the user's default tablespace will be the **SYSTEM** tablespace. Always assign a non-**SYSTEM** default tablespace to the user.

If sort segments are written to the **SYSTEM** tablespace, excessive I/O will result. If a user is created without a temporary tablespace assignment, the user will perform all sorts to disk in the **SYSTEM** tablespace. Always assign a non-**SYSTEM** temporary tablespace to the user.

 Report.txt and **V$FILESTAT** report I/O statistics for the Oracle database files only. If you are running non-Oracle applications on your system, you might want to utilize operating system utilities to track I/O for all files on the system.

# Tuning Contention

Contention occurs when a process competes with another process for the same resource simultaneously. This causes processes to wait for a resource on the Oracle system and can have an effect on performance.

Latch contention can occur for the library cache, buffer cache, and log buffer structures in the SGA. Latch contention is identified in report.txt. In addition, the **V$LATCH** view will provide information about each type of latch in your system. Table 2.13 provides a description of the **V$LATCH** columns.

Contention for rollback segments can also result in poor system performance. Rollback segments are used to store undo information for transactions and for rollback, read consistency, and recovery. Contention problems can occur when transactions experience waits for rollback segments. You must ensure that you have a sufficient number of rollback segments and that the segments are sized properly.

| Table 2.13    V$LATCH view. | |
| --- | --- |
| **Column** | **Description** |
| ADDR | Address of the latch object |
| LATCH# | Latch number |
| LEVEL# | Latch level |
| NAME | Latch name |
| GETS | Number of times obtained wait |
| MISSES | Number of times obtained wait but failed on first try |
| SLEEPS | Number of times slept when wanted wait |
| IMMEDIATE_GETS | Number of times obtained without wait |
| IMMEDIATE_MISSES | Number of times failed to get with no wait |
| WAITERS_WOKEN | Number of waiting processes posted |
| WAITS_HOLDING_LATCH | Number of waits that were holding latches |
| SPIN_GETS | Gets that missed on first try but succeeded on spin |
| SLEEP1 | Waits that slept 1 time |
| SLEEP2 | Waits that slept 2 times |
| SLEEP3 | Waits that slept 3 times |
| SLEEP4 | Waits that slept 4 times |
| SLEEP5 | Waits that slept 5 times |
| SLEEP6 | Waits that slept 6 times |
| SLEEP7 | Waits that slept 7 times |
| SLEEP8 | Waits that slept 8 times |
| SLEEP9 | Waits that slept 9 times |
| SLEEP10 | Waits that slept 10 times |
| SLEEP11 | Waits that slept 11 times |
| SLEEP12 | Waits that slept 12 times |

# Tuning For Application Environments

When tuning an Oracle system, it is important to keep in mind the different tuning goals for the various types of applications. The two primary application environments are online transaction processing (OLTP) and decision support systems (DSSs). A hybrid system is a combination of an OLTP system and a DSS system. With the multithreaded server (MTS) architecture, multiple users share a single server process. The MTS configuration helps to maximize server memory utilization and can be used in conjunction with an OLTP, DSS, or hybrid system.

## Online Transaction Processing Systems

An online transaction processing (OLTP) system is a high-activity system characterized by frequent insert and update transactions. An example of such a system might be a banking system that is accessed by a high number of concurrent users accessing data that is frequently updated. In an OLTP environment, you need to ensure that the potentially large number of users accessing the system simultaneously does not affect system performance. The goals of an OLTP system are availability, speed, concurrency, and recoverability.

Because OLTP systems store frequently changed data, it is important to make sure that your indexing strategy is as efficient as possible. Indexing is important because most of your requests for data will involve indexed retrievals rather than full table scans. However, you should avoid excessive indexing, which will affect performance during inserts, updates, and deletes. Indexes might need to be rebuilt regularly because of their frequent modifications.

Oracle recommends that you try to avoid dynamic space allocation in an OLTP system. To do this, you must be familiar with your data and its projected growth activity so that you can explicitly preallocate space to tables, clusters, and indexes. Preallocating extents will avoid the performance hit encountered when Oracle creates a new extent. In an OLTP system, you should also try to use bind variables whenever possible. By doing so, you can increase the amount of shared code and reduce parse time.

Rollback segments must be configured correctly for an OLTP system. Most transactions in this type of system are likely to be very short. You probably will have enough rollback segment space, but you need to make sure that you have enough rollback segments to prevent contention for rollback segment transaction tables. Oracle recommends that you set **MINEXTENTS** to 20, as the dynamic growth of rollback segments is as much of a performance degradation as dynamic growth of data segments. In an OLTP system, you will probably need more rollback segments that are generally smaller in size than those in other systems.

# Decision Support Systems

A decision support system (DSS) holds large volumes of data (usually historical) and is most frequently used for reporting purposes. Generally, decision support applications perform large queries on data that has been loaded from an OLTP system. Managers and other decision-makers typically use this information to make strategic business decisions. The goals of a decision support system are speed, accuracy, and availability.

Oracle's Parallel Query option is best utilized in DSSs in which large, intense queries (full table scans) are performed. Parallel Query is also useful when a large amount of data is being loaded or indexed, as is the case in most decision support systems.

Oracle recommends that you set **DB_BLOCK_SIZE** to the maximum value that your operating system will support. This is especially true for DSSs because this type of application system performs many full table scans.

Your usage of indexes should be minimal in a decision support system because most data is accessed using full-table scans. If you do use indexes in this type of system, you should use them selectively on a limited number of tables. Bitmapped indexes are especially useful in a DSS in which the column values are of low cardinality. Chapter 3 explains the usage of bitmapped indexes.

You will probably not need as many rollback segments in a DSS, but the segments will need to be larger to support batch transactions and read consistency.

# Hybrid Systems

A hybrid system is a multipurpose configuration that can combine an OLTP system and a DSS system. In most cases, data gathered by the OLTP system is fed into the DSS system. In this type of environment, both systems could use the same database, but the conflicting goals of the two systems could result in performance problems. To resolve this issue, Oracle recommends that an image of the OLTP database be copied into a second database to be used by the decision support application. Because the data may be copied to the DSS system only once a day, this configuration could possibly compromise the DSS's goal of accuracy. However, the resolution of performance issues might be worth the trade-off.

# Multithreaded Server

Oracle provides a multithreaded server (MTS) architecture to allow for environments in which the user load might exceed available memory. MTS allows multiple users to share a single connection process to the database. Generally, Oracle recommends that MTS not be used until the user load exceeds 150 concurrent users. However, many experts agree that MTS can improve performance on systems with limited memory with as few as 50 to 100 concurrent users.

In MTS environments, the DBA must configure the initial number and the maximum number of dispatcher and server processes for the instances. The configuration of MTS is accomplished using the MTS initialization parameters. Table 2.15 describes the major MTS parameters.

When using MTS, servers and dispatchers are automatically brought online to their preset maximum counts as needed to service the user load. However, if you find that you have underestimated the number of servers or dispatchers that you need, you can use the **ALTER SYSTEM** command to temporarily increase the values of **MTS_MAX_DISPATCHERS** and **MTS_MAX_SERVERS** until you can reset their values in the initialization file and reboot. If the values of **MTS_MAX_SERVERS** and **MTS_MAX_DISPATCHERS** are reset, Oracle will bring new dispatchers or servers online

**Table 2.15   The major MTS initialization parameters.**

| Parameter | Example Setpoint | Description |
| --- | --- | --- |
| mts_dispatchers | "TCP, 10" | Sets up minimum number of dispatchers for the specified protocol |
| mts_max_dispatchers | 20 | Sets maximum number of dispatchers for all protocols |
| mts_servers | 10 | Sets minimum number of servers |
| mts_max_servers | 300 | Sets maximum number of servers |
| mts_service | ORCNETP1 | Names service; usually the same as SID |
| mts_listener_address | "(ADDRESS=(PROTOCOL=TCP) (HOST=90.11.244.157) (PORT=1521))" | Sets address information for listeners; one address set per protocol required |

as needed to service new user connections. It should be obvious that the basis for determining how many shared servers will be needed on your system depends solely on the expected number of concurrent processes.

Several files must be configured on your system for MTS to work properly. We have already discussed the initialization file parameters, but two other key files must be set up: tnsnames.ora and listener.ora. The tnsnames.ora file must be set up with the proper instance names and address data for your system because MTS uses SQL*Net for access control. The listener.ora file must contain the proper addresses, which must match the entries for the **MTS_LISTENER_ADDRESS** parameters in the initialization file. If the address values in the initialization file for MTS do not match the entries in the listener.ora file, users will receive dedicated rather than shared connections.

One note of caution about MTS. Because it forces some sorting activity to be done in the shared pool area (specifically, the UGA section that is added for MTS systems), you will need to increase the shared pool to accommodate the additional memory requirements for MTS systems.

# Practice Questions

## Question 1

> You have run the UTLBSTAT/UTLESTAT utility, and report.txt shows a latch hit ratio of 0.99. What does this value indicate about latch activity for the database?
>
> ○ a. Latch contention is high
>
> ○ b. Latch contention is at normal levels
>
> ○ c. The value is not accurate, and report.txt should be regenerated

The correct answer is b. The latch hit ratio for this database is 99 percent, which is an acceptable level. Your goal for the latch contention hit ratio should be at least 98 percent. Anything less could indicate potential latch contention problems.

## Question 2

> A mail order system has a DML-intensive order entry system. Which type of system is this?
>
> ○ a. Data warehouse
>
> ○ b. DSS
>
> ○ c. Hybrid
>
> ○ d. OLTP

The correct answer is d. A characteristic of an OLTP system is that it performs frequent DML operations, such as **INSERT, UPDATE**, and **DELETE**. A DSS system stores large volumes of data that is most frequently used for reporting (**SELECT**) purposes. A hybrid system is a combination of an OLTP and a DSS system.

## Question 3

To which value should you set the Oracle block size when creating a database?

- ○ a. 2K
- ○ b. 4K
- ○ c. 32K
- ○ d. Maximum value allowed by the operating system

The correct answer is d. Oracle recommends that you set your block size to the maximum value allowed by the operating system. This is especially true for decision support systems (DSSs), which perform frequent full table scans.

## Question 4

The inventory application was installed two years ago, and datafiles were striped evenly across the file system. Many datafiles have since been added, and they were placed wherever space was available. You are analyzing the database and see that the new datafiles are not evenly placed. Which area should you consider tuning because of this condition?

- ○ a. Application
- ○ b. Memory
- ○ c. I/O
- ○ d. Contention
- ○ e. Design

The correct answer is c. Proper distribution of I/O can dramatically improve database performance. Once you have determined the current I/O distribution using **V$FILESTAT** or the I/O statistics from report.txt, consult your hardware documentation to determine the capacity limits of your disks. You might need to move one or more heavily accessed files to a less active disk. You should continue this process until you have an even distribution of I/O on all disks.

## Question 5

Which statistics are obtained when UTLBSTAT.SQL is executed?

○ a. Beginning database statistics for that point in time

○ b. Ending database statistics for that point in time

○ c. Beginning database statistics at startup

○ d. Ending database statistics at startup

The correct answer is a. The letter *b* in UTLBSTAT indicates *beginning* statistics, and the letter *e* in UTLESTAT indicates *ending* statistics. UTLBSTAT creates and populates a set of tables with database statistics beginning at the time that UTLBSTAT was submitted. Database statistics are continually gathered until UTLESTAT is submitted, at which time the gathering of these statistics is halted and the report.txt file generated.

## Question 6

In which file can you find information about database events?

○ a. event.log

○ b. alert.log

○ c. alert.trc

○ d. error.log

The correct answer is b. The alert logfile stores information about all major database events within the database. It is located in the destination specified in the **BACKGROUND_DUMP_DEST** parameter of the database initialization file. The event.log, alert.trc, and error.log files are not default files within the Oracle system.

# Question 7

Performance has degraded significantly on your system, and you
discover that paging and swapping is occurring. What is the probable cause of this problem?

○ a. The SGA is too small

○ b. The PGA is too large

○ c. The SGA is too large

○ d. The PGA is too small

The correct answer is c. If paging and swapping is occurring on the system, the
SGA might be too large. This could cause the operating system to temporarily
swap all or portions of the SGA out of main memory to satisfy other memory
requirements.

# Question 8

Which component of Oracle7 protects access to internal structures?

○ a. Transaction locking

○ b. Latches

○ c. Locks

○ d. Roles

○ e. Privileges

The correct answer is b. Latches protect access to internal structures, such as
the library cache, buffer cache, and log buffer. When a process needs to make a
change to one of these structures, it must first acquire a latch.

## Question 9

> Which type of system uses a combination of OLTP and DSS for the same instance?
>
> ○ a. OLTP
>
> ○ b. DSS
>
> ○ c. Client server
>
> ○ d. Hybrid

The correct answer is d. A hybrid system is a combination of an online transaction processing (OLTP) system and a decision support system (DSS), and might require special configurations to meet the performance needs of both types of systems.

## Question 10

> What should your goal be when tuning I/O?
>
> ○ a. To distribute I/O as much as possible
>
> ○ b. To keep Oracle I/O limited to one area of the system
>
> ○ c. To not place any non-Oracle files on the system
>
> ○ d. To reduce writes as much as possible

The correct answer is a. Use the **V$FILESTAT** view to identify file I/O distribution since instance startup. Use the UTLBSTAT and UTLESTAT scripts to check for file I/O distribution during a specific period of time.

# Need To Know More?

 The first place to go for more information is the *Oracle7 Tuning Manual* and the *Oracle7 Server Reference Manual*.

 RevealNet Corporation provides Oracle Administration, a superior software reference tool for Oracle database administration. RevealNet's Web address is www.revealnet.com.

 Aronoff, Eyal, Kevin Loney, and Noorali Sonawalla: *Advanced Oracle Tuning and Administration*. Oracle Press, 1997. ISBN 0-07882-241-6.

 Corey, Michael, Michael Abbey, and Daniel J. Dechichio: *Tuning Oracle*. Oracle Press. 1995. ISBN 0-07881-181-3.

 Corrigan, Peter and Mark Gurry: *Oracle Performance Tuning*. O'Reilly & Associates, Inc., 1993. ISBN 1-56592-048-1.

# Tuning Applications

### Terms you'll need to understand:

√ EXPLAIN PLAN

√ Autotrace

√ SQL Trace

√ TKPROF

√ DBMS_APPLICATION_INFO

√ Optimizer

√ Hints

### Techniques you'll need to master:

√ Creating the PLAN_TABLE and using EXPLAIN PLAN

√ Using SQL Trace and TKPROF

√ Understanding the basics of the DBMS_APPLICATION_INFO package

√ Understanding how to use indexes

√ Using the optimizer and hints

Your biggest return in the area of increasing performance is tuning your application code. Before you begin tuning the Oracle database, you should tune your applications. Regardless of how well you tune your database, poorly written SQL statements will result in poor performance. This chapter explains how to use autotrace, **EXPLAIN PLAN**, SQL Trace, and TKPROF for tuning your SQL statements. This will lead to a discussion of how indexes can be used to increase the performance of your SQL or can result in very poor performance. The chapter concludes with a discussion of using the optimizer and hints to tune your applications further.

# Statement Tuning

Tuning every SQL statement in the application is unrealistic. You need to identify and tune individual SQL statements that are creating problems. Before tuning these statements, you need to understand how Oracle is executing your SQL. Oracle provides several utilities to help you understand the methods it is using to execute your code. Once you know how Oracle is executing your SQL statements, you can look at rewriting the code to improve performance.

The following are some of the most common problems encountered in poorly performing SQL statements:

➤ The optimizer is unable to use an index

➤ The use of a **CONNECT BY** without an index on the **CONNECT BY** and **START WITH** columns

➤ The **GROUP** functions, especially with the use of the **HAVING** clause

➤ The use of a complex view

➤ The use of the **DISTINCT** keyword that causes sorting

➤ The queries that are written differently and do not take advantage of bind variables

The first step to performance tuning the application is to determine the SQL statement or statements that are using the most resources and resulting in the slowest response time. The second step is to obtain information on the execution plan that Oracle is using for the SQL statement and statistical information on the resources used by the SQL statement. **EXPLAIN PLAN** is used to obtain the execution plan. SQL Trace creates a trace file of statistical and performance information that is then formatted with TKPROF.

# EXPLAIN PLAN

**EXPLAIN PLAN** is a command that provides information on how the Oracle database is optimizing and executing your SQL statements. A row for each step in the execution plan is placed into a user-specified table or into the **PLAN_TABLE**. To use **EXPLAIN PLAN**, you must create the **PLAN_TABLE** or a table with the equivalent columns. The **PLAN_TABLE** is created by running the utlxplan.sql script located in the $ORACLE_HOME/rdbms/admin directory (the name of this script can vary, depending on the operating system). Table 3.1 shows the columns in the **PLAN_TABLE**.

To populate the **PLAN_TABLE** with the steps of the execution plan, you must execute the syntax shown in Figure 3.1.

The **SET STATEMENT_ID** specifies the statement ID you want for that execution plan in the **PLAN_TABLE**. The use of a statement ID allows several

| Table 3.1 | Description of the PLAN_TABLE. |
|---|---|
| **Column** | **Definition** |
| statement_id | The identifier assigned at the time the EXPLAIN PLAN statement is issued (optional) |
| timestamp | The date and time that the EXPLAIN PLAN statement was issued |
| remarks | Comments that can be added to the EXPLAIN PLAN by the user |
| operation | The actual operation performed at this step |
| options | Options used for the execution of the statement |
| object_node | Database link used, if any |
| object_owner | Owner of the object referenced |
| object_name | Name of the object referenced |
| object_instance | Position of the object in the SQL statement |
| object_type | Description of the type of object referenced |
| search_columns | Not currently used but might be in the future |
| id | The ID number assigned by Oracle to this step in the plan |
| parent_id | The parent statement for this step of the execution plan |
| position | The order in which this step was performed (If the cost-based optimizer is being used, this value in the first line of the plan represents the cost assigned to this statement; if the rule-based optimizer is being used, this value will be null in the first line of the plan) |
| other | Additional information on this step |

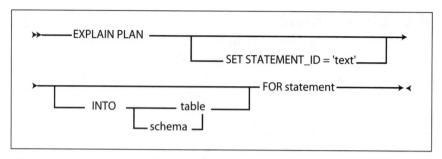

**Figure 3.1** The syntax for the **EXPLAIN PLAN** command.

statements to be placed into the same **PLAN_TABLE**. The **INTO** clause allows you to place the information into a table other than the **PLAN_TABLE**. If no other table is specified with the **INTO** clause, Oracle will assume that the information should be placed in the **PLAN_TABLE**. The statement following the **FOR** keyword is the statement for which you would like to have Oracle generate an execution plan.

The **EXPLAIN PLAN** command does not actually execute the statement. This is helpful when you want to obtain information on a long-running SQL statement and do not want to wait for the statement to execute. To use **EXPLAIN PLAN**, follow these steps:

1. Execute the statement to fill in the **PLAN_TABLE**:

```
EXPLAIN PLAN SET STATEMENT_ID = 'EMPLOYEE_STATE'
FOR
SELECT LAST_NAME, FIRST_NAME, STATE.NAME
FROM EMPLOYEE, STATE
WHERE EMPLOYEE.STATE_CODE = STATE.CODE
AND STATE.CODE = 'VA';
```

2. Execute a query against the **PLAN_TABLE** to obtain the execution plan:

```
select    id, parent_id,
lpad(' ',2*level)||operation  access_plan,
 options, object_name
       from PLAN_TABLE where statement_id = 'EMPLOYEE_STATE'
       connect by prior id = parent_id start with id = 0;
```

3. Review the optimization plan. Table 3.2 shows the resulting optimization plan.

4. Create an index on the **state_code** in the employee table:

```
Create index employee_state on employee(state_code);
```

**Table 3.2     The initial optimization plan.**

| ID | PARENT _ID | ACCESS _PLAN | Options | OBJECT _NAME |
|----|-----------|--------------|---------|--------------|
| 0 |   | SELECT STATEMENT |   |   |
| 1 | 0 | MERGE JOIN |   |   |
| 2 | 1 | SORT |   | JOIN |
| 3 | 2 | TABLE ACCESS | FULL | STATE |
| 4 | 1 | SORT |   | JOIN |
| 5 | 4 | TABLE ACCESS | FULL | EMPLOYEE |

5. Truncate the **PLAN_TABLE** or delete the rows related to that access plan:

```
Truncate table PLAN_TABLE;
Delete from PLAN_TABLE where statement_id = 'EMPLOYEE_STATE';
```

*Note: You can also use a different statement ID for the second execution plan.*

6. Execute the statement to fill in the **PLAN_TABLE** with the new execution plan:

```
EXPLAIN PLAN SET STATEMENT_ID = 'EMPLOYEE_STATE'
FOR
SELECT LAST_NAME, FIRST_NAME, STATE.NAME
FROM EMPLOYEE, STATE
WHERE EMPLOYEE.STATE_CODE = STATE.CODE
    AND STATE.CODE = 'VA';
```

7. Execute a query against the **PLAN_TABLE** to obtain the new execution plan:

```
select    id, parent_id,
lpad(' ',2*level)||operation  access_plan,
   options, object_name
     from PLAN_TABLE where statement_id = 'EMPLOYEE_STATE'
     connect by prior id = parent_id start with id = 0;
```

8. Review the new optimization plan. Table 3.3 shows the new optimization plan.

| ID | PARENT _ID | ACCESS _PLAN | Options | OBJECT _NAME |
|----|-----------|--------------|---------|--------------|
| Table 3.3 | New optimization plan. | | | |
| 0 | | SELECT STATEMENT | | |
| 1 | 0 | NESTED LOOPS | | |
| 2 | 1 | TABLE ACCESS | FULL | STATE |
| 3 | 1 | TABLE ACCESS | BY ROWID | EMPLOYEE |
| 4 | 3 | INDEX | RANGE SCAN | EMPLOYEE_STATE |

The **PLAN_TABLE** is always read from the bottom up and inside out. The second execution plan is performing actions in the following order:

➤ An index range scan using the employee_state index

➤ A table access by rowid of the employee table

➤ A full table scan of the state table

➤ A nested loop operation

➤ The **SELECT** statement

The two different explain plans demonstrate the results of adding an index on a column that is used to join two tables (a foreign key column). The initial query included two full table scans and a sort/merge join. After the index is added, a range scan on the index allowed rowid access on the employee table, reduced the full table scans to one, and used a nested loop access instead of a sort/merge join. Nested loops are much faster than sort/merge joins. In addition, if the employee table is very large, a full table scan should be avoided. The changes in the access path should improve performance for this SQL statement.

## Autotrace

Another way to obtain and display information on the execution plan generated for SQL statements is to use **SET AUTOTRACE ON** within SQL*Plus. Autotrace will place information on the execution plan steps into the **PLAN_TABLE** after execution of each statement. After each SQL statement is executed, information from the **PLAN_TABLE** is displayed along with statistical information on the statement executed. The information in the **PLAN_TABLE** is then deleted.

The advantages to using autotrace are that:

➤ The **PLAN_TABLE** is cleaned up after the information is displayed

➤ The information is displayed automatically

The disadvantage to using autotrace is that it will execute each statement before displaying the information. Listing 3.1 provides an example of using the autotrace utility. After you have completed your performance tuning and use of the autotrace utility, you can turn autotrace off with **SET AUTOTRACE OFF**. If you fail to turn autotrace off, it will remain in effect until you exit and end your session.

## Listing 3.1    Example of using autotrace.

```
set autotrace on;

SELECT LAST_NAME, FIRST_NAME, STATE.NAME  STATE
FROM SCOTT.EMPLOYEE, SCOTT.STATE
WHERE EMPLOYEE.STATE_CODE = STATE.CODE
AND STATE.CODE = 'VA';


LAST_NAME                FIRST_NAME             STATE
------------------       --------------------   --------------------

CANE                     JOHN                   Virginia
ROLLAND                  BILL                   Virginia
CLINTON                  JAKE                   Virginia
ANDERSON                 WAYNE                  Virginia


Execution Plan
----------------------------------------------------------------
   0       SELECT STATEMENT Optimizer=CHOOSE (Cost=2 Card=2
                                              Bytes=84)
   1    0    NESTED LOOPS (Cost=2 Card=2 Bytes=84)
   2    1      TABLE ACCESS (FULL) OF 'STATE' (Cost=1 Card=1
                                              Bytes=15)
   3    1      TABLE ACCESS (BY ROWID) OF 'EMPLOYEE'
   4    3        INDEX (RANGE SCAN) OF 'EMPLOYEE_STATE' (NON-UNIQUE)

Statistics
----------------------------------------------------------------
          0  recursive calls
          2  db block gets
          7  consistent gets
          0  physical reads
          0  redo size
```

```
347  bytes sent via SQL*Net to client
406  bytes received via SQL*Net from client
  3  SQL*Net roundtrips to/from client
  0  sorts (memory)
  0  sorts (disk)
  4  rows processed
```

```
set autotrace off;
```

# SQL Trace And TKPROF

SQL Trace is used to generate statistics into a trace file, which is then format-ted using TKPROF. SQL Trace can be used to identify SQL statements that are consuming the most resources, that are consuming the most resources per row, and that are executing the most often. To use SQL Trace, you must first set **TIMED_STATISTICS=TRUE** in your database initialization parameter file and enable SQL tracing. The default for **TIMED_STATISTICS** is **FALSE**. This parameter can be changed dynamically with an **ALTER SYS-TEM SET TIMED_STATISTICS=TRUE**. Statistics will be timed to 1/100th of a second. SQL Trace will use the **MAX_DUMP_FILE_SIZE** (de-fault 500 blocks) and the **USER_DUMP_DEST** parameters from the database parameter file. These parameters set the maximum size and the location of the trace file.

SQL Trace can be performed for an instance or for a session. Because tracing will affect performance, you should set tracing at the session level. To perform SQL Trace for an instance, you must set **SQL_TRACE=TRUE** in the data-base initialization parameter file. Setting SQL Trace at the instance level enables tracing for all users. To enable tracing for a session, you can execute the **DBMS_SESSION.SET_SQL_TRACE** package or use the **ALTER SES-SION** command.

You can use either of the following commands to enable session-level tracing

```
ALTER SESSION SET SQL_TRACE=TRUE;
```

or:

```
EXECUTE SYS.DBMS_SESSION.SET_SQL_TRACE(TRUE);
```

You can disable tracing for a session by exiting SQL*Plus, or you can use either of the following commands

```
ALTER SESSION SET SQL_TRACE=FALSE;
```

or:

```
EXECUTE SYS.DBMS_SESSION.SET_SQL_TRACE(FALSE);
```

You can use the **DBMS_SYSTEM.SET_SQL_TRACE_IN_SESSION** to start tracing for another user's session. This requires the session ID (the value of the **SID** column in the **V$SESSION** table), the serial ID (the **SERIAL#** column in the **V$SESSION** table), and either **TRUE** or **FALSE**. The following is an example of the code that can be used to obtain information on another user's session:

```
BEGIN
     SYS.DBMS_SYSTEM.SET_SQL_TRACE_IN_SESSION(10,2345,TRUE);
END
```

After the user has completed executing the SQL statements, you should set **SQL_TRACE** to **FALSE** for that user. The following example shows how to turn off SQL Trace for another user:

```
BEGIN
     SYS.DBMS_SYSTEM.SET_SQL_TRACE_IN_SESSION(10,2345,FALSE);
END
```

TKPROF is used to generate a readable report on the basis of the statistical information gathered with SQL Trace.

The following process is used to obtain performance data using SQL Trace and TKPROF:

1. Set the **TIMED_STATISTICS=TRUE** initialization parameter

2. Turn on SQL Trace

3. Execute the application SQL statements

4. Turn off SQL Trace

5. Execute TKPROF to format the trace information

6. Review the results

The statistical information provided by the TKPROF report is listed in Table 3.4. Statistical information is provided for the following stages:

➤ Parse

➤ Execute

➤ Fetch

**Table 3.4    Statistical information provided by TKPROF.**

| Column | Definition |
|---|---|
| count | Number of times the statement was parsed or executed; the number of fetch calls issued |
| CPU | Total CPU used in seconds; if found in the shared pool, this is 0 |
| elapsed | Total seconds in elapsed time |
| disk | Total physical data blocks read from database files; if the blocks are buffered, this will be very low |
| query | Total number of logical buffers retrieved in consistent mode; usually used for SELECT statements |
| current | Total number of logical buffers retrieved in current mode; usually used for DML statements |
| rows | Total number of rows processed, excluding rows processed by a subquery; this is in the fetch phase for SELECT statements and in the execute phase for DML statements |

The TKPROF command is executed at the command line, not within SQL*Plus. The syntax for this command is:

```
tkprof   infile=filename   outfile=filename   [sort=option (,option)]
      [print=integer]   [explain=user/password]
[table=schema.tablename]
      [sys=NO]   [record=filename]   [insert=filename]
```

INFILE is the name of the trace file on which the TKPROF utility will be executed. OUTFILE is the name of the file into which the report will be placed. The SORT option allows the information to be sorted by the options specified by the user before being placed into the OUTFILE. Table 3.5 lists the options that can be used for sorting the SQL trace file. The PRINT option allows the user to limit the number of SQL statements to include in the file. If the PRINT option is omitted, all SQL statements are included. The EXPLAIN option executes an EXPLAIN PLAN for statements issued by the specified user. The TABLE option allows you to specify a table for use by TKPROF. If you specify a TABLE but do not use EXPLAIN, TKPROF will ignore this option. SYS=NO will ignore recursive SQL statements executed as SYS. The RECORD option will record nonrecursive statements into the trace file for use later in replaying the recorded events. The INSERT option creates a SQL script that can be executed to create a table and insert statistics into that table for each SQL statement traced.

| Table 3.5 | Sort options for TKPROF. |
|-----------|--------------------------|
| **Option** | **Definition** |
| PRSCNT | Number of times parsed |
| PRSCPU | CPU time spent parsing |
| PRSELA | Elapsed time spent parsing |
| PRSDSK | Number of physical reads from disk during parse |
| PRSQRY | Number of consistent mode block reads during parse |
| PRSCU | Number of current mode block reads during parse |
| PRSMIS | Number of library cache misses during parse |
| EXECNT | Number of executes |
| EXECPU | CPU time spent executing |
| EXEELA | Elapsed time spent executing |
| EXEDSK | Number of physical reads from disk during execute |
| EXEQRY | Number of consistent mode block reads during execute |
| EXECU | Number of current mode block reads during execute |
| EXEROW | Number of rows processed during execute |
| EXEMIS | Number of library cache misses during execute |
| FCHCNT | Number of fetches |
| FCHCPU | CPU time spent fetching |
| FCHELA | Elapsed time spent fetching |
| FCHDSK | Number of physical reads from disk during fetch |
| FCHQRY | Number of consistent mode block reads during fetch |
| FCHCU | Number of current mode block reads during fetch |
| FCHROW | Number of rows fetched |

Listing 3.2 is an example of output from TKPROF using the following command:

```
tkprof ifile=ora_100334.trc outfile=tkprof_rpt explain=scott/tiger
```

Note that this command does not include **SYS=NO**, which would ignore the recursive SQL statements. In addition, no table was given for use in obtaining the optimizer plan. When no table is specified, TKPROF will create a table named **PROF$PLAN_TABLE**, use this table for the optimizer plan information, and then drop this table. You should also remember that the **EXPLAIN**

**PLAN** results are obtained when the TKPROF utility is executed. If any changes have been made to the objects, such as adding an index, the optimizer access plan might use the new index and might not reflect the plan that was used during the SQL Trace. Therefore, if you want to include the optimizer plan, you should execute the TKPROF utility immediately after you have finished gathering your SQL Trace statistics.

## Listing 3.2    Example of output from a TKPROF report.

```
TKPROF: Release 7.3.3.0.0 - Production on Fri May 22 15:38:04 1998
Copyright (c) Oracle Corporation 1979, 1996.  All rights reserved.
Trace file: ora_100334.trc
Sort options: default
*********************************************************************
count    = number of times OCI procedure was executed
cpu      = cpu time in seconds executing
elapsed  = elapsed time in seconds executing
disk     = number of physical reads of buffers from disk
query    = number of buffers gotten for consistent read
current  = number of buffers gotten in current mode (usually for
                                                       update)
rows     = number of rows processed by the fetch or execute call
*********************************************************************
alter session set sql_trace=true
call    count    cpu     elapsed    disk    query    current    rows
Parse      0     0.00      0.00       0        0         0         0
Execute    1     0.02      0.06       0        0         0         0
Fetch      0     0.00      0.00       0        0         0         0
-------------------------------------------------------------------
total      1     0.02      0.06       0        0         0         0
Misses in library cache during parse: 0
Misses in library cache during execute: 1
Optimizer goal: CHOOSE
Parsing user id: 48  (SCOTT)
*********************************************************************
SELECT LAST_NAME, FIRST_NAME, STATE.NAME
FROM EMPLOYEE, STATE
WHERE EMPLOYEE.STATE_CODE = STATE.CODE
AND STATE.CODE = 'VA'

call    count    cpu     elapsed    disk    query    current    rows
Parse      7     0.02      0.06       0        0         0         0
Execute    7     0.00      0.00       0        0         0         0
Fetch      7     0.00      0.00       0       49        14        28
-------------------------------------------------------------------
total     21     0.02      0.06       0       49        14        28
```

```
Misses in library cache during parse: 1
Optimizer goal: CHOOSE
Parsing user id: 48  (SCOTT)
 Rows   Execution Plan
------   -----------------------------------------------------
    0    SELECT STATEMENT   GOAL: CHOOSE
    4    NESTED LOOPS
   51    TABLE ACCESS   GOAL: ANALYZED (FULL) OF 'STATE'
    4    TABLE ACCESS   GOAL: ANALYZED (BY ROWID) OF 'EMPLOYEE'
    5    INDEX   GOAL: ANALYZED (RANGE SCAN) OF 'EMPLOYEE_STATE'
             (NON-UNIQUE)
**********************************************************************
select  *  from  state
call       count    cpu    elapsed    disk    query    current   rows
Parse        1     0.00     0.00       0        0         0        0
Execute      1     0.00     0.00       0        0         0        0
Fetch        4     0.01     0.01       0        4         2       51
------------------------------------------------------------------
total        6     0.01     0.01       0        4         2       51
Misses in library cache during parse: 1
Optimizer goal: CHOOSE
Parsing user id: 48  (SCOTT)
 Rows   Execution Plan
-----   -----------------------------------------------------
    0    SELECT STATEMENT   GOAL: CHOOSE
   51    TABLE ACCESS   GOAL: ANALYZED (FULL) OF 'STATE'
**********************************************************************
alter session set sql_trace=false
call       count    cpu    elapsed    disk    query    current   rows
Parse        1     0.00     0.00       0        0         0        0
Execute      1     0.00     0.00       0        0         0        0
Fetch        0     0.00     0.00       0        0         0        0
------------------------------------------------------------------
total        2     0.00     0.00       0        0         0        0
Misses in library cache during parse: 1
Optimizer goal: CHOOSE
Parsing user id: 48  (SCOTT)
**********************************************************************
OVERALL TOTALS FOR ALL NON-RECURSIVE STATEMENTS
call       count    cpu    elapsed    disk    query    current   rows
Parse       13     0.03     0.08       0        0         0        0
Execute     14     0.02     0.06       0        0         0        0
Fetch       15     0.02     0.02       0       63        20       91
------------------------------------------------------------------
total       42     0.07     0.16       0       63        20       91
Misses in library cache during parse: 4
```

```
Misses in library cache during execute: 1
OVERALL TOTALS FOR ALL RECURSIVE STATEMENTS
call       count      cpu     elapsed    disk    query    current    rows
Parse          0     0.00      0.00         0        0          0       0
Execute        0     0.00      0.00         0        0          0       0
Fetch          0     0.00      0.00         0        0          0       0
-------------------------------------------------------------------------
total          0     0.00      0.00         0        0          0       0
Misses in library cache during parse: 0
    14   user  SQL statements in session.
     0   internal SQL statements in session.
    14   SQL statements in session.
 3   statements explained in this session.
*************************************************************************
Trace file: ora_100334.trc
Trace file compatibility: 7.03.02
Sort options: default
     1   session in trace file.
    14   user  SQL statements in trace file.
     0   internal SQL statements in trace file.
    14   SQL statements in trace file.
     /   unique SQL statements in trace file.
 3   SQL statements explained using schema:
         SCOTT.prof$PLAN_TABLE
           Default table was used.
           Table was created.
           Table was dropped.
   183   lines in trace file.
```

# DBMS_APPLICATION_INFO Package

You can track performance and resource usage for application modules with the **DBMS_APPLICATION_INFO** package. To use this package, you need to execute the dbmsutil.sql script. This script is called by the catproc.sql script, which is usually executed when the database is created. The application module that is to be tracked must register with the database, after which the performance and use of resources can be tracked.

**DBMS_APPLICATION_INFO** contains the following procedures:

➤ **SET_MODULE** (module, action)

➤ **SET_ACTION** (action)

➤ **SET_CLIENT_INFO** (client)

➤ READ_MODULE (module, action)

➤ READ_CLIENT_INFO (action)

The **SET_MODULE** procedure is used to set the name of the module and to store this information in the **V$SQLAREA**. The **SET_MODULE** can also be used to set the action instead of using the **SET_ACTION** procedure. You should call this procedure when the module starts.

The **SET_ACTION** procedure should be called before each new transaction to set the name of the current action to be traced and to store this information in the **V$SQLAREA**. After the procedure executes, **SET_ACTION** should be set to null.

The **SET_CLIENT_INFO** sets the client information. This additional information is stored in **V$SESSION**.

The **READ_MODULE** and **READ_CLIENT_INFO** procedures read information from **V$SESSION** and **V$SQLAREA**. The **READ_MODULE** reads the **SET_ACTION** and **SET_MODULE** information. The **READ_CLIENT_INFO** is used to read the last client information for the session.

# Indexes

The use of indexes can improve performance or drastically increase the time necessary for a SQL statement to execute. The correct use of indexes will allow the optimizer to choose an efficient path and avoid unnecessary full table scans. An index scan will retrieve data on the basis of the value in one or more indexed columns. The index stores the value of the column or columns specified for the index and the rowid for a row in the table. A full table scan will search every row of the table.

A composite index is one that consists of more than one column. The order of the columns in the index is very important. If a column in the **WHERE** clause references the first column in the index, it will be able to use that index. If a column in the **WHERE** clause references only the column in the second position in the index, that index cannot be used. If the **WHERE** clause references columns at the beginning of the index, it is said to reference the leading edge of the index. Composite indexes should be considered when two or more columns are frequently used together in the **WHERE** clause. The first column in the composite index should be the column most frequently referenced in the **WHERE** clause. If all the columns are equally used, consider ordering the columns from the most selective to the least selective.

# Index Usage

The type of work that end users are performing is a key element in determining when to create an index. For applications that are insert-, update-, and delete-intensive, indexes add additional overhead by requiring values to be added and/or changed in the index as well as the table. For applications that are highly query-intensive, more indexes are usually required. Many data warehouses are very query-intensive during the day and updated with large batch jobs at night. In this hybrid situation, it might be advisable to drop the indexes before executing the batch job and to re-create the indexes after the batch job completes.

When there is no index on a table, Oracle must read every row of the table to determine which rows meet the requirements of the SQL statement. In some cases, a full table scan is the best way to access a table. A full table scan is preferable in the following situations:

➤ When tables are small and have very few values

➤ When SQL statements will change or fetch a large portion of the rows

An index scan is preferable in the following situations:

➤ When selected rows are uniformly located throughout the blocks associated with the table and the number of rows to be selected is less than four percent

➤ When selected rows are randomly located throughout the blocks associated with the table and the number of rows to be selected is less than 25 percent

Even if an index is created on a column or columns, the optimizer might not use it. This might be because of the way the SQL statement is written or because the optimizer has determined that the index should not be used. The following conditions will cause the index to be ignored:

➤ Columns in the **WHERE** clause are selected from the same table for both sides of the qualifier in the **WHERE** clause

➤ The **IS NULL** or **IS NOT NULL** qualifier is used in the **WHERE** clause

➤ The **NOT IN** or != qualifier is used in the **WHERE** clause

➤ The **LIKE** qualifier is used in the **WHERE** clause with a pattern match for the initial character (for example, '%pattern')

➤ The **NOT EXISTS** subquery is used

➤ The index column is modified in some way by a function in the **WHERE** clause

➤ The **WHERE** clause is based on a nonindexed column or a column that is not the leading edge of an index

When trying to decide which columns should be indexed, you should consider how the columns are used. Columns used within queries in the following ways are good candidate columns to be indexed:

➤ Column(s) are used in a **WHERE** clause (especially equality queries)

➤ Column(s) are often used to join tables

➤ Column(s) are not frequently modified

➤ Column(s) are used for referential integrity constraint enforcement

# Types Of Indexes

Several types of indexes can be created on columns and tables. The types of indexes are:

➤ Unique

➤ Nonunique

➤ Bitmapped

➤ Hashkey

When you create a unique or primary key constraint on a column or columns, a unique index is generated to ensure uniqueness. There is no need to create a separate unique index for columns already used in a unique or a primary key constraint. If you have already created a unique index and later alter the table to add a unique or primary key constraint, the unique index will be used by the unique or primary key constraint if an exact match exists. The referenced columns must be the same and must be in the same order. Rather than creating unique indexes, you should consider creating unique or primary constraints for the indexed column or columns.

A nonunique index is an index created on a column or columns that can have multiple rows with the same values.

Both unique and nonunique indexes are usually stored using a B-tree index. Over time, the addition and deletion of data can fragment the B-tree index. The index will grow in width, and SQL code using the index will degrade in performance. Dropping and re-creating or rebuilding the index will resolve this problem.

Bitmapped indexes are often used for a decision support system (DSS) environment or for data warehouses. They work best on large tables with values of low cardinality for the bitmapped columns. When bitmapped indexes are used properly, they result in excellent performance and an indexing scheme that requires much less storage space than the traditional B-tree index structure. A bitmap is created for each value with an entry for each row. Bitmapped indexes are especially useful when used in conjunction with other bitmapped indexes. Bitmapped indexes do not work well for columns in which additional values can be used or the values are updated often. Table 3.6 provides an example of using a bitmapped index.

Hashkey indexes can be used for a single table or for clustering two tables. For more information on clustering two tables, see Chapter 4. In order to use a hashkey index, a column or columns in the table must be designated as the key value. A hash function is applied to the specified key value to determine the hash value. The hash value is then used to determine the location of the row in the table.

## Turning Off Index Usage

In some cases, an individual query will execute faster if the index is not used. You can turn the use of the index off for that individual query in several ways. The **WHERE** clause can be altered to invalidate the use of the index by changing the indexed column referenced in the **WHERE** clause. You can concatenate a null string (two single quotes) to a **varchar** column, add zero to a number column, use a function on the column, or use a hint (discussed later in this chapter). When you are tuning your database for performance, you need to

| Table 3.6 | Example of using a bitmapped index. |
|---|---|
| **EMAIL Column** | **Y=has an email address; N=does not have an email address** |
| Y:<111000111100> | |
| N:<000111000011> | |

| **GENDER Column** | **F=female; M=male** |
|---|---|
| F:<110011100111> | |
| M:<001100011000 | |

**Select \* from employee where email = 'Y' and gender = 'F';**
Result set:<110000100100>

| Table 3.7    Invalidating the use of an index in a query. |
| --- |
| **An index will be used, if available:**<br>SELECT * from department where code = 'ABC'; |
| **The index will be ignored:**<br>SELECT * from department where code\|\|''= 'ABC'; |
| **An index will be used, if available:**<br>SELECT * from class where number = 30; |
| **The index will be ignored:**<br>SELECT * from class where number+0 = 30; |

recognize that the index has been invalidated. You should ask yourself, Was that really what the user intended? For an example of how to invalidate the use of an index, see Table 3.7.

# Optimizer Tuning

Currently, Oracle supports two methods of optimization: rule-based optimizer (RBO) and cost-based optimizer (CBO). Oracle originally started with only an RBO. The CBO was introduced with Oracle7. Eventually, the RBO will no longer be supported by Oracle and only the CBO will be available

The optimizer mode can be set at the instance, session, and statement levels. To set the optimizer at the instance level, the **OPTIMIZER_MODE** parameter is set to either **CHOOSE** or **RULE** in the database initialization parameter file; the default is **CHOOSE**. The **CHOOSE** option will default to **RULE** unless statistics are found for an object. If statistics are found, the default will change to **COST**. If the **OPTIMIZER_MODE** parameter is set to **RULE**, any statistics will be ignored and rule-based optimization will be performed.

An **ALTER SESSION SET OPTIMIZER_GOAL = RULE** or **ALTER SESSION SET OPTIMIZER_GOAL=CHOOSE** will change the optimizer mode used until it is changed again or the user session ends. The **ALTER SESSION SET OPTIMIZER_GOAL** can also be set to either **ALL_ROWS** or **FIRST ROWS**. These options will use the CBO.

To change the optimizer at the statement level, you can use hints (covered later in this chapter).

Rule-based optimization determines the fastest access path on the basis of the **WHERE** clause. Rule-based optimization has a set of rules and each rule is assigned a rank. The lowest rank is the fastest method. The RBO ignores the order of the statements in the **WHERE** clause. If an index can be used, the RBO will always use the index, even if a full table scan would be faster. If your applications were developed under the RBO by developers who understood the use of the optimizer rules, you will probably find that these applications will perform better using the RBO. Table 3.8 lists some of the general access paths used by the RBO from the lowest rank (fastest) to the highest rank (slowest).

The CBO uses statistics on the tables, indexes, and columns to determine the fastest access path. This information is generated using the **ANALYZE** command. The CBO computes the cost of each possible access path and chooses the access path with the lowest cost. It also takes into consideration the estimated resources (especially the number of logical reads), CPU utilization, and memory requirements for each access path considered. Even if an index is available, the CBO might determine that it would be faster to perform a full table scan, the actual cost of which depends on the number of multiblock reads required to scan the entire table. The number of blocks that can be read simul-

**Table 3.8    Access paths used by the RBO (from fastest to slowest).**

| Access Method | Description |
| --- | --- |
| ROWID | Rows are selected on the basis of the rowid |
| UNIQUE | All columns for a unique or primary key index are specified in the WHERE clause using the equals (=) operator |
| COMPOSITE KEY | All the columns of a composite index are specified in the WHERE clause using the equals (=) operator |
| NONUNIQUE | The WHERE clause includes one or more single-table indexes using the equals (=) operator |
| RANGE SCAN | The WHERE clause includes the column indexed in a single-column index or the leading edge column of a composite index |
| SORT/MERGE | A sort/merge is used for a join operation |
| SPECIAL CONDITIONS | The WHERE clause uses MAX or MIN, the statement includes an ORDER BY clause and there is a single-column index, or the leading edge of a composite index can be used (special restrictions might apply) |
| FULL TABLE SCAN | A full table scan |

taneously is determined by the database initialization parameter file entry for **DB_FILE_MULTIBLOCK_READ_COUNT**.

The CBO relies on statistics obtained using the **ANALYZE** command or the **DBMS_UTILITY.ANALYZE_SCHEMA** package. This package requires that the schema and the method (**COMPUTE** or **ESTIMATE**) be supplied. This package will analyze all the objects owned by the specified schema.

The **ANALYZE** command supports two methods to obtain the statistics: **ESTIMATE** and **COMPUTE**. The **ESTIMATE** method uses a sample of the data to determine the statistical information. The **ESTIMATE** option allows you to specify the amount of data to be analyzed (**SAMPLE**). The **SAMPLE** can be either the number of rows to be analyzed or the percent of the object to be analyzed. The **COMPUTE** method provides exact statistics on the object analyzed. The **COMPUTE** option requires more system resources to complete. The process of analyzing an index uses much fewer system resources than does the process of analyzing a table.

It is very important that statistics be updated regularly and after large batch loads; otherwise, the CBO will not have the correct statistics and might choose incorrect access paths that negatively affect performance. In addition, the CBO assumes that the operating system has a very low buffer cache hit rate. If you have a single-user system with a large buffer cache, the CBO will perform differently even if the objects have been analyzed.

When a table, index, or cluster is analyzed, information is placed in the data dictionary. You can view this information using the **DBA** views listed in Table 3.9. Users can access table, column, index, and cluster information for objects they own. In addition, there are the **ALL_TABLES**, **ALL_TAB_COLUMNS**, and **ALL_INDEXES** views for information on objects that are accessible to the user.

| Table 3.9 | Data dictionary views with statistical information. |
|---|---|
| **Column** | **Definition** |
| **DBA_TABLES** | |
| table_name | Name of the table |
| tablespace_name | Tablespace in which the table resides |
| empty_blocks | Number of blocks assigned to the table that have never been used |
| avg_space | Average available freespace in the table |

*(continued)*

**Table 3.9 Data dictionary views with statistical information (continued).**

| Column | Definition |
|---|---|
| **DBA_TABLES** | |
| chain_cnt | Number of chained rows |
| avg_row_len | Average length of the rows in the table, including overhead |
| degree | Degree of parallelism for table scans |
| instances | Number of instances across which the table must be scanned |
| cache | Indicates whether the table is in the buffer cache |
| owner | Owner of the table |
| cluster_name | Name of the cluster to which the table belongs, if applicable |
| pct_free | Minimum percentage of freespace for the blocks |
| pct_used | Maximum percentage of space used for each block before it is placed back on the freelist |
| ini_trans | Initial number of transactions for the table |
| max_trans | Maximum number of transactions for the table |
| initial_extent | Size of the initial extent (bytes) |
| next_extent | Size to be used for the next extent allocated for the table (bytes) |
| min_extents | Minimum number of extents allowed for this table |
| max_extents | Maximum number of extents allowed for this table |
| pct_increase | Percentage of increase to be applied for additional extents on the basis of the current size of the next extent |
| freelists | Number of freelists allocated to this table |
| freelist_groups | Number of freelist groups allocated to this table |
| backed_up | Indicates whether the table has been backed up since last modified |
| num_rows | Number of rows in the table |
| blocks | Number of used data blocks in the table |
| **DBA_TAB_COLUMNS** | |
| table_name | Name of the table to which this column belongs |
| column_name | Name of the column |

*(continued)*

**Table 3.9    Data dictionary views with statistical information (continued).**

| Column | Definition |
|---|---|
| **DBA_TAB_COLUMNS** | |
| owner | Owner of the table |
| data_type | Datatype of the column |
| data_length | Length of the column (bytes) |
| data_precision | Decimal precision for NUMBER datatype; binary for FLOAT, null for all others |
| data_scale | Digits to the right of the decimal point for NUMBER datatypes |
| nullable | Indicates whether null values are allowed |
| column_id | Sequence number assigned to the column by Oracle |
| default_length | Length of the default value |
| num_distinct | Number of distinct values |
| low_value | Smallest value in the column |
| high_value | Highest value in the column |
| density | Measurement of how distinct the values are |
| **DBA_INDEXES** | |
| table_name | Name of the indexed object |
| tablespace_name | Name of the tablespace in which the index resides |
| table_owner | Owner of the indexed object |
| index_name | Name of the index |
| uniqueness | Whether this is a UNIQUE or NONUNIQUE index |
| avg_leaf_blocks_per_key | Average number of leaf blocks per key |
| avg_data_blocks_per_key | Average number of data blocks per key |
| clustering factor | Measurement of the order or disorder of the table associated with this index |
| status | Indicates whether the index is in DIRECT LOAD STATE |
| owner | Owner of the index |
| ini_trans | Initial number of transactions |
| max_trans | Maximum number of transactions |
| initial_extent | Size of the initial extent (bytes) |

*(continued)*

| Table 3.9 | Data dictionary views with statistical information (continued). |
|---|---|

| Column | Definition |
|---|---|
| **DBA_INDEXES** | |
| next_extent | Size of the next extent to be allocated (bytes) |
| pct_increase | Percentage of increase to be applied for additional extents on the basis of the current size of the next extent |
| freelists | Number of freelists allocated to this index |
| pct_free | Minimum percentage of freespace in a block |
| blevel | B-tree level: depth of the index from the root to the leaf blocks; 0 indicates that the root and the leaf block are the same |
| leaf_blocks | Number of leaf blocks in the index |
| distinct_keys | Number of distinct keys in the index |
| **DBA_CLUSTERS** | |
| cluster_name | Name of this cluster |
| tablespace_name | Name of the tablespace in which the cluster resides |
| owner | Owner of the cluster |
| pct_free | Minimum percentage of freespace for the blocks |
| pct_used | Maximum percentage of space used for each block before it is placed back on the freelist |
| ini_trans | Initial number of transactions |
| max_trans | Maximum number of transactions |
| initial_extent | Size of the initial extent (bytes) |
| next_extent | Size to be used for the next extent allocated for this cluster (bytes) |
| min_extents | Minimum number of extents allowed for this segment |
| max_extents | Maximum number of extents allowed for this segment |
| pct_increase | Percentage of increase to be applied for additional extents on the basis of the current size of the next extent |
| freelists | Number of freelists allocated to this segment |
| freelist_groups | Number of freelist groups allocated to this segment |
| key_size | Estimated size of cluster key and associated rows |

*(continued)*

| Table 3.9 | Data dictionary views with statistical information (continued). |
|-----------|-------------------------------------------------------------------|

| Column | Definition |
|--------|------------|
| **DBA_CLUSTERS** | |
| avg_blocks_per_key | Average number of blocks containing rows for the cluster key |
| cluster_type | B-tree or hash cluster |
| function | Hash function, if applicable |
| hashkeys | Number of hash keys (hash buckets), if applicable |
| degree | Degree of parallelism for scans |
| instances | Number of instances across which the cluster must be scanned |
| cache | Indicates whether the table should be cached in the buffer cache |

# Hint Usage

The application developer and end users know more about the data and how it is used than the optimizer the optimizer does. Oracle provides a method known as hints to enable you to tell the optimizer the method to use for the SQL statement. Oracle recommends that hints not be used as the main method of controlling the optimization for SQL statements. Instead, the SQL statement should be appropriately rewritten for better performance.

A SQL statement can have only one comment containing hints. The hint must be placed after the **SELECT, UPDATE,** or **DELETE** in the SQL statement. It should be preceded by /*+ and followed by */. An alternate approach is to precede the hint with --+. If multiple hints are used, they must be separated by spaces. Figure 3.2 shows the syntax for a hint.

If hints are incorrectly specified, Oracle will treat the hint as a comment and will ignore it during SQL statement optimization. You will not receive an error message. If multiple hints exist, Oracle will ignore those with syntax errors but will use those that are correctly included in the statement. If any of the hints provide conflicting optimization requests, Oracle will not choose between them, and conflicting hints will be ignored.

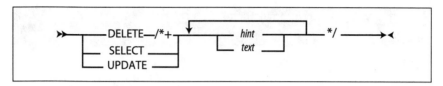

**Figure 3.2** Syntax diagram for hints.

Hints are categorized as follows:

➤ Optimization mode and goals

➤ Access methods

➤ Join operations

➤ Parallel query execution

The four types of hints for optimization mode and goals are:

➤ **CHOOSE**

➤ **RULE**

➤ **ALL_ROWS**

➤ **FIRST_ROWS**

The **CHOOSE** and **RULE** hints specify whether the CBO or the RBO should be used. Correctly specified hints will override the optimizer mode specified. If an optimization approach is specified, that approach will be used regardless of the initialization parameter setting for **OPTIMIZER_MODE** or the session setting for **OPTIMIZER_GOAL**. If statistics are present for even one table and the hint specifies **CHOOSE**, the optimizer will use the CBO. If no statistics are available, the optimizer will use the RBO. The use of the **RULE** hint will cause the optimizer to ignore any other hints specified.

Both the **ALL_ROWS** and the **FIRST_ROWS** use the CBO. If no statistics are available, the optimizer will use whatever storage information is available. The **ANALYZE** command should be used to provide statistics before using either the **ALL_ROWS** or the **FIRST_ROWS** hint. If a hint specifying an access path or join operation is also specified, it will be given precedence over the **ALL_ROWS** and **FIRST_ROWS** hints.

The **ALL_ROWS** hint concentrates on the best throughput with the minimum total resource consumption. **FIRST_ROWS** optimizes with the goal of the best response time and the minimum resource usage necessary to return the first row. The **FIRST_ROWS** hint will be ignored for **DELETE** and **UPDATE** statements. Because the following statements require that all rows be accessed before any results are returned, the **FIRST_ROWS** hint will be ignored if the SQL statement contains:

➤ Set operators (**UNION, UNION ALL, INTERSECT, MINUS**)

➤ The **GROUP BY** clause

➤ The **FOR UPDATE** clause

➤ Group functions

➤ The **DISTINCT** operator

If the described access method requires an index that does not exist, the hint will be ignored. The table must be specified in the hint the same as it is in the SQL statement. If an alias is used for the table, the table specified in the hint must use the table alias instead of the table name. You cannot use the schema name for the table, even if the table is fully qualified with the schema name in the **FROM** clause. Table 3.10 lists the hints that can be used for specification of the access method.

The syntax for the **FULL** hint is:

```
FULL(table)
```

| Table 3.10 | Table access method hints. |
|---|---|
| **Hint** | **Description** |
| FULL | Full table scan |
| ROWID | Full table scan using rowid |
| CLUSTER | Cluster scan |
| HASH | Hash scan |
| INDEX | Specifies the index to be used |
| INDEX_ASC | Specifies the index to be used; if applicable, it will perform a range scan of the specified index in ascending order; this is equivalent to the INDEX hint (at this time) |
| INDEX_DESC | Specifies the index to be used; if applicable, it will perform a range scan of the specified index in descending order; useful only for single-table SQL statements |
| AND_EQUAL | Merges the scans on several single-column indexes |
| USE_CONCAT | Changes the OR conditions in a WHERE clause into UNION ALL operations |

The syntax for the **ROWID** hint is:

```
ROWID(table)
```

The syntax for the **CLUSTER** hint is:

```
CLUSTER(table)
```

The syntax for the **HASH** hint is:

```
HASH(table)
```

The syntax for the **INDEX** hint is shown in Figure 3.3.

If the **INDEX** hint specifies more than one index, the optimizer will use one or all of the specified indexes and will ignore any other indexes. If this hint does not include a specific index, the optimizer will choose which index to use.

The syntax for the **INDEX_ASC** hint is shown in Figure 3.4.

The syntax for the **INDEX_DESC** hint is shown in Figure 3.5.

The syntax for the **AND_EQUAL** hint is shown in Figure 3.6.

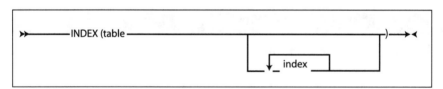

**Figure 3.3**   The syntax for **INDEX** hint.

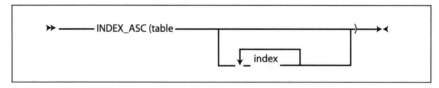

**Figure 3.4**   The syntax for **INDEX_ASC** hint.

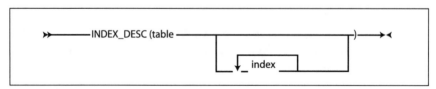

**Figure 3.5**   The syntax for **INDEX_DESC** hint.

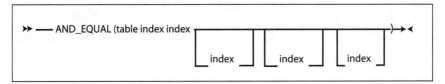

**Figure 3.6**   The syntax for **AND_EQUAL** hint.

| Table 3.1 | Join hints. |
|---|---|
| **Hint** | **Description** |
| ORDERED | Joins tables in the order specified in the FROM clause |
| USE_NL | Specifies the use of nested loops; requires that the ORDERED hint and specification of the table be used for the inner table |
| USE_HASH | Specifies the use of a hash join |
| USE_MERGE | Specifies the use of a sort_merge join; requires the ORDERED hint |

Hints can be used to specify the order in which join operations are performed. Table 3.11 describes the join hints.

The syntax for the **USE_NL** hint is shown in Figure 3.7.

The syntax for the **USE_HASH** hint is shown in Figure 3.8.

The syntax for the **USE_MERGE** hint is shown in Figure 3.9.

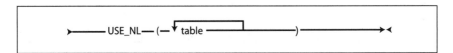

**Figure 3.7**   The syntax for **USE_NL** hint.

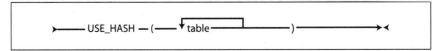

**Figure 3.8**   The syntax for **USE_HASH** hint.

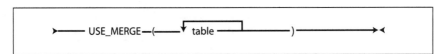

**Figure 3.9**   The syntax for **USE_MERGE** hint.

| Table 3.12 | Hints available for parallel query execution optimization. |
|---|---|
| **Hint** | **Description** |
| PARALLEL | Specifies the number of parallel query servers to be used |
| NOPARALLEL | Disables parallel scanning; overrides degree of parallelism specified when the table was created |
| CACHE | Places the blocks for that table at the most recently used end of the LRU |
| NOCACHE | Places the blocks for that table at the least recently used end of the LRU |
| PUSH_SUBQ | Evaluates subqueries at the first opportunity instead of as the last step; will be ignored for remote tables and merge join operations |

Table 3.12 describes the hints available for parallel query execution optimization.

The syntax for the **PARALLEL** hint is shown in Figure 3.10.

The first value in the syntax for the **PARALLEL** hint specifies the degree of parallelism for the specified table; the second value is used for a **PARALLEL SERVER** to specify the split between the two servers.

The syntax for the **NOPARALLEL** hint is:

```
NOPARALLEL(table)
```

The **NOPARALLEL** hint can also be specified by using the **PARALLEL** hint and setting the degree of parallelism to 1.

The syntax for the **CACHE** hint is:

```
CACHE(table)
```

The syntax for the **NOCACHE** hint is:

```
NOCACHE(table)
```

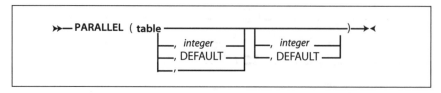

**Figure 3.10** The syntax for **PARALLEL** hint.

# Practice Questions

## Question 1

> Which facility within Oracle7 is used to format the output of a SQL Trace session?
>
> ○  a. The **ANALYZE** command
>
> ○  b. TKPROF
>
> ○  c. **EXPLAIN PLAN**
>
> ○  d. Server Manager

The correct answer is b. The TKPROF utility is used at the operating system command line to format information obtained using SQL Trace. The ANALYZE command is used to create statistics for the cost-based optimizer. EXPLAIN PLAN is used to obtain information on the execution plan for the SQL statement. The Server Manager is the utility for performing database maintenance and recovery functions.

## Question 2

> Which script must be executed to create the **PLAN_TABLE**?
>
> ○  a. utlexcpt.sql
>
> ○  b. utlmontr.sql
>
> ○  c. utlxplan.sql
>
> ○  d. utlsidsx.sql

The correct answer is c. Oracle usually makes the script name self-explanatory. The utlxplan.sql is used to create the PLAN_TABLE, which is used by the EXPLAIN PLAN command. An exception to this is the dbmsutil.sql script, which creates several utility packages, including DBMS_APPLI-CATION_INFO.

## Question 3

> If SQL statements are not performing well, what can sometimes be done to improve performance?
>
> ○ a. Create larger redo logfiles
>
> ○ b. Resize the shared pool to a small value
>
> ○ c. Create indexes where appropriate

The correct answer is c. Creating indexes can improve performance provided that they are created on the appropriate columns. Improperly sized redo logs affect the database as a whole, not only specific SQL statements. Resizing the shared pool to a smaller value usually has a negative effect on performance.

## Question 4

> Which Oracle7 facility can you use to identify SQL areas that might be causing performance problems?
>
> ○ a. utlestat.sql
>
> ○ b. TKPROF
>
> ○ c. **EXPLAIN PLAN**
>
> ○ d. SQL Trace

The correct answer is d. SQL Trace is the Oracle7 facility that actually traces the SQL statement execution performance, including the access plan and statistical information. The utlestat.sql script is used to obtain statistics on database activity for the instance. TKPROF is used to generate a report on the information obtained using SQL Trace. **EXPLAIN PLAN** provides information on the access plan for the query.

## Question 5

> You run the SQL Trace utility to trace a user session. What will the formatted output contain?
>
> ○ a. All user process information for the specified period
>
> ○ b. User process information for the specified user
>
> ○ c. Database activity information for the specified period
>
> ○ d. SQL activity for all user processes

The correct answer is b. The SQL Trace utility can be used at both the instance and the session level. When used at the session level, it will trace the processes for the user until that user turns off SQL Trace or ends the session. Because the question specifies a user session, you can eliminate the answers that include "all user" processes. The **SQL_TRACE** command does not have a parameter to set a time period.

# Question 6

What is an important factor when examining SQL statements for performance purposes?

○ a. Change SQL statements only after users have been notified

○ b. Consider using alternative queries to achieve the same results with less overhead

○ c. Do not change any application code

○ d. Do not change any SQL statements that include DML

The correct answer is b. The first thing to examine when a performance problem is encountered is the SQL statement. It is important to remember that SQL is very flexible and supports alternative ways to obtain the same information. SQL statements can be written in alternative ways, allowing you to change the statement without the need to notify all users.

# Question 7

You want to run the SQL Trace facility to gather performance information. How long should you run the process before stopping it and analyzing the output?

○ a. Until the database is restarted

○ b. Until the user session is completed

○ c. Until all user sessions are completed

The correct answer is b. The SQL Trace parameter can be dynamically changed for the database and does not require that the database be restarted. Setting SQL Trace at the instance level to trace all user sessions will cause excessive overhead. Therefore, the answer is to perform a SQL Trace for a user session, executing the SQL statements that are having performance problems.

## Question 8

> Which TKPROF option would be set to ignore recursive SQL?
>
> ○ a. **EXPLAIN**
> ○ b. **SORT**
> ○ c. **INSERT**
> ○ d. **SYS**
> ○ e. **RECORD**

The correct answer is d. Recursive SQL are the SQL statements performed by SYS. By setting **SYS=NO** when formatting the results of a SQL Trace, recursive SQL will be excluded from the report. The **EXPLAIN** option is used to set the user and password for statements for which an explain plan will be generated. **SORT** allows sorting by options. **RECORD** places a record of the nonrecursive statements into the trace file. The **INSERT** option creates a SQL script to store the trace file statistics in the database.

## Question 9

> Which two things can you track using the **DBMS_APPLICATION_INFO** package provided by Oracle7? [Check all correct answers]
>
> ❑ a. User information
> ❑ b. Performance
> ❑ c. Resource usage
> ❑ d. Network information
> ❑ e. Database files
> ❑ f. Error information

The correct answers are b and c. A variety of tables are provided for user information and database files. For error information, the log and trace files are very useful. Because **DBMS_APPLICATION_INFO** is an Oracle-stored package, it does not trace network information. The built-in **DBMS_APPLICATION_INFO** package is provided by Oracle to obtain information specifically on performance and resource consumption.

# Need To Know More?

 The first place to go for more information is the *Oracle7 Tuning Manual* and the *Oracle7 Server Reference Manual*.

 Aronoff, Eyal, Kevin Loney, and Noorali Sonawalla: *Advanced Oracle Tuning and Administration*. Oracle Press, 1997. ISBN 0-07882-241-6. Pay particular attention to Chapters 10 and 11.

 Corey, Michael, Michael Abbey, and Daniel J. Dechichio: *Tuning Oracle*. Oracle Press, 1995. ISBN 0-07881-181-3. Chapter 7 is a good chapter to pay close attention to.

 Corrigan, Peter and Mark Gurry: *Oracle Performance Tuning*. O'Reilly & Associates, Inc., 1993. ISBN 1-56592-048-1. Chapters 6 and 12 should be read carefully.

 Feuerstein, Steven, Charles Dye, and John Beresniewicz: *Oracle Built-in Packages*. O'Reilly & Associates, 1998. ISBN 1-56592-375-8. Pay particular attention to Chapters 7, 10, and 11.

# Database
# Configuration

. . . . . . . . . . . . . . . . . . . . . . . . . . . . . . . . . . . . . . . . . . .

## Terms you'll need to understand:

√ RAID

√ Striping

√ Multithreaded server (MTS)

√ PCTUSED and PCTFREE

√ High water mark

√ FREELISTS

√ Optimal Flexible Architecture (OFA)

√ Chaining and migration

√ Clusters

√ Parallelism

√ Raw devices

## Techniques you'll need to master:

√ Understanding how to balance I/O

√ Understanding the differences between manual and operating system striping

√ Understanding storage parameters and how to use them

√ Understanding the types of Oracle tablespaces and the appropriate uses of each

Regardless of how well you have tuned your application, I/O will limit its performance, and you will have performance problems if significant disk contention exists. Oracle provides several methods of configuring your database to reduce I/O bottlenecks. This chapter focuses on performance tuning from the I/O perspective.

# Optimal Flexible Architecture

Oracle's Optimal Flexible Architecture (OFA) is a recommended standard for database configuration. It includes recommendations for the following:

➤ Naming standards

➤ Security issues

➤ Raw devices

➤ Managing upgrades

➤ File distribution

The naming standards presented by OFA provide a method of organizing files so that files for each database and the types of file (log, database, or control) can be identified easily. The OFA recommends using operating system profiles and separating Oracle files from user files to address security issues. It also provides an overview of the use of raw devices (addressed in more detail later in this chapter). The OFA makes recommendations on directory structures that support multiple versions of Oracle on a single server, making upgrades easier to manage.

The OFA makes several recommendations on file distribution. According to Cary V. Millsap of the Oracle National Technical Response Team (as quoted from and with the permission of the authors of RevealNet), the OFA is based on the following three rules:

1. Establish an orderly operating system directory structure in which any database file can be stored on any disk resource.

2. Separate groups of segments (data objects) with different behavior into different tablespaces.

3. Maximize database reliability and performance by separating database components across different disk resources.

# File Placement

The placement of files belonging to an Oracle database is very important for performance reasons and for backup and recovery issues. Every server is limited in the number of processes that can simultaneously access any disk. Your goal in file placement should be to have I/O evenly spread across the available disk drives to minimize simultaneous access to each disk. The **V$FILESTAT** view provides statistical information on physical reads (**PHYRDS**) and writes (**PHYWRTS**) by file number (**FILE#**). The total I/O for a physical disk is the sum of the **PHYRDS** and **PHYWRTS**. The rate of I/O is calculated by dividing the total physical I/O by the time interval during which the statistics were gathered (for more detailed information on the **V$FILESTAT** view, see Chapter 2).

You need to consider non-Oracle activity and how your operating system handles cache and I/O. If possible, separate Oracle files and non-Oracle files, as this will reduce I/O contention between Oracle and non-Oracle activities. You can use operating system monitoring tools to determine the I/O and memory activity on the server for both Oracle and non-Oracle activities.

Where you place your database files has a major effect on the amount of I/O. When tuning I/O, it is important to review statistics on physical reads and writes to determine which files are very active. Highly active files should be placed on a separate disk or striped across several disks to reduce I/O (striping is addressed in more detail later in this chapter).

For backup and recovery, it is very important that you have copies of your control file and online redo logfiles on separate disks. It is also important to have sufficient space for archive logs if **ARCHIVELOG** mode is in use. Insufficient space for your archive logs can cause your database to hang.

## Physical Files

An Oracle database consists of five types of physical files:

➤ Database files

➤ Control files

➤ Online redo logfiles

➤ Offline archived redo logfiles

➤ Parameter files

Database files (or datafiles) are the physical operating system files that make up each tablespace. A datafile can belong to only one tablespace. However, a tablespace can contain many datafiles. Although a table can belong to only one tablespace, that tablespace can have multiple datafiles on several physical disks.

A control file is a small binary file used by Oracle to synchronize all the datafiles and to keep track of all the files belonging to the database. The control file is updated continuously by Oracle. Oracle recommends having a minimum of two copies, placed on different physical disk drives.

Every database must have at least two online redo logs. These logs contain all the changes made to data. Redo logs are written to in a circular fashion (redo logs are covered more extensively in Chapter 6).

Offline archive redo logfiles are created when a database is placed in **ARCHIVELOG** mode. These logfiles are historical copies of redo logs (the use of **ARCHIVELOG** mode is covered extensively in Chapter 11). When planning how to place files on the available disks, it is very important that archive redo logfiles be placed on a separate disk. As stated earlier, online redo logs are written to in a circular fashion. When **ARCHIVELOG** mode is used, each redo log must be archived before it can be used again. If the file system for the archive logs becomes full, additional archive logs cannot be created and the Archiver will wait until there is sufficient freespace in the file system to write the new archive log files. If this space problem is not resolved before the online redo logs fill up, the database will not be able to reuse the redo logs because they are waiting to be archived. By placing the archive logs on a separate disk, it will be easier for you to ensure that sufficient space is always available for creating new archive log files.

The parameter file contains information read by Oracle at startup to determine the database initialization settings. If no parameter file is specified when the database is started, the default is to look for an init<SID>.ora file. On Unix systems, the default location is the $ORACLE_HOME/dbs directory. This file is referenced only when the database is started, and the name of this file is not stored within the Oracle database.

## Disk Configuration

As a rule of thumb, the more disks you have available, the better you will be able to spread out the I/O activity. Rather than having all your files on one or two gigabyte-size disks, Oracle recommends that you have a minimum of five disks. Table 4.1 shows a minimal five-disk configuration based on recommendations in RevealNet and in Oracle's OFA.

The configuration for file placement in Table 4.1 is a minimum configuration for all but the smallest Oracle databases. This configuration does not include a second member for each redo log group. Because redo logs are vital for recovery of your database, it is very important that they be mirrored (that is, two members per group on different disks). Oracle will write to all the redo logs in parallel to reduce the overhead. This minimum configuration does not provide flexibility for placing highly active tables on a separate disk. Additional disks provide more flexibility for balancing I/O.

| Table 4.1 | File placement configuration using five disks. |
|---|---|
| **Disk 1** | **Files** |
| | Oracle executables |
| | User files |
| | TEMPORARY tablespace |
| | One copy of the control file |
| | Redo logs |
| | SYSTEM tablespace |
| **Disk 2** | **Files** |
| | Data |
| | One copy of the control file |
| **Disk 3** | **Files** |
| | Indexes |
| | One copy of the control file |
| **Disk 4** | **Files** |
| | Rollback segments |
| | Export files |
| **Disk 5** | **Files** |
| | Archive logfiles |

# Tablespaces

Oracle recommends a minimum configuration of the following six tablespaces:

➤ SYSTEM

➤ TEMPORARY

➤ ROLLBACK

➤ USERS

➤ DATA

➤ INDEX

Each of these tablespaces represents a different type of data, and Oracle benefits in performance if each type of tablespace can be separated onto different physical drives. Even if they cannot be separated physically, the type of data placed into each tablespace is different and should be not be mixed.

The **SYSTEM** tablespace should contain only data dictionary tables. When you issue the **CREATE DATABASE** statement, Oracle creates these data dictionary tables using the sql.bsq script. You can modify the storage parameters in this file to create the data dictionary tables with sizes more appropriate to your requirements. However, you must not drop, add, or rename any columns or tables. In addition, you should not decrease the storage parameters (with the exception of **PCTINCREASE**).

Only objects owned by the SYS and SYSTEM accounts should be placed in the **SYSTEM** tablespace. Oracle places all package definitions in the **SYSTEM** tablespace as well. If no default and temporary tablespaces are specified for a user, the **SYSTEM** tablespace will be used. This can negatively affect performance and result in a highly fragmented **SYSTEM** tablespace, which cannot be defragmented without dropping and re-creating the database. When reviewing statistics, such as the report.txt file obtained from the utlbstat/utlestat utility, look for heavy reads and writes for the **SYSTEM** tablespace. This is an indication that users are defaulting to the **SYSTEM** tablespace for data, sorting, or both.

The **TEMPORARY** tablespace is used for sorting when the sort cannot be performed in memory. Chapter 8 contains in-depth information on turning sorts. Placing the **TEMPORARY** tablespace on a separate disk drive will prevent sorting activities from competing with reads and writes for other Oracle files. User data should never be placed in the **TEMPORARY** tablespace. You can designate a tablespace as being a temporary tablespace only if no permanent objects are in the tablespace.

Rollback segments should be created in a separate **ROLLBACK** tablespace. Rollback segments are used to store before images of changed data. You cannot use multiple tablespaces unless you have first created and brought online at least one rollback segment, in addition to the initially created rollback segment in the **SYSTEM** tablespace. Rollback segments are used to roll back transactions (that is, reverse the action of an insert, update, or delete), for recovery, and for read consistency. Because of the heavy I/O generated by DML activity in an OLTP environment, you should try to separate the **ROLLBACK** tablespace on a separate physical disk. You should be aware that you cannot take a tablespace offline if it contains an active rollback segment. Oracle recommends naming the **ROLLBACK** tablespace **RBS**.

In some Oracle environments, end users might need to do more then insert, update, and delete data from application tables. They might need to create tables and other Oracle objects. A **USERS** tablespace should be created and used as the default for end users. Placing user objects in a separate tablespace makes maintenance easier. If possible, place the **USERS** tablespace on a separate physical disk to spread the I/O.

The **DATA** tablespace should be used for objects that contain the data for the application. The **INDEX** tablespace should be used only for indexes. The separate tablespaces created for data and indexes should be placed on different physical drives. If data and indexes are placed on the same disks, much more contention for resources will exist.

# Striping Tables

Striping is a method of spreading data for a single table across several physical disks. Striping can be performed either by the operating system or by hand, though the former is easier than the latter. Striping can improve performance for applications that perform many full table scans and databases using the parallel query option. When determining the size of each stripe, you need to consider both the **DB_BLOCK_SIZE** and **DB_FILE_MULTIBLOCK_READ_COUNT**, as specified in your database initialization parameter file. Oracle can only allocate space by blocks (**DB_BLOCK_SIZE**). The number of blocks that are read at one time for a full table scan is determined by the **DB_FILE_MULTIBLOCK_READ_COUNT** parameter. By making the size of your database stripes a multiple of the **DB_FILE_MULTIBLOCK_READ_COUNT** and the **DB_BLOCK_SIZE**, you will be sizing your stripes to match the amount of database blocks that Oracle will read at one time. This will maximize the effect of striping by reducing I/O for full table scans.

## Striping With The Operating System

Striping performed by the operating system is accomplished using Redundant Arrays of Inexpensive Disks (RAID). Special hardware is required for RAID striping. Table 4.2 lists the most-often-used forms of RAID. RAID devices can be very useful in read-intensive systems. The most commonly used versions of RAID are RAID 1 and RAID 5.

| Table 4.2    Frequently used RAID options. | |
|---|---|
| **RAID Level** | **Description** |
| 0 | Standard file structure |
| 1 | Disk mirroring |
| 0 + 1 | Combination of disk striping and mirroring |
| 3 | Striping with one dedicated parity disk |
| 5 | Striping with distributed parity |

RAID 0 is the normal file structure in which no mirroring or operating system striping has been used. All striping on a RAID 0 configuration is performed by hand. RAID 0 configurations can provide excellent performance. Because no mirroring is performed, a disk crash will cause all the datafiles on that disk to be lost.

RAID 1 provides a mirrored copy of each disk. If a disk is lost, the mirrored copy becomes available automatically. If a file is corrupted by software or end-user error, the mirrored copy of the file is also corrupted. Using RAID 1 requires twice as many disks. One erroneous assumption often made about RAID 1 is that if you are mirroring every file, you do not need multiple members for each redo log group and multiple copies of the control file. Even if RAID 1 mirror-ing is used, Oracle recommends that you still have a second member in every redo log group. If one of the redo log members is corrupted, the mirror may also be corrupted. In the event that a redo logfile can no longer be read by Oracle and there is a second member in the redo log group, Oracle will be able to use the second member of the redo log group. Because of the importance of the control file, you should have at least one additional control file placed on a second physical drive in case of file corruption.

RAID 0 + 1 uses a combination of mirroring some disks and having some disks unmirrored.

RAID 3 uses error correction codes (ECCs), also called parity, for data protec-tion and redundancy. The data is distributed across several disks. RAID 3 stores all the ECCs on one physical disk.

RAID 5 is the most common form of operating system striping. It uses ECCs that are stored with the data. Data is distributed across several disks. RAID 5 can provide good performance for read-only applications. However, if an ap-plication is write intensive, the constant calculation of ECCs makes write operations much slower. An additional disadvantage of using RAID 5 is that recovery operations are more time consuming. If you need to recover a striped tablespace because of file corruption, all the disks over which the tablespace is striped must be involved in the recovery process.

If you determine that you must stripe your data across multiple drives, operat-ing system striping is much easier to do than striping by hand. The use of a RAID configuration is transparent to Oracle. For randomly accessed files, such as datafiles and archive logs, a RAID 5 device can improve performance in a read-only application system without additional effort on your part. However, files that must be accessed sequentially should never be placed on a RAID 5 device. Redo logs and the **TEMPORARY** tablespace are read sequentially and therefore should not be placed on a RAID 5 device.

# Striping By Hand

Striping by hand is performed by creating a tablespace with datafiles that are located on different physical drives. Striping by hand is very labor-intensive and requires an in-depth knowledge of the data and how it is used. Two ways to stripe tables and indexes across the datafiles are through tablespace storage default and table extent allocation.

With the tablespace storage default method, you create the table or index with multiple extents in which each extent is slightly smaller than the size of each datafile. The following code is an example of setting up a striped table with this method:

```
CREATE TABLESPACE employee_ts
DATAFILE '/db01/employee_01.dbf' size 161M,
                '/db02/employee_02.dbf' size 161M,
                '/db03/employee_03.dbf' size 161M
DEFAULT STORAGE (initial 160M next 160M min extents 2)';
CREATE TABLE employee
(first_name          varchar2(20)
, last_name          varchar2(20)
, middle_name        varchar2(20)
, address_line1      varchar2(20)
, address_line2      varchar2(20)
, address_line3      varchar2(20)
, state_code         varchar2(2)
, zip_code           number(5))
TABLESPACE    employee_ts;
```

With the table extent allocation method, you explicitly indicate which datafile is to be used for each extent allocated. The following code is an example of using this method:

```
ALTER TABLE employee
ALLOCATE EXTENT (DATAFILE '/db01/employee_02.dbf' SIZE 160M);
```

# Storage Parameters

The smallest unit of I/O in Oracle is a block, the size of which is determined by the **DB_BLOCK_SIZE** parameter in the database initialization parameter file at the time the database is created. Although you cannot change the **DB_BLOCK_SIZE** after the database is created, storage parameters can be used to determine how much data is stored in each block. Each extent is made up of blocks, and you can use storage parameters to control the number of extents and size of each.

The **ANALYZE** command can be used to obtain statistics on space usage for tables and indexes. Table 4.3 lists the columns in the **DBA_TABLES** view that are relevant to analyzing space used for each table. You can also access this information with the associated **USER_TABLES** and **ALL_TABLES** views. It is important to note that the **EMPTY_BLOCKS** column references the number of blocks that have never been used, not the number of blocks currently empty. If the number of empty blocks is high, you should consider reorganizing the table to release this space for use by other objects.

Oracle provides both tablespace and object parameters that can be used to determine space usage. If an individual table does not include explicit storage parameters, the defaults specified for the tablespace are used. If no default storage parameter is specified for the tablespace, the Oracle tablespace defaults are used.

If you decide to reorganize a table, you can use either the export/import method or the create/rename method. In the export/import method, you will need to export the table, drop the table, re-create the table with more appropriate storage parameters, and import the data with the **IGNORE=Y** option. In the create/rename method, you will need to create a new table using the **CREATE TABLE...AS...** command, drop the old table, and rename the new table to the original name. The second option can be used only if you have sufficient space for two copies of the table.

The parameters set for your tablespaces and objects determine how space is used by Oracle blocks. The storage parameters, along with the block size, can determine how efficient your database reads and writes data. Although resetting some of these parameters might require reorganizing a table or index, all the options discussed in this section can be changed without re-creating the database. Table 4.4 lists the storage parameters and the default for each.

| Table 4.3 | Data dictionary view columns relevant to space used by a table. |
|-----------|------------------------------------------------------------------|
| **Column** | **Description** |
| num_rows | Number of rows in the table |
| blocks | Number of used blocks (blocks below the high water mark) |
| empty_blocks | Number of blocks that have never been used (blocks above the high water mark) |
| avg_space | Average available freespace below the high water mark (in bytes) |
| avg_row_len | Average length of a row (including overhead) |
| chain_cnt | Number of chained and migrated rows |

**Table 4.4    Storage parameter defaults.**

| Parameter | Default |
|---|---|
| INITIAL EXTENT | Five Oracle data blocks |
| NEXT EXTENT | Five Oracle data blocks |
| MINEXTENTS | 2 for rollback segments, 1 for all other objects |
| MAXEXTENTS | Vary, depending on the operating system |
| PCTINCREASE | 50 percent |
| FREELISTS | 1 |
| FREELIST GROUPS | 1 |
| OPTIMAL | Null (used only for rollback segments) |
| INITRANS | 1 for clusters and indexes, 1 for all other objects |
| MAXTRANS | Operating system dependent |
| PCTFREE | 10 percent |
| PCTUSED | 40 percent (not applicable for indexes) |

# Chaining And Row Migration

Chaining and row migration cause additional I/O because more than one block must be read to obtain the data for a single row. When a row is too large to fit in a single Oracle block, it must be spread across blocks. Rows spread across two or more blocks are referred to as chained rows. Chained rows are inevitable if the **DB_BLOCK_SIZE** is smaller than the largest row. For example, if your **DB_BLOCK_SIZE** is 4096 (4K) and your row is equal to 5120 (5K), the row will need to be spread across two blocks. The **AVG_ROW_LEN** column in the **DBA_TABLES, ALL_TABLES,** or **USER_TABLES** will provide you with information on the average length of a row in the table. If the number of bytes in the **AVG_ROW_LEN** is larger than your **DB_BLOCK_SIZE**, you will have a problem with row chaining. The only way to resolve this is to re-create the database with a larger block size.

A more manageable problem is row migration. If a row that has been inserted into a block is updated to a size that will no longer fit into that block, the row must be moved to another block that will hold the entire row. When rows are moved from one block to another, they are referred to as migrated rows. Oracle sets a pointer at the block that originally contained the row to indicate the new block location for the row. This increases I/O when an index goes to the block to retrieve the specified row and then must go to another block to actually obtain the row. Rows can be migrated more than once. For example, suppose that a row is initially inserted in a block. That row is later updated and can no longer fit into the block. The row is moved to a new block that has sufficient freespace for the entire row, and an indicator is left to point to the new location for the row. If the row is updated again in the new location and can no longer fit into that block, an indicator is placed in the second block and the row moved to another block. With each move of the row, additional I/O is needed to locate the row.

Row migration can be detected, resolved, and prevented. To obtain information on chained and migrated rows, you can execute the **ANALYZE** command. When a table is analyzed, information on the number of chained rows is provided. You can view the **CHAIN_CNT** column in the **DBA_TABLES**, **ALL_TABLES**, or **USER_TABLES** to see the number of chained and migrated rows. You can also use the **ANALYZE** command to obtain specific information on which rows are chained (the syntax for this command is given in Chapter 2). The following code is an example of the **ANALYZE** command that is used to obtain information on specific chained and migrated rows:

```
ANALYZE TABLE sandy.employee LIST CHAINED ROWS;
```

By default, the results are placed in the **CHAINED_ROWS** table. You can specify another table to hold the results. If you prefer to use another table, it must match the column structure of the **CHAINED_ROWS** table, described in Table 4.5. This table is created by the utlchain.sql script.

Once you have identified the migrated rows, you can use one of two methods to resolve this problem. You can export the table and then either truncate the table or re-create the table with more appropriate parameters and import the rows. The alternate way is to reorganize only the rows listed in the **CHAINED_ROWS** table. Before you begin this process, you should have an export of the table in case you encounter a problem and need to start over. The following steps are used to reorganize the chained rows:

**Table 4.5 Data dictionary view for information on chained and migrated rows.**

| Column | Definition |
| --- | --- |
| owner_name | Table owner |
| table_name | Name of the table |
| cluster_name | Name of the cluster, if applicable |
| head_rowid | The rowid of the chained row |
| timestamp | Date and time of the ANALYZE command used to obtain this information |

1. Execute the **ANALYZE** command to fill in the **CHAINED_ROWS** table:

```
ANALYZE TABLE employee LIST CHAINED ROWS;
```

2. Create a new table to temporarily store the chained rows:

```
CREATE TABLE chained_employee AS
SELECT * FROM employee
WHERE rowid IN
        (SELECT head_rowid FROM chained_rows);
```

3. Delete the chained rows from the table:

```
DELETE FROM employee
WHERE rowid in
        (SELECT head_rowid FROM chained_rows);
```

4. Insert the rows back into the table:

```
INSERT INTO employee
SELECT * FROM chained_employee;
```

5. Drop the intermediate table:

```
DROP TABLE chained_employee;
```

To prevent further row migration, you should adjust the **PCTFREE** parameter to allow sufficient space for updates to the rows.

Although indexes do not have chained or migrated rows, you will have increased I/O if the number of levels for a B-tree index exceeds 2. You can analyze your indexes and then look at the **BLEVEL** in **DBA_INDEXES, ALL_INDEXES,** or **USER_INDEXES.** If the **BLEVEL** is zero, the root and leaf blocks are the same. If the **BLEVEL** is greater than 2, you can rebuild the index to reduce the number of levels. Rebuilding your indexes regularly can decrease I/O and improve performance significantly.

The **VALIDATE STRUCTURE** keyword in the **ANALYZE COMMAND** is another way to obtain information on the space used by your indexes. The following is an example of this syntax:

```
ANALYZE INDEX employee_name_ind VALIDATE STRUCTURE;
```

This command will check for corruption and provide important statistics on the index. If your index is corrupted, you should drop and rebuild it. Statistical information on your indexes can be found in the **INDEX_STATS** view, described in Table 4.6. Depending on the type of application, you might want to rebuild the index if the total number of deletions is more than 20 percent of the total number of current rows. You can use the following code to determine this percentage:

```
SELECT (del_lf_rows_len / lf_rows_len) * 100 FROM index_stats;
```

| Table 4.6 | Data dictionary view for statistical information on indexes. |
|---|---|
| **Column** | **Description** |
| height | Height of the B-tree index (levels) |
| blocks | Number of blocks allocated to this index |
| name | Name of the index |
| lf_rows | Number of values (leaf rows) in the index |
| lf_blks | Number of B-tree leaf blocks |
| lf_rows_len | Total length (in bytes) of all the rows in the B-tree index |
| lf_blk_len | Usable space in a leaf block |
| br_rows | Number of branch rows in the B-tree index |
| br_blks | Number of branch blocks in the B-tree index |
| br_rows_len | Total of the lengths of all the branch blocks in the B-tree index |
| br_blk_len | Usable space in a branch block |
| del_lf_rows | Number of deleted rows |
| del_lf_rows_len | Total length (in bytes) of the deleted rows |
| distinct_keys | Number of distinct keys (sometimes includes deleted rows) |
| most_repeated_key | Number of repetitions for the most repeated key (sometimes includes deleted rows) |
| btree_space | Total allocated space for the B-tree index |
| used_space | Total space used for the B-tree index |
| pct_used | Percentage of allocated space being used |
| rows_per_key | Average number of rows per distinct key |
| blks_gets_per_access | Estimate for the number of consistent mode block reads necessary to access a row in the B-tree index |

When building an index, you can reduce the required I/O with the **UNRE-COVERABLE** option. This option builds the index without using the redo logs and therefore reduces I/O. When you build an index with this option, any failure will mean that you must reexecute the SQL command to build the index. Because indexes do not contain data, you can easily rebuild the index with a SQL command.

# High Water Mark

The high water mark is the top limit for the number of blocks that have been used for a table. The high water mark is recorded in the segment header and is incremented five Oracle blocks at a time as rows are inserted into blocks. The high water mark is important because of the effect it has when a full table scan is performed. When performing a full table scan, Oracle will read all the blocks below the high water mark even if they are empty blocks. Having many unused blocks below the high water mark degrades performance for full table scans with additional, unnecessary I/O.

You should use the **ANALYZE** command to obtain statistics on your tables. Table 4.3 lists the relevant columns in the **DBA_TABLES** view. Compare the number of blocks that contain rows with the number of blocks that are available below the high water mark. This will help you determine the proportion of underused space below the high water mark. You can use the following formula

$1 - r/h$

where $r$ represents the number of blocks with rows and $h$ represents the number of blocks below the high water mark.

You can find the number of blocks with rows with the following statement:

```
SELECT count(distinct substr(rowid, 15,4) || substr(rowid, 1,8) )
FROM schema.table;
```

The number of blocks below the high water mark is in the **BLOCKS** column in the **DBA_TABLES** view.

If the result from the formula is zero, you do not need to rebuild your table. If the result is greater than zero, you should consider your environment and application before deciding whether to reorganize your table.

If your application is well indexed and rarely performs full table scans, empty blocks below the high water mark, although consuming space, are not being accessed. If you receive different results from this formula at different times, this might be only a temporary problem that does not require reorganization.

You also need to consider the time you have, the available space, and whether this is a priority.

Oracle also provides the built-in **DBMS_SPACE** package, which can be used to help you determine your high water mark and space usage. The **DBMS_SPACE** package is created with the dbmsutil.sql script, which is called by the catproc.sql script.

The **DBMS_SPACE** package contains two procedures: **UNUSED_SPACE** and **FREE_BLOCKS**. These are described in Table 4.7. The **UNUSED_SPACE** procedure returns information on the unused space for a segment.

**Table 4.7    DBMS_SPACE procedures.**

**DBMS_SPACE.UNUSED_SPACE**

unused_space(

| | | |
|---|---|---|
| segment_owner | IN | varchar2, |
| segment_name | IN | varchar2, |
| segment_type | IN | varchar2, |
| total_blocks | OUT | number, |
| total_bytes | OUT | number, |
| unused_blocks | OUT | number, |
| unused_bytes | OUT | number, |
| last_used_extent_file | OUT | number, |
| last_used_extent_block_id | OUT | number, |
| last_used_block | OUT | number |

)

---

**DBMS_SPACE.FREE_BLOCKS**

free_blocks(

| | | | |
|---|---|---|---|
| segment_owner | IN | varchar2 | |
| segment_name | IN | varchar2, | |
| segment_type | IN | varchar2, | |
| freelist_group_id | IN | varchar2, | |
| free_blks | OUT | number, | |
| scan_limit | IN | number | DEFAULT NULL |

)

The **FREE_BLOCKS** procedure returns information on the free blocks for a segment. To execute these procedures, the user must have the **ANALYZE ANY** system privilege.

The high water mark is set at the beginning of the segment when the table is created. Deleting rows will never reset the high water mark even if all the rows are deleted from the table. Only the **TRUNCATE** command will reset the high water mark. You can delete empty blocks that have never been used (blocks that are above the high water mark) with the **ALTER TABLE** command. The syntax for this command is:

```
ALTER TABLE  table_name DEALLOCATE UNUSED;
```

Blocks above the high water mark are ignored and have no effect on performance. However, this wastes space. If space is an issue, you should reclaim the empty blocks.

## INITIAL EXTENT

The **INITIAL EXTENT** parameter specifies the space allocated for the very first extent of an object when it is created. Once an object is created, you cannot change the initial extent size. You can, however, change the tablespace default storage parameter for initial extents. The new tablespace default storage parameter will be used for any new tables that are created without a storage specification.

If your **INITIAL EXTENT** parameter is sized for full expected growth of each object, you will waste space in the early stage of database population and will not improve performance. Instead, Oracle recommends that **INITIAL EXTENT** and **NEXT EXTENT** be sized the same.

## NEXT EXTENT

The **NEXT EXTENT** parameter specifies the size of the next extent that is allocated for that object. When a block cannot be found in which to insert a new row or to place a migrated row, Oracle will add an extent to the object on the basis of the size specified in this parameter. The space for each **NEXT EXTENT** must be one contiguous section of disk. An extent map is used to track the location of all the extents allocated to an object. This extent map is located in the segment header and contains the disk address for each extent allocated to an object.

Oracle does not view the total number of extents as impacting I/O for an index or a table. To improve performance, you should make all extents (both initial and next for indexes and tables) a multiple of the database initialization parameter for **DB_FILE_MULTIBLOCK_READ_COUNT** multiplied by the **DB_BLOCK_SIZE**. The only SQL command that will take longer if there are multiple extents is the **DROP TABLE** command.

## MINEXTENTS

The **MINEXTENTS** parameter is the minimum number of extents that will be allocated when the segment is initially created. You can reduce the overhead involved in creating new extents by allocating additional extents when an object is created. Rollback segments are always created with a minimum of two extents.

## MAXEXTENTS

The **MAXEXTENTS** parameter specifies the maximum number of extents that can be allocated for a segment. Once this number is reached, no new extents can be created, and the user will receive an error message. Oracle7.3 allows this to be set to **UNLIMITED**. The **UNLIMITED** setting should never be used for rollback segments.

## PCTINCREASE

The **PCTINCREASE** parameter is used to determine the percentage by which the extents will increase as new extents are allocated. Once the **NEXT EXTENT** is allocated, the new value for **NEXT EXTENT** is determined by multiplying the **PCTINCREASE** by the value of **NEXT EXTENT**. The **PCTINCREASE** for rollback segments should always be set to zero and cannot be increased. If the **PCTINCREASE** is set to zero at the tablespace level, Oracle will assume that the tablespace contains rollback segments and will not automatically coalesce space for that tablespace. **PCTINCREASE** should normally be set to zero for most application tables.

## FREELISTS

The **FREELISTS** parameter specifies the number of freelists. Freelists are lists of the free blocks that are available for insertion of new rows into an object. At least one freelist is maintained in every segment header. When the amount of space in a block drops below the **PCTUSED**, that block is added to the **FREELISTS**. If the high water mark for a table changes, blocks can also be added to the **FREELISTS**. When the space available reaches the **PCTFREE**, new rows are no longer inserted into that block, and the block is removed from the **FREELISTS**. If the size of a new row would fill the block over the **PCTFREE**, the row is not inserted into that block.

Oracle will search through all blocks on the **FREELISTS** until it finds a block where the row can be inserted. If no block will allow the row to be inserted without exceeding the **PCTFREE**, a new extent will be created. Because Oracle will search through all the **FREELISTS** for a block to hold the new row, it is important that the **PCTFREE** and **PCTUSED** be sized correctly; otherwise, the **FREELISTS** will contain a growing number of blocks that cannot be used. The resulting overhead negatively affects performance when new rows are inserted. There will also be additional overhead if blocks are continuously placed on and then removed from the **FREELISTS**. If the **PCTFREE** and **PCTUSED** equal 100 percent, blocks will be continuously placed on and taken off the **FREELISTS**. The gap between **PCTFREE** and **PCTUSED** should be greater than the average row size for the segment. If no space is left in the blocks and no empty transaction slots exist, the application will hang. Although this might appear to be a locking problem, it is actually a space problem.

If there are many inserts and deletes for a table, contention for access to the **FREELISTS** can result in waits for the **FREELISTS**. The **V$WAITSTAT** view indicates whether contention exists for the **FREELISTS**. However, this view does not indicate which table or index has the problem. The following SQL statement can be used to obtain the number of waits for **FREELISTS**:

```
SELECT class, count  FROM v$waitstat
WHERE class = 'free list';
```

The following SQL statement can be used to obtain the total number of requests:

```
SELECT sum(value)  FROM v$sysstat
WHERE name in ('db block gets', 'consistent gets');
```

You should compare the number of free block waits with the total number of requests. If this is more than 1 percent, you need to determine which tables have a problem with **FREELISTS** and increase the **FREELISTS** for those tables. You must rely on your knowledge of the application to determine which tables have a high number of inserts and deletes and would therefore be candidates for **FREELISTS** contention.

The number of **FREELISTS** associated with a table or index cannot be changed with an **ALTER** command. The maximum value depends on the **DB_BLOCK_SIZE**. If you attempt to create an object with a **FREELISTS** value that is too high, Oracle will generate an error message. To change the number of **FREELISTS**, you must export the table, drop the table, re-create the table with the new value for **FREELISTS**, and import the data.

FREELISTS for index segments are handled slightly different than FREELISTS for tables. When an index block becomes empty, it is placed on the FREELISTS. As long as the block contains even one entry, it will be maintained separately and not placed on the FREELISTS.

## FREELIST GROUPS

The FREELIST GROUPS parameter is valid only if you are using the parallel server option in parallel mode. This parameter specifies the number of FREELIST GROUPS that can be associated with a segment.

## OPTIMAL

The size a rollback segment will dynamically shrink back to is specified by the OPTIMAL parameter. This can be specified in bytes, kilobytes, or megabytes. The minimum for OPTIMAL cannot be less than the space initially allocated with the INITIAL, NEXT, and MINEXTENTS parameters as specified in the CREATE ROLLBACK SEGMENT command. You need to combine the space requirements specified in these storage parameters to determine the minimal OPTIMAL setting. The maximum value is operating system dependent.

If OPTIMAL is not specified, Oracle will still allocate extents for active transactions as needed; but it will not deallocate extents when they are no longer needed. If the OPTIMAL setting is used, Oracle will deallocate extents only down to the OPTIMAL setting. You can use the OPTIMAL parameter to allow more efficient use of disk space for infrequent, large transactions. If OPTIMAL is used, it must be set high enough to accommodate the majority of the transactions. If OPTIMAL is set too low, the rollback segment will continually allocate and deallocate extents, causing additional overhead.

## INITRANS

The INITRANS parameter specifies the initial number of transaction entries that are allocated for each block associated with a table. This value should usually remain at the default value of 2 for indexes and clusters and 1 for other objects. Each update requires a transaction entry in the block header. Transaction entries are used to control the number of concurrent updates to a block. The number of transactions is allocated and deallocated dynamically. The size of a transaction is operating system dependent.

## MAXTRANS

The MAXTRANS parameter is the maximum number of transactions updating a block concurrently. You should not change the value for MAXTRANS.

When the **MAXTRANS** value is reached, Oracle will not make additional updates to the block even if additional freespace is available.

# PCTFREE And PCTUSED

The **PCTFREE** (percent free) and **PCTUSED** (percent used) parameters allow you to control the amount of space allocated for updates and inserts into a block. These parameters are used together to optimize space utilization for blocks. It is important that you consider both **PCTFREE** and **PCTUSED** when you plan the storage parameters for each object in your database.

The **PCTFREE** parameter specifies the percentage of the block that is to be retained for updates to rows in the block. Row migration will result if the **PCTFREE** is insufficient for the increased size of the rows in the block. When inserting rows into a table, the **PCTFREE** controls when new rows can be inserted and when they must be placed in a new block or a block that is on the **FREELISTS**. For very static tables with very few updates, the **PCTFREE** should be lower to allow more rows to be inserted into each block. Because all the blocks below the high water mark for a table are read for full table scans, performance will be improved and I/O decreased if each block contains the maximum amount of data. However, if **PCTFREE** is set too low, rows that are updated will become chained, and performance will be negatively affected.

Use the following formula to determine a correct setting for **PCTFREE**

```
PCTFREE = 100 * a/(a+b)
```

where $a$ represents the average amount added for an update and $b$ represents the average size of the initial row.

**PCTFREE** can be changed with the **ALTER** command. Changing **PCTFREE** does not affect existing blocks. However, all future DML will use the new **PCTFREE** parameter.

The **PCTUSED** parameter specifies the percentage of the block below which the block usage must drop in order for the block to be added to the **FREELISTS**. PCTUSED is relevant only to tables in which rows are deleted. For example, data is inserted into a block until it reaches the specified **PCTFREE**. That block is taken off the **FREELISTS** until data is deleted down to the setting for **PCTUSED**. When the **PCTUSED** setting is reached again, the block is placed back on the **FREELISTS**, and data is once again inserted into the block until the **PCTFREE** setting is reached. A high **PCTUSED**, in conjunction with a low **PCTFREE**, can lead to blocks being taken on and off the **FREELISTS** continually, which increases the overhead.

For tables that have many inserts and few deletes, you should set the **PCTUSED** to a higher number. A higher **PCTUSED** in conjunction with a lower **PCTFREE** will pack each block and increase performance by decreasing the number of blocks that need to be read for full table scans (decreasing I/O).

**PCTUSED** can be changed with the **ALTER** command. Changing **PCTUSED** does not affect existing blocks. However, all future DML will use the new **PCTUSED** parameter.

# Other Database Configuration Options

File placement, striping, and adjusting object storage parameters are important to database configuration. There are several other advanced database configuration options that can be used for specific types of database environments. This includes the use of raw devices, clustering tables, parallelism, multithreaded server (MTS), pinning packages, and caching tables. It is important to carefully review your application server and individual requirements before using any of these options.

## Raw Devices

A raw device is a Unix-character special file that Oracle can read and write directly without Unix I/O buffering. From Oracle's perspective, tablespaces are created the same regardless of whether the operating system file is a raw device or a datafile. Oracle addresses the advantages and disadvantages of using raw devices in its OFA. Raw devices require expert system and database administration to set up and administer. It is possible to mix the use of raw devices for highly active OLTP-related tablespaces with standard file systems for other tablespaces and files.

In a few specific situations, Oracle recommends the use of raw devices. If you are using the Oracle parallel server for multiple nodes that are using a single database on a shared disk array, you must use Unix raw devices. You cannot mount a shared disk simultaneously on multiple servers. If you are using a non-Unix server that does not have asynchronous I/O, a raw device will enhance performance. Raw devices can also be used to improve performance for write-intensive redo logs.

There are several disadvantages with using raw devices. Raw devices are much more difficult to administer. The following operations are much more complex when raw devices are used:

➤ Backup and recovery

➤ I/O load balancing

➤ Adding files to the database

Oracle discourages the use of raw devices in any database environment in which you cannot practice backup and recovery operations before the database is used for production. In addition, you must be able to leave two or more large unformatted disk slices available to accommodate an increase in the size of your database or to perform load balancing. You should always try to identify and resolve I/O bottlenecks as much as possible before you consider using raw devices. Remember that using raw devices does not negate the recommendations for placement of Oracle files on the server.

# Clustering Tables

Clustering allows the rows in two tables to be stored together in the same block on the basis of the common value in both tables. The deciding factor for determining whether to cluster tables is how they are accessed by users of your application. Tables should be clustered only if they are referenced in the same SQL statement using a join with an equality condition.

If you often perform full table scans of the individual tables, a cluster will actually increase I/O. When a full table scan is performed on a cluster, it will be necessary to read all the blocks associated with the cluster even if the block is empty. If the clustered tables are accessed separately in a SQL statement, clustering will negatively affect performance because many more blocks will need to be read.

Another deciding factor is the size of your data blocks in relation to the size of the cluster key. When Oracle reads data from a cluster, it must read all the blocks that are associated with that cluster key. If it is necessary to read several blocks of data to read one row, using a cluster will involve more physical reads than accessing an unclustered table with a primary key index.

It is important to determine a baseline for performance of SQL statements using a join and indexes before clustering tables. This baseline will give you a basis by which to compare the effect of using a cluster. The application code should be thoroughly tested to determine whether using a cluster will increase performance in one area but will negatively affect other application code.

To cluster two tables, you must first decide on the cluster key for your data. A cluster key should consist of the common column or columns that are used in the **WHERE** clause with an equality condition. You must determine how much the clustered tables will grow and allow sufficient space for this growth. Remember that if the tables outgrow the space allocated, you will need to re-create the cluster. In addition, the cluster key should be composed of columns that are rarely, if ever, updated. The time required to modify the cluster can be significant if the change to the key causes the data to be moved to another block in the cluster. If too few cluster keys are specified, you will have collisions (that is, two rows having the same cluster key value). For Oracle to identify the correct row for clusters with the same cluster key value, it is necessary to evaluate all the rows in all the blocks with that value. This slows the performance for scans of clustered tables.

# Parallelism

If your server has more than one CPU, you can take advantage of the parallel query option. The parallel query option allows multiple processes to work on retrieving the data. Application of parallelism on massively parallel, clustered, symmetric multiprocessing (SMP) servers or on tables that take advantage of striping can significantly improve performance. The default for degree of parallelism is **NOPARALLEL.**

A parallel query is performed using a query coordinator and multiple query servers. Parallelism is used for both scanning and sorting. Separate query servers are used for these operations. The number of query servers for each process is equal to the **DEGREE** of parallelism specified. Because there are two processes (sorting and scanning), the number of parallel query processes is 2 multiplied by the **DEGREE** of parallelism specified. The query coordinator dispatches the query servers to perform the query against parts of the table and coordinates the results of the multiple query servers. This speeds up full table scans and sort operations. You can alter the degree of parallelism for a table with the following syntax:

```
ALTER TABLE table_name PARALLEL (DEGREE integer);
```

For example:

```
ALTER TABLE employee PARALLEL (DEGREE 5);
```

This example would enable queries against the employee table to use 5 query servers for sorting and 5 query servers for scanning, for a total of 10 query processes.

The following types of SQL statements can be performed with the parallel query option:

➤ **SELECT**

➤ Subqueries in **UPDATE, INSERT,** and **DELETE**

➤ CREATE TABLE...AS SELECT...

➤ CREATE INDEX

➤ REBUILD INDEX

The syntax for the parallel clause is shown in Figure 4.1.

The query server is responsible for determining which parts of a SQL statement can be performed in parallel. The query server will determine what can be performed in parallel on the basis of hints, the database initialization file parameters, and the table definition. Table 4.8 specifies the relevant database initialization file parameters. The default is operating system-dependent with the exception of **PARALLEL_MIN_PERCENT** and **PARALLEL_MIN_SERVERS**, both of which default to zero.

You can also take advantage of Oracle's parallel query option to build indexes. Two sets of query servers are used when building an index in parallel. One set retrieves the column and row information from the table. The other set performs the sorting and builds the B-tree index.

When parallelism is used in creating a table or an index, the storage allocated by Oracle for the initial extent is equal to the **degree** of parallelism multiplied by the size of the **INITIAL EXTENT**. Each of the query servers will be allocated disk space in the table's default tablespace equal to the size of the initial extent. When the query servers return the results to the query coordinator, all the results will be combined into the required number of initial extents and trimmed, as determined by the query coordinator. For example, if you create a table with **INITIAL 10M** using **PARALLEL DEGREE 5**, the resulting space requirements in the table's tablespace could be as much as 50MB.

The parallel server option is different from the parallel query option in that the former supports multiple servers accessing the same database. The database is placed on a shared disk array that can be accessed by multiple servers in a

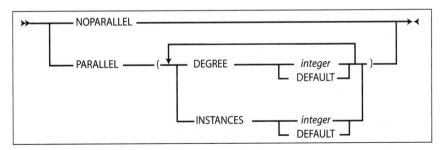

**Figure 4.1**  Syntax for defining parallelism.

**Table 4.8    Database initialization parameters for parallelism.**

| Parameter | Description |
|---|---|
| PARALLEL_DEFAULT_MAX_INSTANCES | Number of instances to be used for the parallel operation |
| PARALLEL_DEFAULT_MAX_SCANS | Obsolete with Oracle7.3 |
| PARALLEL_DEFAULT_SCANSIZE | Obsolete with Oracle7.3 |
| PARALLEL_MAX_SERVERS | Maximum number of servers |
| PARALLEL_MIN_PERCENT | Minimum number of query servers (slaves) required |
| PARALLEL_MIN_SERVERS | Number of query servers initiated at startup |
| PARALLEL_SERVER_IDLE_TIME | The number of minutes a query server can be idle before it is terminated |

parallel server configuration. In such a configuration, placing data is even more important. Because all the nodes can access the same data, data contention becomes a key point, and distribution of the datafiles is vital.

# Multithreaded Server Configuration

Oracle supports two types of database connections: dedicated and shared. Each dedicated connection to Oracle requires a process on the server. Dedicated connections are required for Server Manager. Application connections can use either dedicated connections or shared connections. Shared connections are made using the multithreaded server (MTS) configuration. Connections using MTS reduce the number of processes executing on the server. This is especially useful when many end users are accessing the system at the same time and the server is approaching the limits for processes and semaphores. Users performing large batch processes or database-intensive work will find no advantage to using MTS. The use of MTS affects the shared pool (for information on tuning the shared pool for an MTS configuration, see Chapter 5).

If you look at the users who are connected to a database, you will see that the session is usually inactive. The only time the session is active is when Oracle is executing a **SELECT, INSERT, UPDATE,** or **DELETE** command. The time period during which a user process is inactive is usually referred to as think time. Think time is when a user is typing data onto a screen, composing a SQL query, reviewing the data returned by a SQL query, and so on. The shared server concept is based on the idea of optimizing the active time for all connections. With MTS, users share database servers, and database dispatchers coordinate the process.

To use MTS, you must set the database initialization parameters and then shut down and start up the database. Table 4.9 lists the database initialization parameters that are associated with MTS. The MTS option requires the use of SQL*Net version 2. The SQL*Net listener process should always be started before the databases using MTS are started so that the databases can register with the listener process on startup. Once the database is started using MTS, all connections will use shared servers and dispatchers automatically, unless the connection is specified as a dedicated connection. The only exception is Server Manager, which always creates a dedicated connection.

When a user logs on to a database that is using MTS, a dispatcher picks up the connection request and places it in a request queue located in the SGA. Shared server processes constantly check the request queue for new requests. A shared server picks up the request and performs all the calls necessary to satisfy that request. The results are placed in a response queue for the dispatcher from which the request was initiated. The dispatcher process picks up the response and sends the information to the user. As more users log on to the database, additional dispatchers and servers will be created dynamically up to the **MTS_MAX_DISPATCHERS** and **MTS_MAX_SERVERS** limits. As users log off the database, the number of dispatchers and servers is dynamically

**Table 4.9    Multithreaded server database initialization parameters.**

| Parameter | Default | Description |
| --- | --- | --- |
| MTS_DISPATCHERS | Null | Number of dispatchers at database startup for each network protocol supported |
| MTS_LISTENER_ADDRESS | Null | Network protocol address as specified in the SQL*Net listener.ora file |
| MTS_MAX_DISPATCHERS | 5 | Maximum number of dispatchers |
| MTS_MAX_SERVERS | 20 | Maximum number of servers |
| MTS_MULTIPLE_LISTENERS | FALSE | Indicates multiple MTS_LISTENER_ADDRESS parameters in one consolidated list |
| MTS_SERVERS | 0 | Number of servers at database startup |
| MTS_SERVICE | DB_NAME | Connect string to be used if no dispatcher is available; value of the SID in the CONNECT_DATA clause of the tnsnames.ora file |

| Table 4.10    V$MTS data dictionary view. | |
|---|---|
| **Column** | **Description** |
| maximum_connections | Maximum number of connections each dispatcher can support (based on the operating system) |
| servers_started | Total number of additional shared servers started since the database started (excluding those specified during startup) |
| servers_terminated | Total number of shared servers stopped since instance startup |
| servers_highwater | The highest number of servers at any time |

decreased down to the number specified by the **MTS_SERVERS** and **MTS_DISPATCHERS** database initialization parameters. The **V$MTS** view, described in Table 4.10, contains information on the MTS connections. If the **SERVERS_HIGHWATER** column is equal to the **MTS_MAX_SERVERS** value in the database initialization parameter file, you should consider increasing the value of the **MTS_MAX_SERVERS** parameter.

When using MTS, you need to be aware that you could encounter artificial deadlocks. When a user tries to commit and the process hangs, it might appear to the end user that there is a deadlock situation. However, the real problem is that the **COMMIT** command cannot be executed because of a problem with MTS. Artificial deadlocks are encountered when the maximum number of shared servers has been reached and no additional requests can be processed (including **COMMIT** and **ROLLBACK** statements).

If the database is configured to use the MTS option, you need to monitor the dispatchers and shared servers. You should establish a baseline and then monitor the MTS dispatchers and shared servers when users are accessing the database. You should increase the maximum number of dispatchers and shared servers when contention exists for these processes. The following three views are important in monitoring your dispatchers and shared servers for MTS:

➤ V$DISPATCHER

➤ V$QUEUE

➤ V$SHARED_SERVER

These views are available only to the SYS user and to users with the **SELECT ANY TABLE** system privilege.

You can use the **V$DISPATCHER** view to monitor your dispatchers. Table 4.11 describes the **V$DISPATCHER** view, and Table 4.12 lists the possible

## Table 4.11     V$DISPATCHER data dictionary view.

| Column | Description |
|---|---|
| name | Name of this dispatcher process |
| network | Network protocol (that is, TCP or DECNET) |
| paddr | Process address |
| status | Status of the dispatcher |
| accept | YES to indicate that this dispatcher is accepting new connections; NO to indicate that this dispatcher is not accepting new connections |
| messages | Number of messages processed by this dispatcher |
| bytes | Total number of bytes for the messages processed by this dispatcher |
| breaks | Number of breaks that have occurred in this connection |
| owned | Number of circuits owned by this dispatcher |
| created | Number of circuits created by this dispatcher |
| idle | Total idle time (hundredths of a second) |
| busy | Total busy time (hundredths of a second) |
| listener | Last error number received from the listener process |

## Table 4.12     STATUS column values for the V$DISPATCHER view.

| Status | Meaning |
|---|---|
| WAIT | Idle |
| SENT | Currently sending a message |
| RECEIVE | Currently receiving a message |
| CONNECT | Establishing a connection |
| DISCONNECT | Processing a request to disconnect |
| BREAK | Processing a break |
| OUTBOUND | Establishing an outbound connection |

values for the **STATUS** column of the **V$DISPATCHER** view and the meaning for each. The **IDLE** and **BUSY** columns are the most important items to monitor for the dispatcher. The following query can be used to determine the total busy rate for the dispatcher for each network:

```
SELECT network,
       sum(busy) / (sum(busy) + sum(idle)  )
```

```
FROM V$DISPATCHER
GROUP BY network;
```

If the total busy rate is greater than 50 percent, you should add additional dispatcher processes. You can do this with the following command:

```
ALTER SYSTEM SET mts_dispatchers = 'protocol, number';
```

This will increase the number of dispatchers for use by new connections. However, it will not increase the number of dispatchers available to users who are already logged on to the database.

Table 4.13 describes the columns in the **V$SHARED_SERVER** view. Table 4.14 lists the possible values for the **STATUS** column of the **V$SHARED_ SERVER** view and the meaning for each. You can determine the number of shared servers that are currently running with the following query:

```
SELECT COUNT(*) FROM V$SHARED_SERVERS
WHERE status != 'QUIT';
```

If the number of shared servers is approaching the **MTS_MAX_SERVERS** limit, you might be able to improve performance by increasing this database initialization parameter. If you determine that you have set too many shared servers at database startup, you can reduce the number of shared servers. The syntax to increase or reduce the number of shared servers is:

**Table 4.13    V$SHARED_SERVER data dictionary view.**

| Column | Description |
| --- | --- |
| name | Name of this server process |
| paddr | Process address |
| status | Status of this shared server |
| messages | Number of messages processed by this server |
| bytes | Total number of bytes in all the messages |
| breaks | Number of breaks |
| owned | Number of circuits |
| circuit | Address for the current circuit being served |
| idle | Total idle time (hundredths of a second) |
| busy | Total busy time (hundredths of a second) |
| requests | Total number of requests serviced from the common queue since this server was created |

**Table 4.14    Status information for the V$SHARED_SERVER view.**

| Status | Meaning |
|---|---|
| EXEC | Executing a SQL statement |
| WAIT(ENQ) | Waiting for a lock |
| WAIT(SEND) | Waiting to send data to a user |
| WAIT(COMMON) | Waiting for a user request to service |
| WAIT(RESET) | Waiting for a circuit to reset after a break |
| QUIT | Terminating |

```
ALTER SYSTEM SET MTS_SERVERS = integer;
```

Because Oracle will increase the number of shared servers dynamically, Oracle recommends starting with a low number of servers (1 per 100 users) and increasing the number of shared servers as needed.

**V$QUEUE** provides information on the MTS queues for the dispatcher and shared servers. Table 4.15 describes the **V$QUEUE** view. The following query can be used to determine the average wait time for a connection that is waiting in the response queue for a dispatcher process:

```
SELECT network,
       DECODE (SUM(totalq), 0, 'NO RESPONSES',
              SUM(wait)/SUM(totalq) )
FROM V$QUEUE, V$DISPATCHER
WHERE v$queue.type = 'DISPATCHER'
AND   v$queue.paddr = v$dispatcher.paddr
GROUP BY network;
```

**Table 4.15    V$QUEUE data dictionary view.**

| Column | Description |
|---|---|
| paddr | Address of the process that owns the queue |
| type | COMMON for queues processed by servers; OUTBOUND for queues used by remote server's dispatcher |
| queued | Number of items in the queue |
| wait | Total time that all items have been queued |
| totalq | Total number of items that have been in the queue |

To determine the average wait time for each shared server request, you can execute the following query:

```
SELECT DECODE( totalq, 0, , 'NO RESPONSES',
               wait/totalq)
FROM V$QUEUE
WHERE type = 'COMMON';
```

Remember that these **V$** views represent cumulative statistics since the last time the database was shut down and restarted.

Both the **MTS_DISPATCHERS** and the **MTS_SERVERS** parameters can be changed with the **ALTER SYSTEM** command. However, you cannot interactively change the **MTS_MAX_DISPATCHERS** and **MTS_MAX_SERVERS** parameters.

If there is a problem with a specific process in the database, you can use the **V$CIRCUIT** view to obtain information on the specific user. Table 4.16 describes the **V$CIRCUIT** view. The **SADDR** column of the **V$CIRCUIT** view provides the session address that corresponds to the **SADDR** column in the **V$SESSION** view. The **V$SESSION** view contains the user name and

**Table 4.16    V$CIRCUIT data dictionary view.**

| Column | Description |
| --- | --- |
| circuit | Circuit address |
| dispatcher | Current dispatcher process address |
| server | Current server address |
| waiter | Address of server process waiting for an available circuit |
| saddr | Address of session |
| status | BREAK for interrupted; EOF for about to be removed; OUTBOUND for outward link to a remote database; NORMAL |
| queue | COMMON if waiting to be picked up by a shared server; SERVER if currently being serviced; OUTBOUND if waiting to establish a connection; DISPATCHER if waiting for a dispatcher; NONE if idle |
| message0 | Size in bytes of first message buffer |
| message1 | Size in bytes of second message buffer |
| messages | Total number of messages that have gone through this circuit |
| bytes | Total number of bytes that have gone through this circuit |
| breaks | Total number of interruptions for this circuit |

operating system user information.

If you are using MTS, you should never kill a user process at the operating system prompt. Because connections are shared, other user processes will be killed as well. In addition, you need to be sure that the setting for the **PRO-CESSES** database initialization file parameter includes the total number of all the dispatchers and shared servers that might be active (up to the maximum).

## Pinning Packages In The Shared Pool

Oracle provides a built-in package, **DBMS_SHARED_POOL**, that can be used to pin packages into the shared pool, therefore reducing I/O. The **DBMS_SHARED_POOL** package is created with the dbmspool.sql and prvtpool.pbl scripts, which are located in the $ORACLE_HOME/rdbms/admin directory on a Unix server.

The **DBMS_SHARED_POOL.KEEP** procedure will pin the package in the shared pool and prevent it from being aged out or flushed out of the shared pool. The package is not immediately read into the shared pool when this procedure is executed. Rather, it is kept in the shared pool once it has been accessed. The package will stay in the shared pool until the **DBMS_SHARED_POOL.UNKEEP** procedure is executed or the database is shut down. Once the **UNKEEP** procedure has been executed, the package will age out of the shared pool normally (for more information on pinning and unpinning objects in the shared pool, see Chapter 5).

## Cache Tables In The Shared Pool

If you have a table that is frequently accessed, especially with a full table scan, you can cache the table in the shared pool. This does not permanently read the table into the shared pool or prevent it from being aged out. Full table scans usually result in the table being placed at the least recently used (LRU) end of the LRU list and then being quickly aged out. Caching the table will place it on the most frequently used end of the LRU list instead of the least recently used end. The **CACHE** keyword can be used when creating the table to cache it in the shared pool. You can also use hints (for detailed information on hints, see Chapter 3) or the **ALTER TABLE** command to cache a table in the shared pool. The following is an example of how to **CACHE** a table in the shared pool with an **ALTER TABLE** command:

```
ALTER TABLE state_codes CACHE;
```

# Practice Questions

## Question 1

> Which two conditions might make it worthwhile for you to manu-
> ally stripe tablespaces across the file system? [Check all correct
> answers]
>
> ☐ a. The application is performing many full table scans
>
> ☐ b. There is limited operating system memory
>
> ☐ c. The application is performing few full table scans
>
> ☐ d. The server is running in parallel query mode

The correct answers are a and d. Manually striping tablespaces across a file
system is very labor-intensive and complex. Striping will increase performance
only if there are many full table scans and if the degree of parallelism is greater
than 1 (parallel query mode). If the operation is performing well and not executing full table scans, the time and effort involved in striping is not justified.

## Question 2

> What should be your goal when tuning I/O?
>
> ○ a. Distribute I/O as much as possible
>
> ○ b. Keep Oracle I/O limited to one area of the system
>
> ○ c. Do not place any non-Oracle files on the system
>
> ○ d. Reduce writes as much as possible

The correct answer is a. Oracle recommends that the files be distributed across
as many drives as possible. Although it is beneficial to have only Oracle files on
a system, this might not be realistic. Keeping Oracle I/O limited to one area
would mean limiting the number of drives for Oracle files and is opposite to
Oracle's recommendations. Reducing the number of writes would not reduce
the number of physical reads.

# Question 3

Which strategy should you follow when your system contains Oracle and non-Oracle files?

○  a. Store the files on separate devices

○  b. Store files in separate directories

○  c. Make sure that the files contain distinct names

○  d. Remove all non-Oracle files from the system as soon as possible

The correct answer is a. The best answer is to separate Oracle and non-Oracle files on different physical drives whenever possible. Storing Oracle and non-Oracle files in the same directory will not reduce the I/O contention if both directories are on the same physical disk. Naming conventions will not affect I/O, and removing non-Oracle files might not be reasonable for most applications.

# Question 4

When designing a database, which objects should be stored in the **RBS** tablespace other than rollback segments?

○  a. User-created objects

○  b. Database triggers

○  c. Temporary segments

○  d. None

The correct answer is d. Rollback segments tend to have high I/O and should be stored on separate disks whenever possible. Oracle recommends separate tablespaces for user-created objects for ease of maintenance. Database triggers are stored in the **SYSTEM** tablespace. Temporary segments should be stored in their own tablespace, which should be designated as a temporary tablespace.

## Question 5

> You want to prevent row migration on the **PARTS** table. Which action should you take?
>
> O a. Increase **PCTUSED**
>
> O b. Decrease **PCTUSED**
>
> O c. Increase **PCTFREE**
>
> O d. Decrease **PCTFREE**

The correct answer is c. Row migration results from insufficient freespace for updates. Therefore, the obvious answer is to increase the **PCTFREE** to allow more space for updates. as Decreasing **PCTFREE** would only increase row migration. The **PCTUSED** is relevant only to deletions.

## Question 6

> Which view can you query to determine if contention for the free-list Is high?
>
> O a. **V$SESSION**
>
> O b. **V$WAITSTAT**
>
> O c. **V$RESOURCE**
>
> O d. **V$LOADSTAT**

The correct answer is b. The **V$WAITSTAT** will provide information on waits for the freelist. However, this view will not indicate which tables are affected by waits for freelist. It is up to the DBA to review the application and determine which tables are performing multiple insert and delete operations.

## Question 7

> What is increased when the database contains migrated rows?
>
> O a. **PCTUSED**
>
> O b. I/O
>
> O c. **SHARED_POOL_SIZE**
>
> O d. **PCTFREE**

The correct answer is b. It is important to read this question carefully. It is asking what is increased by row migration, not how to reduce row migration. The **PCTUSED** and **PCTFREE** parameters are not increased by migrated rows. The **SHARED_POOL_SIZE** is also not increased automatically by row migration. When a row is migrated, an indicator is set at the previous block location to point to the new location. This increases I/O because the original block in which the row was located must be read, as must the new block containing the row. The **PCTUSED** and **PCTFREE** parameters are used to regulate space in blocks, and inappropriate settings can lead to row migration problems.

## Question 8

You issue this command:

```
ANALYZE TABLE inventory.item COMPUTE STATISTICS;
```

Which column in the **DBA_TABLES** view can you query to see the number of migrated rows in the **INVENTORY.ITEM** table?

○ a. **BLOCKS**

○ b. **CHAIN_CNT**

○ c. **AVG_ROW_LEN**

○ d. **NUM_ROWS**

The correct answer is b. The **CHAIN_CNT** column lists the number of both chained and migrated rows. Chained rows result from having a block size that is too small for the row to fit into a single block. Because the block size can be changed only by re-creating the database, this problem is not easily fixed. Migrated rows are the result of insufficient space in a block for updates. Once the migrated rows have been identified, they can be removed and reinserted.

## Question 9

> Which statement type can you use to reset the high water mark on a table?
>
> ○ a. **DELETE**
>
> ○ b. **TRUNCATE**
>
> ○ c. **UPDATE**
>
> ○ d. **INSERT**

The answer is b. You need to read this question carefully. Inserting and updating data in a table can cause the high water mark to change (increase). However, this is done implicitly, only when Oracle determines that it is necessary, and does not reset the high water mark. The **DELETE** command will remove all the rows but will not reset the high water mark. The only SQL command that will reset the high water mark is the **TRUNCATE** command.

# Need To Know More?

 The first place to go for more information is the *Oracle7 Tuning Manual* and the *Oracle7 Server Reference Manual*.

 Alomari, Ahmed: *Oracle and Unix Performance Tuning.* Prentice-Hall, 1997. ISBN 0-13-849167-4. The important chapter in this book is Chapter 3.

 Aronoff, Eyal, Kevin Loney, and Noorali Sonawalla: *Advanced Oracle Tuning and Administration.* Oracle Press, 1997. ISBN 0-07882-241-6. Pay special attention to Chapters 4, 5, and 12.

 Corrigan, Peter and Mark Gurry: *Oracle Performance Tuning.* O'Reilly & Associates, Inc., 1993. ISBN 1-56592-048-1. Chapters 11, 13, and 17 are good chapters to look at closely.

 Feuerstein, Steven, Charles Dye, and John Beresniewicz: *Oracle Built-in Packages.* O'Reilly & Associates, Inc., 1998. ISBN 1-56592-375-8. Pay special attention to Chapter 12.

# Tuning
# The SGA

## Terms you'll need to understand:

√ System global area (SGA)

√ Database buffer cache

√ Shared pool

√ Library cache

√ Dictionary cache

√ Redo log buffer

√ User global area (UGA)

## Techniques you'll need to master:

√ Understanding the performance impact of a correctly sized database block size

√ Determining the optimal configuration for the primary SGA parameters, shared pool, database buffer cache, and redo log buffer

√ Evaluating the additional SGA requirements when implementing the Oracle multithreaded server (MTS) option

An Oracle instance consists of the background processes (for example, SMON, PMON, DBWR, and LGWR) and the system global area (SGA). Both the background processes and the SGA are allocated when the instance is started and deallocated when the instance is shut down. The SGA is a highly tunable shared memory area that stores information for a particular instance. Several initialization file parameters determine the size of the SGA at instance startup. Access to information in memory is always faster than disk access. Therefore, the ideal scenario is to use the cached information in the SGA to satisfy multiple requests for shared data, performing as few physical reads as possible. Proper sizing and allocation of the SGA is vital to achieving this goal.

The SGA consists of three memory structures:

➤ Database buffers

➤ Shared pool

➤ Redo log buffer

This chapter explains how to tune Oracle's shared memory structure: the SGA. This discussion includes proper sizing of the Oracle block size to maximize system performance. The tuning process for the main components of the SGA are detailed first, followed by an explanation of the additional SGA memory requirements when using the multithreaded server (MTS).

# Tuning The Oracle Block Size

The Oracle database block size is the smallest logical unit of database storage. When a request is made to read or write data, this value indicates the minimum chunk of data transferred between physical disk and memory. One database block corresponds to a specific number of bytes of physical storage for an Oracle datafile. The Oracle block size is set during database creation by the **DB_BLOCK_SIZE** database initialization parameter. The default for **DB_BLOCK_SIZE** varies, depending on the operating system, but is typically 2K or 4K. A database block size should be a multiple of the operating system's block size.

Once the database has been created, a block size has been established for that database and the database block size should *never* be changed unless the database is re-created. Changes to the **DB_BLOCK_SIZE** parameter without database re-creation could result in database corruption. To re-create the database, you should perform a full cold backup of all database files and then use the Export utility to export the full database. The database can then be re-created using the new **DB_BLOCK_SIZE** initialization file parameter. The Import utility can then be run to import the data into the new database.

You will find that several initialization file parameters are allocated in database blocks. When you re-create an Oracle database with a new **DB_BLOCK_SIZE** parameter, you should consider the additional initialization file parameters that might need to be altered to accommodate the change in the database block size. For example, if the database is re-created to increase the Oracle block size from 4K to 8K and the **DB_BLOCK_BUFFERS** parameter is not altered, you have essentially doubled the size of the database buffer cache. The database buffer cache is explained later in this chapter.

In many cases, a block size larger than the default will provide greater I/O efficiency when transferring data between physical disk and the SGA and, therefore, better system performance. This is especially true for decision support systems (DSSs). Oracle recommends that in a DSS environment you size the database blocks as large as the operating system will allow, even if it means re-creating the database. A larger block size takes advantage of read-intensive (full table scan) operations that are typical in a DSS system. A larger block size is also recommended for a large system with a substantial amount of memory and fast disk drives. The performance gain from a correctly sized database block size (or the performance loss from an incorrectly sized database block size) is substantial. Some tests have revealed a 40 percent increase in performance when using the correct block size. Whenever possible, you should create multiple databases and test performance statistics with various database block sizes to determine the optimal block size for your database.

# Tuning The Shared Pool

The shared pool is an area of the SGA that contains two main memory structures:

➤ Library cache

➤ Dictionary cache

The efficiency of the shared pool is determined mainly by its hit ratio. The hit ratio reveals how often the information requested by a process was already located in the shared pool, without requiring physical reads from disk.

The size of the shared pool is determined by the **SHARED_POOL_SIZE** initialization file parameter. The default size of the shared pool is 3,500,000 bytes; this size is generally inadequate for most systems. The size of the shared pool should be large enough to achieve a good hit ratio on the library cache and dictionary cache. However, it should not be so large that it wastes memory or causes paging and swapping to occur because of memory constraints that cannot accommodate such a large shared pool size.

If the database is using the MTS architecture, additional memory considerations are required for proper sizing of the shared pool. This is because some user information is stored in the shared pool with an MTS configuration. These requirements are covered later in this chapter.

## Library Cache

The library cache is the most tunable component of the shared pool. It stores SQL statements and PL/SQL blocks, including procedures, packages, and triggers issued in the database. These statements are parsed and ready for execution. SQL entries in the library cache are managed by a least recently used (LRU) algorithm. When memory is insufficient to store a new SQL statement, the LRU algorithm ages the least recently used SQL statements out of the library cache first. Proper sizing of the library cache will help to prevent shared SQL statements from being prematurely aged out of memory.

Each SQL statement in the library cache has an entry in the shared SQL area and an entry in the private SQL area.

The shared SQL area of the library cache contains a parse tree and an execution plan for each SQL statement. A primary goal of tuning the library cache is to keep parsing to a minimum by reusing SQL statements in the shared SQL area. When a SQL statement is issued, Oracle searches the shared SQL area for the identical SQL code before loading that statement into the library cache. To identify the exact statement, the SQL is translated to the numeric value of the ASCII text, and a hash function is used to locate the statement. If the statement is found from a previous request, Oracle will discard the new SQL statement and reuse the parsed and executable SQL statement already in the shared SQL area. A statement must be an exact match for Oracle to use the same shared SQL area. For example, the following statements are not considered identical by Oracle:

```
SELECT * FROM dept;

SELECT    * FROM dept;

SELECT * FROM Dept;

SELECT * FROM DEPT;
```

Whenever possible, SQL statements should use bind variables rather than constants to maximize the reusable database code. Packages are also recommended to increase the efficiency of the library cache because they always use generic code and are loaded into the shared SQL area when any section of them is accessed. In environments in which many packages or stored procedures are used, the shared SQL area of the library cache can consume a significant amount of memory. The method to determine the amount of sharable memory utilized by existing objects in the library cache is covered later in this chapter.

For each SQL statement, each user must have a separate entry in the private SQL area of the library cache. A private SQL area is the part of the library cache that contains data such as runtime buffers and bind information. Multiple private SQL areas can be associated with one shared SQL area. A private SQL area consists of two memory components:

➤ Persistent area

➤ Runtime area

The persistent area uses memory in the library cache for the span of an open cursor. This portion of the private SQL area continues to exist until the corresponding cursor is closed. If a statement is reused frequently, it might be efficient to leave the cursor open, provided you can afford the additional memory in your shared pool. However, if cursors are left open unnecessarily after SQL processing for the cursor has completed, the private SQL area could result in inefficient memory usage.

The runtime area contains information that is required while a SQL statement is executing. The size of the runtime area depends on the complexity of the SQL statement and the size of the rows that are processed by that statement. The runtime memory area is released immediately after an **INSERT, UPDATE,** or **DELETE** statement has completed execution. For **SELECT** statements, runtime area memory is released only after all rows have been fetched or the query is canceled.

The number of private SQL areas that a user can allocate is limited by the **OPEN_CURSORS** initialization file parameter. The value for this parameter indicates the maximum number of cursors that a user process can have open at any one time. The default value for **OPEN_CURSORS** is 50. Trying to open a cursor beyond the maximum will result in the error message "ORA-01000 Maximum open cursors exceeded." The resolution for this error is to modify the program to use fewer open cursors or increase the value of **OPEN_CURSORS** in the initialization file and restart the instance.

Several **V$** views provide statistics about the library cache. These views can be used to provide detailed information about the library cache area of the shared pool and can help identify the SQL being executed and its frequency, the database objects cached, and the hit ratio of the library cache objects since instance startup. To select from these views, you must have the SELECT ANY TABLE system privilege. The dynamic views of the library cache include:

➤ **V$LIBRARYCACHE**

➤ **V$SQLAREA**

➤ **V$SQLTEXT**

➤ **V$DB_OBJECT_CACHE**

➤ **V$SGASTAT**

The **V$LIBRARYCACHE** view, described in Table 5.1, reflects statistics about the library cache activity since instance startup. This view is used to determine the overall performance of the library cache. The **PINS** column indicates the number of times the system issued a pin request for objects in the cache in order to access them. The **RELOADS** column reveals whether parsed statements have been aged out of the shared SQL area, essentially becoming unavailable to other requests without reparsing the statement. Ideally, the **RELOADS** column should be zero but should never be more than 1 percent of the value of the **PINS** column.

The **V$LIBRARYCACHE** view is also useful in identifying the percentage of parse calls that found a cursor to share in the library cache. Table 5.2 provides an example of the query results from the **V$LIBRARYCACHE** view.

```
SELECT namespace, gethitratio
   FROM V$LIBRARYCACHE
   WHERE namespace = 'SQL AREA';
```

The **GETHITRATIO** for the namespace **SQL AREA** in the library cache should be in the high 90s. If sufficient space is allocated to the shared pool and the hit ratio is not in this range, the application code should be evaluated for efficiency. An additional consideration might be that the statistics reflected in the **V$LIBRARYCACHE** view are from instance startup to the current time. If you want library cache statistics for a specific time period, remember to run utlbstat/utlestat after the instance has been up and running with activity for a period of time sufficient to populate the SGA. This will discount expected misses in the library cache immediately after instance startup.

The **V$SQLAREA** view gives full statistics on the shared cursor cache. Each row stores statistics on one shared cursor. This view lists the first 80 characters of the SQL statement. This view is useful for determining the most frequently used SQL statements and the number of times that a SQL statement has been

**Table 5.1    The V$LIBRARYCACHE view.**

| Column | Description |
| --- | --- |
| NAMESPACE | Library cache namespace: SQL AREA, TABLE/PROCEDURE, BODY, TRIGGER, INDEX, CLUSTER, OBJECT, PIPE |
| GETS | Number of times a lock was requested for the namespace objects |
| GETHITS | Number of times the object's handles are already allocated in the cache |
| GETHITRATIO | Number of GETHITS divided by GETS; values close to 1 indicate that most of the handles that the system has attempted to acquire are cached |
| PINS | Number of times a pin was requested for the namespace objects |
| PINHITS | Number of times all the metadata pieces of the library object were already allocated and initialized in the cache |
| PINHITRATIO | Number of PINHITS divided by number of PINS |
| RELOADS | Number of times library objects must be reinitialized and reloaded with data because they have been aged out or invalidated |
| INVALIDATIONS | Number of times objects in the namespace were marked invalid because of the modification of a dependent object |
| DLM_LOCK_REQUESTS | Number of GET lock instance locks; DLM indicates the distributed lock manager, which is used for parallel server |
| DLM_PIN_REQUESTS | Number of pin-distributed lock manager locks |
| DLM_PIN_RELEASES | Number of releases on a pin by the distributed lock manager |
| DLM_INVALIDATION_REQUESTS | Number of distributed lock manager requests for invalidation instance locks |
| DLM_INVALIDATIONS | Number of invalidation pins, received from other instances |

**Table 5.2    Sample results of query on V$LIBRARYCACHE.**

| NAMESPACE | GETHITRATIO |
| --- | --- |
| SQL AREA | .965208231 |

executed since instance startup. It also lists the number of users currently executing a SQL statement from the **USERS_EXECUTING** column of the view. Table 5.3 describes the **V$SQLAREA** view.

The **V$SQLTEXT** view lists the full SQL statement, without truncation, of each SQL cursor in the shared SQL area of the SGA. Multiple rows can exist in this view for one SQL statement if necessary. This view is useful if you need to obtain the full SQL statement for input to an **EXPLAIN PLAN** execution. Table 5.4 describes the **V$SQLTEXT** view.

**Table 5.3    The V$SQLAREA view.**

| Column | Description |
| --- | --- |
| SQL_TEXT | First 80 characters of the SQL statement for the current cursor |
| SHARABLE_MEM | Amount of memory in bytes that is sharable between users |
| PERSISTENT_MEM | Amount of memory in bytes that persists for the life of the cursor |
| RUNTIME_MEM | Amount of memory in bytes that is needed only during execution |
| SORTS | Number of sorts performed by the SQL statement |
| VERSION_COUNT | Number of different versions of this cursor; the same SQL text might be used by different users, each on their own version of a table |
| LOADED_VERSIONS | Versions of the cursor that are currently fully loaded with no parts aged out |
| OPEN_VERSIONS | Number of versions on which some user has an open cursor |
| USERS_OPENING | Number of users who currently have this SQL statement parsed in an open cursor |
| EXECUTIONS | Total number of times this SQL statement has been executed |
| USERS_EXECUTING | Number of users currently executing this cursor |
| LOADS | Number of times the object was loaded or reloaded |
| FIRST_LOAD_TIME | Timestamp when object was first loaded into the SGA |
| INVALIDATIONS | Sum of invalidations |
| PARSE_CALLS | Number of times users executed a parse call for this cursor |
| DISK_READS | Number of disk reads by this cursor |

*(continued)*

**Table 5.3    The V$SQLAREA view *(continued)*.**

| Column | Description |
|---|---|
| BUFFER_GETS | Number of buffer gets by this cursor and all cursors caused to be executed by this cursor |
| ROWS_PROCESSED | Total number of rows returned by the statement |
| COMMAND_TYPE | Oracle command-type definition |
| OPTIMIZER_MODE | The optimizer mode: RULE, CHOOSE, FIRST_ROWS, or ALL_ROWS |
| PARSING_USER_ID | The user that parsed the statement the first time the statement was run |
| PARSING_SCHEMA_ID | Schema ID that was used for the initial parse |
| KEPT_VERSIONS | Number of child versions that have been pinned in the library cache using the DBMS_SHARED_POOL package |
| ADDRESS | Used with HASH_VALUE to select the full text of the SQL statement from V$SQLTEXT |
| HASH_VALUE | Used with ADDRESS to select the full text of the SQL statement from V$SQLTEXT |
| MODULE | Contains the name of the module that was executing at the time that the SQL statement was first parsed as set by calling DBMS_APPLICATION_INFO.SET_MODULE |
| MODULE_HASH | The hash value of the module that is named in the MODULE column |
| ACTION | Contains the name of the action that was executing at the time that the SQL statement was first parsed as set by calling DBMS_APPLICATION_INFO.SET_ACTION |
| ACTION_HASH | The hash value of the action that is named in the ACTION column |
| SERIALIZABLE_ABORTS | The number of times the transaction fails to serialize, producing ORA-8177 errors, per cursor |

**Table 5.4    The V$SQLTEXT view.**

| Column | Description |
|---|---|
| ADDRESS | Used with hash value to identify a uniquely cached cursor |
| HASH_VALUE | Used with ADDRESS to identify a uniquely cached cursor |
| PIECE | Number used to order the pieces of SQL text |
| COMMAND_TYPE | Code for the type of SQL statement (for example, SELECT or INSERT) |
| SQL_TEXT | Column contains one piece of the SQL text |

The **V$DB_OBJECT_CACHE** view lists the database objects in the library cache. These objects include tables, indexes, clusters, synonym definitions, PL/SQL procedures, packages, and triggers. Columns of particular importance in this view are the **LOADS** and **EXECUTIONS**. An object that is frequently executed and must be reloaded often might indicate that the **SHARED_POOL_SIZE** is too small. Objects might also benefit from being pinned in the library cache using the **DBMS_SHARED_POOL.keep** procedure. The **KEPT** column has a value of **YES** if the object has been pinned in the library cache. Table 5.5 describes the **V$DB_OBJECT_CACHE** view.

The **V$SGASTAT** view lists sizes of all structures within the SGA. Table 5.6 describes the **V$SGASTAT** view.

**Table 5.5 The V$DB_OBJECT_CACHE view.**

| Column | Description |
|---|---|
| OWNER | Owner of the object |
| NAME | Name of the object |
| DB_LINK | Database link name, if any |
| NAMESPACE | Library cache namespace of the object: TABLE/PROCEDURE BODY, TRIGGER, INDEX, CLUSTER, OBJECT |
| TYPE | Type of object: INDEX, TABLE, CLUSTER, VIEW, SET, SYNONYM, SEQUENCE, PROCEDURE, FUNCTION, PACKAGE, PACKAGE BODY, TRIGGER, CLASS, OBJECT, USER, DBLINK |
| SHARABLE_MEM | Amount of sharable memory in the shared pool consumed by the object |
| LOADS | Number of times the object has been loaded; this count also increases when an object has been invalidated |
| EXECUTIONS | Total number of times this object has been executed |
| LOCKS | Number of users currently locking this object |
| PINS | Number of users currently pinning this object |
| KEPT | YES if the object has been pinned in the shared pool using DBMS_SHARED_POOL.keep; NO if the object is not pinned |

**Table 5.6 The V$SGASTAT view.**

| Column | Description |
|---|---|
| NAME | SGA component name |
| BYTES | Size of the memory area in bytes |

## Determining The Size Of The Library Cache For An Existing Application

To calculate the size required for the library cache on an existing application, Oracle recommends that you start by setting the shared pool to a very large size. This might be at the expense of other structures if additional memory is limited. Run the application at a time that provides the best representation of normal to high application usage. Be sure to allow sufficient time after the application is started for the library cache to be loaded with shared SQL statements and for multiple requests to be issued for those statements. A series of database queries is then submitted to determine the optimal size for the library cache for that particular application. The collective sum of the query results will provide a good estimate of the optimal size of the library cache. If dynamic SQL is used in the database, additional memory will be required for the library cache to accommodate those statements. The following shows an example of the queries required to estimate the size of the library cache:

➤ Determine the sharable memory that is currently used for cached objects such as packages and views:

```
SELECT SUM(sharable_mem)
   FROM V$DB_OBJECT_CACHE;
```

Here is a sample result of the query:

```
SUM(sharable_mem)
         489400
```

➤ Determine the amount of sharable memory that is currently used for shared SQL statements that have been executed more than five times since instance startup:

```
SELECT SUM(sharable_mem)
     FROM V$SQLAREA
     WHERE executions > 5;
```

Here is a sample result of the query:

```
SUM(sharable_mem)
       392707
```

➤ Determine the amount of sharable memory required for the user's open
cursors; 250 bytes of memory for each open cursor is recommended:

```
SELECT SUM(250 * users_opening)
   FROM V$SQLAREA;
```

Here is a sample result of the query:

```
SUM(250 * users_opening)
                   66750
```

This example indicates that the existing application will require a minimum of
948,857 bytes in the library cache to sufficiently support the application.

> *Note: In some environments, especially in a DSS system, dynamic SQL
> can consume a significant amount of the library cache memory. If the
> application is operating in an environment that also generates dynamic
> SQL, the library cache size requirements will be greater.*

The library cache is indirectly sized by the **SHARED_POOL_SIZE** database initialization file parameter. It is important to note that this single parameter
specifies the total memory allocation for the library cache and the dictionary
cache. In addition, if you are using the MTS architecture, you must allocate
additional memory in the shared pool to accommodate some user session information. The maximum value for **SHARED_POOL_SIZE** is operating
system-dependent.

## The *DBMS_SHARED_POOL* Package

The **DBMS_SHARED_POOL** package is provided by Oracle and allows
PL/SQL objects to be pinned, or kept, in the shared SQL area. Once an object
is pinned in the library cache, it will remain in shared memory and not be aged
out. Packages, procedures, triggers, and cursors can be pinned in the library
cache area of the shared pool. An object that is pinned can never be flushed out
of memory until it is explicitly unpinned or the database shut down. The performance advantage of a pinned object is realized when the object is accessed
by multiple processes. The object will always be found in memory.

The dbmspool.sql and prvtpool.sql scripts are executed to create the package
specification and package body for **DBMS_SHARED_POOL** package.
These scripts are not called by the catproc.sql script, so the database adminis-
trator must run these scripts manually before executing the
**DBMS_SHARED_POOL** package. To pin an object in memory, the
**EXECUTE** privilege must be granted to the user account that owns

the **DBMS_SHARED_POOL** package. Normally, this user is SYS. This privilege is required because packages and procedures are executed with the privileges of the user that created the object, not the person executing the package or procedure.

The **DBMS_SHARED_POOL.KEEP** procedure is used to pin an object in the shared pool. The following statement illustrates an example of pinning a package into the library cache area of the shared pool:

```
EXECUTE DBMS_SHARED_POOL.keep ('scott.GL_package');
```

As stated earlier, a pinned object will remain in the shared pool until the database is shut down or the object unpinned from the shared pool. The following statement illustrates how to unpin a package from the shared pool:

```
EXECUTE DBMS_SHARED_POOL.unkeep ('scott.GL_package');
```

The following steps outline the procedure to pin a PL/SQL area using the **DBMS_SHARED_POOL** package:

1. Determine which objects are to be pinned in memory.

2. Start up the database.

3. Reference the object to cause it to be loaded into the library cache. You cannot reference a package or procedure without executing it. However, when any part of a package is executed, the entire package is loaded into the library cache. To pin a package in the library cache after instance startup, include a dummy variable definition in every package that can be referenced without making any undesired changes to the database. This will result in the entire package being loaded into the library cache. To reference a trigger, issue a statement that causes the trigger to fire, if it is possible to do so without making undesired changes to the database.

4. Execute the **DBMS_SHARED_POOL.KEEP** to pin the object.

The following large Oracle packages should be pinned in the SGA at instance startup. This will increase the likelihood that contiguous memory will be available to store these packages. Ensure that your database is using these packages before pinning them in the SGA. Many DBAs include scripts for loading these packages in their database startup routines.

➤ SYS.STANDARD

➤ SYS.DBMS_STANDARD

➤ SYS.DBMS_DESCRIBE

➤ SYS.DBMS_UTILITY

➤ SYS.DBMS.LOCK

➤ SYS.DBMS_PIPE

➤ SYS.DBMS_OUTPUT

The **V$DB_OBJECT_CACHE** view is useful to identify the objects loaded in the library cache. These objects include tables, clusters, indexes, PL/SQL procedures, packages, and triggers. If the value of the **KEPT** column is **YES**, the object is pinned in the library cache. Table 5.7 provides a sample of partial query results for the **V$DB_OBJECT_CACHE** view. Issue the following query to identify objects that are loaded in the library cache, the sharable memory consumed by each object, and whether the object has been pinned with **DBMS_SHARED_POOL.KEEP**:

```
SELECT owner, name, type, sharable_mem, kept
   FROM V$DB_OBJECT_CACHE;
   ORDER BY kept DESC;
```

**Table 5.7   Sample of query results for the V$DB_OBJECT_CACHE view.**

| OWNER | NAME | TYPE | SHARABLE _MEM | KEPT |
|---|---|---|---|---|
| SCOTT | MB_REQUISITION_PKG4 | PACKAGE BODY | 11,394 | YES |
| SCOTT | IB_NOTIFICATIONS_SR23 | PACKAGE BODY | 20,713 | YES |
| SCOTT | KO_CUST | PACKAGE BODY | 5,392 | YES |
| SCOTT | EB_CUSTOM_WITH_PKG | PACKAGE | 10,930 | YES |
| SCOTT | BB_ASL_ATTRIBUTES_THS | PACKAGE | 14,978 | YES |
| SCOTT | EINBR_DISC | PACKAGE BODY | 5,221 | YES |
| SCOTT | RB_NOTIFICATIONS_SR244 | PACKAGE BODY | 8,849 | YES |
| SCOTT | AB_MESSAGES_PKG | PACKAGE BODY | 6,677 | YES |
| SCOTT | RO_ONLINE_REPORT | PACKAGE | 12,401 | YES |
| SCOTT | DB_REQUISITION_DESC_PKG6 | PACKAGE BODY | 11,230 | YES |
| SCOTT | IB_AUTOMATIC_CLEAR_PKG | PACKAGE BODY | 14,990 | YES |
| SCOTT | LB_FUNDS_CONTRL_PKG8 | PACKAGE BODY | 60,421 | YES |
| SCOTT | OB_FLEX_MASTER | PACKAGE | 15,673 | YES |
| SCOTT | VF_PRICE_LIST | SYNONYM | 467 | NO |
| SCOTT | EVEN_LINE_DETAIL | SYNONYM | 478 | NO |
| SYSTEM | YEAR_PROFILE | TABLE | 470 | NO |
| SCOTT | OET_PRIMARY_SS | TABLE | 220 | NO |

*(continued)*

**Table 5.7    Sample of query results for the V$DB_OBJECT_CACHE view (continued).**

| OWNER | NAME | TYPE | SHARABLE _MEM | KEPT |
|---|---|---|---|---|
| SCOTT | USER_CHECKS | VIEW | 854 | NO |
| ARPR | AXA_TERMS | TABLE | 587 | NO |
| ABREF | DEPT_FOLDER | TABLE | 474 | NO |
| SCOTT | RBC_PENDING_ITEM | VIEW | 228 | NO |
| SCOTT | IBC_TRANSACTIONS_INT | TABLE | 231 | NO |
| SCOTT | ABC_UNITS_OF_MEASURE | SYNONYM | 473 | NO |
| SCOTT | NO_ORDER_TYPES | VIEW | 1,155 | NO |
| PO | BO_REFR_VENDORS | TABLE | 217 | NO |
| SCOTT | RBC_ATTCH_BLK_ENTITIES | SYNONYM | 480 | NO |
| SCOTT | OFR_OPTX_VALIDATION_ | SYNONYM | 235 | NO |
| SCOTT | WFR_TRANS_VLD | SYNONYM | 479 | NO |
| SCOTT | NXCG_REPORTS | TABLE | 215 | NO |
| SCOTT | TTLXP_PLANNERS | TABLE | 217 | NO |
| AR | HO_VENDOR_CONTACTS | TABLE | 597 | NO |
| AR | AA_CUST_TRX_TYPES | TABLE | 472 | NO |
| OE | NO_REPORT_PARAMETERS | TABLE | 471 | NO |
| AR | KA_DEPT_TRANS | TABLE | 370 | NO |
| OE | SECTIONS | TABLE | 422 | NO |

## Initialization File Parameters For The Library Cache

Several important database initialization file parameters affect the library cache. Properly configuring these parameters is vital to optimizing the performance of the library cache:

➤ SHARED_POOL_SIZE

➤ SHARED_POOL_RESERVED_SIZE

➤ SHARED_POOL_RESERVED_MIN_ALLOC

➤ CURSOR_SPACE_FOR_TIME

The **SHARED_POOL_SIZE** parameter indicates the size, in bytes, of the shared pool buffer in the SGA. This pool stores shared SQL and PL/SQL blocks, packages, procedures, functions, triggers, the data dictionary cache, and user session information when using the MTS option.

The **SHARED_POOL_RESERVED_SIZE** parameter specifies the shared pool space that is reserved for large objects. This memory area is referred to as the reserve list. The minimum size that defines a large object is specified by the **SHARED_POOL_RESERVED_MIN_ALLOC** parameter. This parameter can be used to help reduce fragmentation in the shared pool because smaller objects are not stored in this area, reducing the possibility of fragmentation in the reserve list. The default value for this parameter is 0 bytes. The **SHARED_POOL_RESERVED_SIZE** must be greater than the **SHARED_POOL_RESERVED_MIN_ALLOC** for a reserved list to be created. The **SHARED_POOL_RESERVED_SIZE** can be specified by a numerical value or a number followed by the suffix K or M.

The **SHARED_POOL_RESERVED_MIN_ALLOC** parameter indicates the minimum size of a large object that can occupy space in the reserve list. The larger the size of this parameter, the more restrictive it is in allowing objects into this memory area. The default value for this parameter is 5,000 bytes. The **SHARED_POOL_RESERVED_MIN_ALLOC** parameter can be specified by a numerical value or a number followed by the suffix K or M.

The **CURSOR_SPACE_FOR_TIME** is a Boolean parameter that indicates when shared SQL areas are aged out of the library cache. The default value for this parameter is **FALSE**. If this parameter is set to **TRUE**, shared SQL areas are kept pinned in the shared pool and private SQL areas not deallocated until all cursors referencing them are closed. If this parameter is set to **FALSE**, Oracle must verify whether the SQL statement is located in the shared SQL area of the library cache. This parameter should not be changed from the default value unless the value of **RELOADS** in the **V$LIBRARYCACHE** view is consistently zero. If any dynamic SQL is used in the database, this parameter should not be changed from the default value (**FALSE**).

## Dictionary Cache

The data dictionary is a collection of tables and views that contain extensive information about the Oracle database. This information includes the names and detailed information of all objects in the database, including user information and privileges. The data dictionary must be referenced each time a user issues a request for data.

The data dictionary cache, or dictionary cache, is an area of the shared pool that contains data dictionary information in memory. When Oracle allocates memory to the various components of the shared pool, it gives precedence to the dictionary cache. Therefore, if the library cache is tuned for optimum performance, the dictionary cache will most likely perform well also. The dictionary cache is sized only indirectly by the **SHARED_POOL_SIZE** database initialization file parameter. The objective for the data dictionary cache is to keep as much of the information regarding the database structures and objects in memory, reducing the frequency of disk reads as much as possible. As with the library cache, the performance of the dictionary cache is gauged by its hit ratio.

The following query will determine the hit ratio of the dictionary cache. You should not expect the **GETMISSES** value to be zero. Oracle must load the object definition into the cache when an initial request is issued after instance startup. The ratio of the collective sum of **GETMISSES** to the collective sum of **GETS** should be less than 15 percent. Table 5.8 provides a sample of the results of the query on **V$ROWCACHE**.

| Table 5.8 Sample results of query on V$ROWCACHE. | | | |
| --- | --- | --- | --- |
| **PARAMETER** | **GETS** | **GETMISSES** | **Miss Percent** |
| dc_free_extents | 9,841 | 829 | 8.4239407 |
| dc_used_extents | 606 | 305 | 50.330033 |
| dc_segments | 177,014 | 10,988 | 6.2074186 |
| dc_tablespaces | 17,020 | 16 | .09400705 |
| dc_tablespaces | 338 | 6 | 1.7751479 |
| dc_users | 49,391 | 70 | .14172623 |
| dc_rollback_segments | 2,257 | 7 | .31014621 |
| dc_objects | 90,209 | 6,496 | 7.2010553 |
| dc_object_ids | 150,692 | 5,032 | 3.3392615 |
| dc_tables | 327,423 | 3,697 | 1.1291204 |
| dc_synonyms | 31,885 | 1,212 | 3.8011604 |
| dc_sequences | 4,374 | 87 | 1.9890261 |
| dc_usernames | 108,592 | 42 | .03867688 |
| dc_histogram_defs | 733 | 263 | 35.879945 |
| dc_users | 1,716 | 12 | .6993007 |
| dc_columns | 5,992,323 | 120,263 | 2.0069512 |
| dc_table_grants | 326,371 | 13,382 | 4.1002417 |
| dc_indexes | 144,702 | 7,137 | 4.9322055 |
| dc_constraint_defs | 19,673 | 2,445 | 12.428201 |
| dc_sequence_grants | 3,865 | 131 | 3.389392 |
| dc_user_grants | 34,255 | 27 | .07882061 |

```
SELECT parameter,
       gets,
       getmisses,
       (getmisses / gets * 100) "Miss Percent"
  FROM v$rowcache
 WHERE gets > 100
 AND GETMISSES > 0;
```

Each row in the **V$ROWCACHE** view contains statistics for a single parameter of the dictionary cache since instance startup. The **PARAMETER** column specifies the particular data dictionary item. The **GETS** column specifies the total number of requests for that dictionary item. The **GETMISSES** column specifies the number of requests that resulted in a cache miss.

# Tuning The Buffer Cache

The database buffer cache is an area of the SGA that stores copies of Oracle database blocks in memory. These blocks are available to be shared by all users and contain data from tables, clusters, indexes, rollback segments, and sequences. There can be several copies of a database block in the buffer cache at any given time. One current copy of the block will always exist, and Oracle might keep one or more read-consistent copies of the block using rollback segment data.

When the server receives a request for a particular block, it first checks the buffer cache to determine whether the block is already in memory. Oracle uses a hash function to make this determination, much like the process that is used to locate a statement in the library cache. If the block is not found in the buffer cache, the server process must perform a physical read from disk to retrieve the block from the appropriate datafile.

The performance of the buffer cache is generally gauged by its hit ratio. As with other structures of the SGA, the objective of the buffer cache is to keep as much of the requested data blocks in memory, therefore reducing the frequency of cache misses. Oracle recommends that the hit ratio on the buffer cache be 80 percent during normal processing and 90 percent if your system is using raw devices on a Unix platform.

Obtaining a good buffer cache hit ratio is more important in OLTP environments than it is in historical environments, such as DSSs or data warehouse systems. DSS and data warehouse applications typically perform many full table scans, increasing the amount of physical reads and reducing the probability of a high buffer cache hit ratio. With these types of application environments, it is vital to concentrate your tuning efforts on minimizing I/O.

Three system statistics are used to measure the hit ratio of the database buffer cache:

➤ **DB BLOCK GETS**

➤ **CONSISTENT GETS**

➤ **PHYSICAL READS**

The **DB BLOCK GETS** value indicates the access to current copies of the data blocks. The **CONSISTENT GETS** value indicates the access to the read-consistent copies of the blocks, built from the rollback segments. The sum of the **DB BLOCK GETS** and **CONSISTENT GETS** will provide the total number of logical reads. The **PHYSICAL READS** value indicates the total number of physical reads from disk. Table 5.10 shows several queries that can be issued against **V$SYSSTAT** to determine the buffer cache hit ratio since instance startup. The first query is more complex and will calculate the cache hit ratio. The second query it is easier to remember and provides the database statistics needed to calculate the buffer cache hit ratio manually.

➤ Query on **V$SYSSTAT** to calculate the buffer cache hit ratio:

```
SELECT (1-(phy.value / (cur.value + con.value))) * 100
"Buffer Cache Hit Ratio"
   FROM V$SYSSTAT cur,
        V$SYSSTAT con,
        V$SYSSTAT phy
   WHERE cur.name = 'db block gets'
   AND con.name = 'consistent gets'
   AND phy.name = 'physical reads';
```

Here is a sample result of the query:

```
Buffer Cache Hit Ratio
            96.115
```

➤ Query on **V$SYSSTAT** to provide statistics to calculate buffer cache hit ratio manually:

```
SELECT name,
       value
   FROM V$SYSSTAT
   WHERE name IN ('db block gets', 'consistent gets',
                  'physical reads');
```

Here is a sample result of the query:

```
NAME              VALUE
db block gets     142924
consistent gets   124556
physical reads     10394
```

➤ Use the following calculation to calculate the buffer cache hit ratio manually:

```
Hit Ratio = 1 - (physical reads / (db block gets +
                 consistent gets))
```

The calculation on these statistics results in a .96 (96 percent) buffer cache hit ratio.

The report.txt file also provides information that you can use to determine the buffer cache hit ratio. The statistics provided are from the time that utlbstat was submitted until the time that utlestat was submitted. These statistics can present a truer picture of the buffer cache hit ratio than **V$SYSSTAT** because you can control the monitoring time period, bypassing statistics such as initial buffer cache load after instance startup.

The size of the buffer cache is determined by two database initialization file parameters:

➤ DB_BLOCK_SIZE

➤ DB_BLOCK_BUFFERS

The **DB_BLOCK_SIZE** parameter multiplied by the **DB_BLOCK_BUFFERS** parameter will determine the size of the buffer cache in bytes. The **DB_BLOCK_SIZE** is specified at database creation and should not be altered unless the database is re-created. Therefore, unless the database is re-created, the only parameter that can be modified to alter the size of the buffer cache is **DB_BLOCK_BUFFERS**.

When an index access is used, Oracle always reads only one block at a time into the buffer cache. When a full table scan access is used, multiple blocks are read into the cache at one time. The number of blocks read during full table scans is determined by the **DB_FILE_MULTIBLOCK_READ_COUNT** database initialization file parameter.

The buffers in the cache consist of two lists: the dirty list and the LRU list. The dirty list contains dirty buffers that have been modified in memory but have not yet been written to disk. The LRU list keeps the most recently used blocks in memory. When any process accesses a database buffer, the buffer is moved to the most recently used end of the LRU list. Blocks that are not frequently referenced are moved to the least recently used end of the LRU list and are eventually aged out of the buffer cache. The LRU list contains free buffers, pinned buffers, and dirty buffers that have not yet been moved to the dirty list. It is the responsibility of the DBWR background process to write dirty buffers to disk, working from the least recently used end of the LRU list. This process helps ensure that free buffers are found in the buffer cache for current and subsequent user processes.

Generally, when full table scans are performed, the batch of blocks retrieved are placed on the least recently used end of the LRU list. This process tends to age full table scan blocks out of the buffer cache earlier than blocks retrieved by index access. The logic behind this approach is that multiple blocks are retrieved from a full table scan, and these blocks potentially can consume a substantial amount of memory in the buffer cache. It is also unlikely that the full set of blocks will be requested again by another process. Full table scan blocks are moved out of the buffer cache as soon as possible to free the cache for more frequently used blocks.

If full table scans are frequently performed on static tables, you might want to alter the default behavior and place those blocks on the most recently used end of the LRU list so that the scanned blocks are not aged out as quickly. You can do this on a table-by-table basis by using the **CACHE** clause when creating or altering a table or cluster. You can also code a **CACHE** hint clause in the **SELECT** statement to obtain the same results. The **CACHE_SIZE_ THRESHOLD** initialization file parameter specifies the maximum number of cached blocks for each table. If a table or cluster exceeds the number of blocks specified in this parameter, the number of blocks cached in the buffer will be limited to the quantity specified in **CACHE_SIZE_THRESHOLD**.

Access to the buffer cache is managed by LRU chain latches. Latches are internal locks that are used to protect access to shared data structures, such as the buffer cache. Single-processor computers have only one LRU latch. However, if you have a symmetric multiprocessor (SMP) computer, you have the ability to set the number of LRU latches for the buffer cache with the **DB_BLOCK_LRU_LATCHES** database initialization file parameter. The default for this parameter is half the number of CPUs for the computer. The maximum setting for this parameter is two times the number of CPUs. It is recommended that you reset this parameter only in a system with high activity. Each latch should have a minimum of 50 buffers to its set.

## Determine The Impact Of Increasing The Buffer Cache

If your buffer cache hit ratio is low, Oracle can collect statistics that will estimate the hit ratio if you were to increase the size of the buffer cache. This test will allow you to determine the likelihood of additional cache hits if the **DB_BLOCK_BUFFERS** parameter was increased by $x$ number of buffers.

The statistics gathered to determine the effect of increasing the number of buffers are placed in the SYS-owned virtual table **X$KCBRBH**. Each row in this table shows the relative performance gain of adding one buffer to the buffer cache. The columns of the **X$KCBRBH** table include:

➤ INDX

➤ COUNT

The value of the **INDX** column is one less than the number of proposed buffers to be added to the buffer cache. The value of the **COUNT** column is the number of additional cache hits that would be achieved if you were to add the **INDX**+1 buffers to the cache. For example, the value of **INDX** in the first row of X$KCBRBH is zero, and the value of **COUNT** is the number additional cache hits gained by adding one buffer to the cache.

To perform the test of a larger cache size, you must set the **DB_BLOCK_LRU_EXTENDED_STATISTICS** database initialization file parameter to the number of rows you want to collect in the **X$KCBRBH** table. For example, if you set the value of this parameter to 200, 200 rows of statistics will be collected in **X$KCBRBH**. Each row will reflect the addition of adding one buffer, up to 200 rows. The default value for **DB_BLOCK_LRU_EXTENDED_STATISTICS** is zero. The database must be stopped and restarted for new value of this parameter to take effect.

To determine the additional buffer cache hits that would occur by adding 50 buffers to the cache, issue the following query:

```
SELECT SUM(count) ACH
    FROM sys.X$KCBRBH
    WHERE indx < 50;
```

You can then determine how those additional hits would affect the cache hit ratio by hard-coding the value of ACH (additional cache hits) into the following database query on **V$SYSSTAT**:

```
SELECT (1- ( phy.value - ACH) / ((cur.value +
    con.value))) * 100 "Buffer Cache Hit Ratio"
    FROM V$SYSSTAT cur,
        V$SYSSTAT con,
        V$SYSSTAT phy
    WHERE cur.name = 'db block gets'
    AND    con.name = 'consistent gets'
    AND    phy.name = 'physical reads';
```

If you use the **DB BLOCK GETS, CONSISTENT GETS,** and **PHYSI-CAL READS** statistics from report.txt, use the following formula to estimate the buffer cache hit ratio with the increased buffer size:

```
Hit Ratio = 1 - (physical reads - ACH / (db block gets + consistent
                gets))
```

Another way to evaluate the statistics in **X$KCBRBH** is to separate the additional buffers into groups. Table 5.9 shows a sample of the results from the following query:

```
SELECT 100*TRUNC(indx/100)+1||' to '||100*(TRUNC(indx/100)+1)
"Interval",
    SUM(count) "Buffer Cache Hits"
        FROM sys.X$KCBRBH
        GROUP BY TRUNC(indx/100);
```

On the basis of the results of the query on **X$KCBRBH,** as shown in Table 5.9, adding 100 buffers to the cache would result in 14,500 additional cache hits. Adding 100 additional buffers, for a total of 200 buffers, would increase the buffer cache hits by 24,721 (14,500 + 10,221). The increase from 200 to 300 buffers would result in only 540 additional cache buffer hits. Use these statistics to determine how many buffers to add to the cache to obtain the most performance gain for the memory resources allocated. To make the buffer cache larger, increase the value of the **DB_BLOCK_BUFFERS** database

**Table 5.9   Sample results of query on the X$KCBRBH table.**

| Interval | Buffer Cache Hits |
| --- | --- |
| 1 to 100 | 14,500 |
| 101 to 200 | 10,221 |
| 201 to 300 | 540 |
| 301 to 400 | 9,215 |

initialization file parameter by the number of buffers you want to add to the cache and restart the instance.

## Determine The Impact Of Decreasing The Buffer Cache

If your buffer cache hit ratio is consistently high, Oracle offers the ability to collect statistics on the effect of reducing the size of the buffer cache. This will allow you to determine whether the desired cache hit ratio can be maintained if you reduce the cache by a specific number of buffers. The statistics collected will help you identify overallocated memory to the buffer cache that might be applied more efficiently to other Oracle memory structures.

The statistics gathered to determine the effect of decreasing the number of buffers in the cache are placed in the SYS-owned virtual table **X$KCBCBH**. These statistics estimate the performance effect of a smaller buffer cache. The columns of the **X$KCBCBH** table include:

➤ INDX

➤ COUNT

The value of the **INDX** column is the potential number of buffers in the cache. The value of the **COUNT** column is the number of cache hits that can be credited to the buffer number **INDX**. The total number of rows in the **X$KCBCBH** table is equal to the number of buffers in the cache, as specified in the **DB_BLOCK_BUFFERS** parameter. The first row of this table is not used for statistics. The **INDX** value is zero, and the **COUNT** value is the total number of blocks moved into the first buffer cache, rather than the number of hits.

To perform the test of a smaller cache size, you must set the **DB_BLOCK_LRU_STATISTICS** database initialization file parameter to **TRUE**. The default value is **FALSE**. The database must be stopped and re-started for the new value of this parameter to take effect.

You can use the statistics in the **X$KCBCBH** table to determine the number of additional cache misses that would occur if you reduced the size of the buffer cache. For example, if you currently have 120 buffers in your cache and you want to find out how many cache misses would occur if you reduced the cache buffers to 100, issue the following query on the **X$KCBCBH** table:

```
SELECT SUM(count) ACM
    FROM X$KCBCBH
    WHERE indx >= 100;
```

You can then determine how those additional misses would affect the cache hit ratio by including the value of ACM (additional cache misses) in the following formula:

```
Hit Ratio = 1 - (physical reads + ACM / (db block gets +
                 consistent gets))
```

The statistics for **PHYSICAL READS, DB BLOCK GETS**, and **CONSISTENT GETS** can be determined from **V$SYSSTAT** or a current report.txt file.

Another way to evaluate the statistics in **X$KCBCBH** is to separate the additional buffers into groups. Table 5.12 shows a sample of the results from the following query:

```
SELECT 50*TRUNC(indx/50)+1||' to '||50*(TRUNC(indx/50)+1)
       "Interval",
    SUM(count) "Buffer Cache Hits"
       FROM sys.X$KCBCBH
       WHERE indx > 0
       GROUP BY TRUNC(indx/50);
```

On the basis of the results of the query on **X$KCBCBH**, as shown in Table 5.10, the first 50 buffers in the cache contribute 3,600 cache hits. The second 50 buffers in the cache contribute an additional 2,200 cache hits. The third 50 buffers are responsible for an additional 2,400 cache hits. The fourth 50 buffers are responsible for only 120 additional cache buffer hits. On the basis of these statistics, if memory is limited on your system, you might want to decrease the buffer cache by 50 buffers and allocate the memory more efficiently to other Oracle structures. To make the buffer cache smaller, decrease the value of the **DB_BLOCK_BUFFERS** database initialization file parameter by the number of buffers you want to eliminate from the cache and restart the instance. The collection of statistics for the buffer cache increase should be activated only when you are tuning the buffer cache and disabled once the statistical collection is completed to reduce performance overhead.

**Table 5.10    Sample results of query on the X$KCBCBH table.**

| Interval | Buffer Cache Hits |
| --- | --- |
| 1 to 50 | 3,600 |
| 51 to 100 | 2,200 |
| 101 to 150 | 2,400 |
| 151 to 200 | 120 |

# Tuning The Redo Log Buffer

The redo log buffer is an area of the SGA that stores redo information in memory before it is written to the physical redo log files. The redo log buffer also stores all changes made to the database. These modifications include all data definition language (DDL) and all **INSERT, UPDATE**, and **DELETE** statements issued in the database. Redo entries contain the information needed to rebuild, or redo, the changes to the database if recovery is necessary.

The redo log buffer should be sized large enough so that user processes do not have to wait to access it. The size of the redo log buffer, in bytes, is determined at database startup and specified by the **LOG_BUFFER** database initialization file parameter. The default for this parameter is operating system-specific and is usually far too low for a high-activity system.

The **V$SYSTEM_EVENT** view contains information on the systemwide waits for an event. The **TIME_WAITED** and **AVERAGE_WAIT** columns will have a zero value on platforms that do not support a fast timing mechanism. If you are running on one of these platforms and want to reflect true wait times, you must set the **TIMED_STATISTICS** database initialization file parameter to **TRUE**. Table 5.11 describes the **V$SYSTEM_EVENT** view.

To determine whether any waits have occurred for the redo log buffer, query **V$SYSTEM_EVENT** for the log buffer space event. Waits for this event indicate that waits for space in the redo log buffer have been occurring. You should check your log buffer several times while your application is active. If you notice a high or increasing number of waits, you should consider increasing the size of the redo log buffer by increasing the value of the **LOG_BUFFER** parameter.

| Table 5.11 | The V$SYSTEM_EVENT view. |
|---|---|
| **Column** | **Description** |
| EVENT | Name of the wait event |
| TOTAL_WAITS | Total number of waits for the event |
| TOTAL_TIMEOUTS | Total number of timeouts for the event |
| TIME_WAITED | Total amount of time waited for the event in hundredths of a second |
| AVERAGE_WAIT | Average amount of time waited for the event in hundredths of a second |

# MTS And The SGA

In an MTS environment, some user session information is stored in the shared pool rather than in the memory area of the user processes. The information stored in the SGA under the MTS architecture includes private SQL areas, cursor state information, and sort areas. Because server processes are shared in an MTS environment, this user information must be stored in an area where any server can access any user's information at any time. This area of the SGA is called the user global area (UGA). The **SHARED_POOL_SIZE** parameter value must be configured to accommodate the additional shared pool memory requirements of the UGA when using the MTS architecture.

The **V$SESSTAT** and **V$STATNAME** views can be queried to calculate the additional space required by the UGA. Issue the following query at a time of high activity to determine how much UGA memory is currently in use:

```
SELECT SUM(value)||' bytes ' "Total Session Memory"
    FROM v$sesstat a, v$statname b
    WHERE name = 'session uga memory'
    AND a.statistic# = b.statistic#;
```

The result of this query provides a good estimate of how much larger you will need to make the shared pool if you use the MTS architecture.

# Practice Questions

## Question 1

Which component of the SGA stores copies of data blocks that can be shared by all users?

○ a. Shared pool

○ b. Data dictionary cache

○ c. Library cache

○ d. Database buffer cache

The correct answer is d. The database buffer cache is an area of the SGA that stores data from tables, indexes, clusters, rollback segments, and sequences. This database information can be shared by all users requesting the same data as long as it remains in the buffer cache. The shared pool is an area of the SGA that stores the data dictionary cache and the library cache at a minimum. The data dictionary cache stores data dictionary information in the shared pool. The library cache stores SQL and PL/SQL objects in the shared pool.

## Question 2

Which situation would cause an object definition to be aged out of the library cache?

○ a. The user process was terminated

○ b. The process timed out

○ c. New objects definitions that needed more space were loaded

○ d. The object definitions were invalid

The correct answer is c. Objects are aged out of the library cache using a least recently used (LRU) algorithm. When memory is insufficient to store a new SQL statement, the LRU algorithm ages the least recently used SQL out of the library cache to make room for the new statement.

## Question 3

In which part of the shared pool are shared SQL and PL/SQL stored?

- ○ a. Dictionary cache
- ○ b. Database buffer cache
- ○ c. Library cache
- ○ d. User global area (UGA)

The correct answer is c. The library cache is the area of the shared pool that stores all cached SQL and PL/SQL objects.

## Question 4

You review your company's current system and believe that the database buffer cache is inadequately sized. How can this condition affect applications?

- ○ a. Applications might not load properly
- ○ b. Applications might generate errors
- ○ c. Applications might run slowly
- ○ d. Applications can halt during certain processing

The correct answer is c. Inadequate sizing of the database buffer cache causes an insufficient number of database blocks to be cached into memory. Although this constraint negatively affects the performance of the application, it will not halt or generate errors. The application will simply run slowly.

## Question 5

Which parameter can you reset to increase the size of the database buffer cache?

- ○ a. **DB_BLOCK_SIZE**
- ○ b. **DB_FILES**
- ○ c. **DB_BLOCK_CHECKPOINT_BATCH**
- ○ d. **DB_BLOCK_BUFFERS**

The correct answer is d. The size of the database buffer cache is determined by multiplying **DB_BLOCK_SIZE** by **DB_BLOCK_BUFFERS**. Both of these parameters determine the size of the buffer cache. However, the **DB_BLOCK_SIZE** parameter should never be altered or reset after database creation unless the database is re-created. Read the question carefully. It asks which parameter can be reset to increase the size of the buffer cache. The only parameter that can be reset to change the size of the buffer cache (without re-creation of the database) is **DB_BLOCK_BUFFERS**.

## Question 6

Where does Oracle7 store user session and cursor state information in a multithreaded server (MTS) environment?

○ a. User global area (UGA)

○ b. Program global area (PGA)

○ c. System global area (SGA)

The answer is a. The UGA is an area of the shared pool that stores user session information when using the MTS option. The shared pool does not have a UGA in a non-MTS environment.

## Question 7

Which Oracle package can you use to pin large PL/SQL packages in the library cache?

○ a. **DBMS_STANDARD**

○ b. **DBMS_SHARED_POOL**

○ c. **STANDARD**

○ d. **DIUTIL**

The correct answer is b. **DBMS_SHARED_POOL.KEEP** is used to pin a package in the shared pool. **DBMS_SHARED_POOL.UNKEEP** is used to unpin a package from the shared pool.

# Question 8

A user issues a SQL statement, and Oracle7 places it into the library cache. Another user issues the same SQL statement. How does Oracle handle the statement issued by the second user?

○ a. Oracle7 removes the first statement and uses the second statement because it is more recent.

○ b. Oracle7 uses the cached version and need not process the second request.

○ c. Oracle7 cannot process both statements at the same time, so the second statement waits for the first statement to complete.

○ d. Oracle7 caches the second statement into the library cache and processes each statement separately.

The correct answer is b. If Oracle finds an identical SQL statement from a previous request, the new statement will be discarded, and Oracle will use the parsed and executable version of the SQL statement already in the library cache.

# Question 9

Which objects can you pin into the library cache using the **DBMS_SHARED_POOL** package? [Check all correct answers]

❑  a. Triggers

❑  b. Procedures

❑  c. SQL statements

❑  d. PL/SQL packages

❑  e. Cursors

❑  f. Data blocks

The correct answers are a, b, d, and e. Triggers, procedures, PL/SQL packages, and cursors can be pinned in the shared pool. Remember, the "pinning" of an object refers to the library cache, not the buffer cache.

## Question 10

> What does Oracle use to manage the SQL and PL/SQL in the library cache?
>
> ○ a. Program global area (PGA)
>
> ○ b. User global area (UGA)
>
> ○ c. Clusters
>
> ○ d. Database buffer cache
>
> ○ e. LRU algorithm

The correct answer is e. Oracle uses a least recently used (LRU) algorithm to manage the library cache. An LRU algorithm is used also to manage the buffer cache.

## Question 11

> Your application has large PL/SQL packages, and you want to accommodate these in the library cache. Which parameter can you set to accomplish this task?
>
> ○ a. **SHARED_POOL_SIZE**
>
> ○ b. **SHARED_AREA_SIZE**
>
> ○ c. **SHARED_POOL_RESERVED_SIZE**
>
> ○ d. **CURSOR_SPACE_FOR_TIME**

The correct answer is c. **SHARED_POOL_RESERVED_SIZE** indicates the bytes in the shared pool that you want to reserve solely for large objects. Smaller objects will not be allowed to occupy this area of the library cache. **SHARED_POOL_RESERVED_MIN_ALLOC** defines the size of "large" in bytes. **SHARED_POOL_RESERVED_SIZE** must be greater than **SHARED_POOL_RESERVED_MIN_ALLOC** for a reserved list to be created.

# Question 12

> Which view can you query to check the amount of sharable memory used by a cached PL/SQL object?
>
> ○ a. **V$DB_OBJECT_CACHE**
> ○ b. **V$ROWCACHE**
> ○ c. **V$SQLAREA**
> ○ d. **V$LIBRARYCACHE**

The correct answer is a. **V$DB_OBJECT_CAHCE** lists objects that are cached in the library cache. These objects include tables, clusters, indexes, PL/SQL procedures, packages, and triggers.

# Question 13

> What is the recommended number of bytes to allow in the shared pool per user per open cursor?
>
> ○ a. 100
> ○ b. 250
> ○ c. 50
> ○ d. 10

The correct answer is b. When calculating the size of the library cache, Oracle recommends that you allocate 250 bytes per user per open cursor.

# Question 14

> Which occurrence places blocks in the database buffer cache?
>
> ○ a. System startup
> ○ b. LGWR process reading blocks into the buffer
> ○ c. DBWR process reading blocks into the buffer
> ○ d. Server process reading blocks into the buffers for users

The correct answer is d. The server process places blocks in the database buffer cache. Your first inclination might be to choose the DBWR background process. DBWR writes data from the buffer cache but does not read data into the cache.

# Need To Know More?

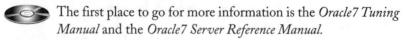

The first place to go for more information is the *Oracle7 Tuning Manual* and the *Oracle7 Server Reference Manual*.

RevealNet Corporation provides Oracle Administration, a superior software reference tool for Oracle database administration. RevealNet's Web address is www.revealnet.com.

Aronoff, Eyal, Kevin Loney, and Noorali Sonawalla: *Advanced Oracle Tuning and Administration*. Oracle Press, 1997. ISBN 0-07-882241-6. Pay close attention to Chapters 3 and 6.

Corey, Michael, Michael Abbey, and Daniel J. Dechichio: *Tuning Oracle*. Oracle Press, 1995. ISBN 0-07-881181-3. Chapter 2 is a good chapter to focus on.

Corrigan, Peter and Mark Gurry: *Oracle Performance Tuning*. O'Reilly & Associates, Inc., 1993. ISBN 1-56592-048-1. Be sure to read Chapters 2, 13, and 14 carefully.

# Tuning Rollback Segments And Redo Logs

**6**

## Terms you'll need to understand:

- √ Redo
- √ Undo
- √ Rollback
- √ Contention
- √ Redo allocation latch
- √ Redo copy latch
- √ Gets
- √ Misses
- √ Sleeps
- √ Hit ratio
- √ Checkpoint
- √ Mirroring
- √ Public
- √ Private

## Techniques you'll need to master:

- √ Sizing redo logs
- √ Sizing rollback segments
- √ Monitoring redo logs
- √ Monitoring rollback segments
- √ Monitoring contention
- √ Tuning redo logs
- √ Tuning rollback segments

One of Oracle's strengths is its recoverability, which it owes to the built-in redo log and rollback segment technology. Redo logs act as transaction journals that record all data-changing transactions that occur in the database. Rollback, or undo, segments act as before-image journals that keep copies of all data before it is altered. Redo logs allow for roll forward during recovery operations by recovering committed and uncommitted transactions up to the time the database crashes. Rollback segments allow for the rollback (or the undo) of uncommitted transactions.

Delayed transaction rollback was introduced in Oracle7.3 to speed instance recovery after instance-type failures. Delayed transaction rollback simply means that rather than perform a roll forward (application or redo logs and archived redo logs) and then a rollback at instance startup or recovery (removing uncommitted transaction changes), rollback is not performed until the data that needs rollback is accessed by a transaction.

Redo logs and rollback segments require a great deal of planning and tuning in a well-constructed database. Significant performance gains for large transactions are realized from properly sized, placed, and tuned redo and rollback processes. For this reason, the tuning exam has many questions concerning redo log and rollback segment tuning.

# Rollback Segments

Rollback segments act as before-image journals and are critical for rollback operations during normal operations and during instance and database recovery. Rollback segments are internal structures, meaning that they are stored in tablespaces. They can be either private (recommended) or public. Private rollback segments must be specified in the initialization file (using the initialization parameter **ROLLBACK_SEGMENTS**) to be brought automatically online at startup. Public rollback segments remain offline until the calculation

```
TRANSACTIONS/TRANSACTIONS_PER_ROLLBACK_SEGMENT
```

tells the Oracle server to bring another online.

Rollback segments are usually stored in their own tablespace (other than the single **SYSTEM** rollback segment, which is in the **SYSTEM** tablespace) for two reasons. First, a tablespace cannot be taken offline if it contains even a single online rollback segment. Second, rollback segments grow and shrink as needed (assuming that the **OPTIMAL** setting is used, which is discussed shortly), and, with dynamic table extension, this could result in severe tablespace fragmentation.

Rollback segments allow for the rollback of uncommitted transactions and for the rollback of uncommitted changes during recovery operations and read consistency for transactions (read-consistent images of data being altered are maintained in the rollback segment).

## Sizing Rollback Segments

Rollback segments are created using the **CREATE ROLLBACK SEGMENT** command. This command has an optional **STORAGE** clause. If this clause is not specified in the **CREATE ROLLBACK SEGMENT** command, the default storage for the rollback segment tablespace is used instead. The parameters specified in the **STORAGE** clause for a **CREATE ROLLBACK SEGMENT** are:

➤ **INITIAL** Sets the size of the initial extents

➤ **NEXT** Sets the size of subsequent extents

➤ **MINEXTENTS** Sets the number of initial extents (must be set to a minimum of 2)

➤ **MAXEXTENTS** Sets the maximum number of extents allowed for the rollback segment

➤ **PCTINCREASE** Set to zero (before version 7.3)

➤ **OPTIMAL** Sets the size to which the rollback segment will shrink if it grows beyond **OPTIMAL** in size (should be set to at least **MINEXTENTS * DB_BLOCK_SIZE**; otherwise, it will be ignored)

The sizing of rollback segments depends on many factors, such as the number of concurrent users, the size of the average transaction, the size of the largest expected transaction, and the available space. Let's examine how each of the **STORAGE** clause parameters should be derived. A critical dynamic performance view for rollback segments, the **V$ROLLSTAT** view, contains dynamic data about actual rollback segment statistics. The **V$ROLLSTAT** view has the following columns that are used to size rollback segments:

➤ **HWMSIZE** The largest transaction

➤ **SHRINKS** The number of times that this rollback segment grew beyond **OPTIMAL** and was forced to shrink

➤ **WRAPS** The number of times that this rollback segment was forced to write over its own data for a given transaction

➤ **EXTENDS** The number of times that this rollback segment had transactions that outgrew a single extent into a second, third, or more extent (incremented for each extend into a new extent)

➤ **AVESHRINK** The average amount that this rollback segment has shrunk

➤ **AVEACTIVE** The average transaction size of this rollback segment

The **V$ROLLSTAT** view provides vital data for the proper sizing of rollback segments.

### Sizing Rollback Segment *INITIAL* Setpoint

The **INITIAL** parameter setpoint sets the size of the initial extents for the rollback segment. The value of the **INITIAL** setpoint should be set to the size of the average transaction. Usually, the **INITIAL** value will need to be reset by dropping and re-creating the first-try rollback segment after operational experience is gained during system testing.

For **INITIAL**, the critical value in the **V$ROLLSTAT** table is **AVEACTIVE**, averaged over the online rollback segments. Set **INITIAL** equal to the average **AVEACTIVE** value.

### Sizing Rollback Segment *NEXT* Setpoint

**NEXT** is probably the easiest of the parameters to set. The **NEXT** setpoint should always be equal to the **INITIAL** setpoint for rollback segments.

### Sizing Rollback Segment *MINEXTENTS* Setpoint

The **MINEXTENTS** setpoint is determined on the basis of the number of expected concurrent DML transactions balanced against the number of desired rollback segments. For example, if you have a potential for 200 concurrent DML transactions and want to have 10 online rollback segments, set **MINEXTENTS** to 20. Each DML transaction will use one extent in a rollback segment, and multiple transactions can use a single rollback segment simultaneously.

### Sizing Rollback Segment *MAXEXTENTS* Setpoint

The **MAXEXTENTS** setpoint is set to the result of the calculation

```
MAXEXTENTS = CEILING(Largest HWMSIZE / INITIAL) + 1
```

which takes the largest high water mark (largest recorded transaction for any of the online rollback segments), divides it by the size of your initial extent (be sure to convert the **INITIAL** size to bytes), and adds 1 to the result to allow for growth. The **CEILING** statement indicates to round up to the nearest integer. Be sure that the rollback segment tablespace is sized appropriately for expected transactions. Large transactions fail mainly because they run out of space in the rollback segment tablespace. They also fail when the **MAX-EXTENTS** setpoint for the table being updated or inserted into is reached.

### Sizing Rollback Segment *OPTIMAL Setpoint*

Sizing the **OPTIMAL** setpoint can be problematic. The best method the authors have found is to set it to twice the size of your **INITIAL** value; monitor the values for wraps and shrinks and adjust as needed. Essentially, you want to increase it until wraps and shrinks are minimized. You should reach a setting at which wraps stays at or near zero and you get only a few shrinks that coincide to large transactions. Remember that **OPTIMAL** must be a multiple of the **INITIAL** setpoint.

### Sizing Rollback Segment *PCTINCREASE Setpoint*

Prior to Oracle7.3, you were allowed to set the **PCTINCREASE** setpoint for a rollback segment. Setting **PCTINCREASE** to anything other than zero was (and still is if you are using an earlier version than 7.3) a bad idea because it resulted in multiple, perhaps oddly sized, extents that could not be reused.

 For purposes of the exam, **PCTINCREASE** should always be set to zero for rollback segments.

# Using Multiple Rollback Segments Of Different Sizes

In some environments, you might periodically need extremely large rollback segments. If the size of the rollback segments needed for a large transaction exceeds the maximum **MAXEXTENTS** on the basis of extent sizes sized for your average transaction, you must resort to having several larger rollback segments. When you find yourself in a situation such as an OLTP (online transaction processing) system during the day and a large batch load operation at night, you can benefit by having two sets of rollback segments.

The first set of rollback segments is normally online and sized as discussed previously, using concurrent DML transaction count and sizing statistics. The second set of rollback segments is normally offline and sized strictly to take into account the large transaction requirements. Remember that on some systems (such as Sun), a rollback segment larger than 2GB can cause errors even when spread across several discrete datafiles. Using the **ALTER ROLL-BACK** command allows you to toggle the online and offline rollback segments as required.

A large transaction, such as a large batch load of data, can be forced to use a specific rollback segment through the **SET TRANSACTION USE ROLL-BACK SEGMENT** seg_name; command. Remember to commit just before using the **SET TRANSACTION** command; any commits will force reuse of the **SET TRANSACTION** command to reassign the rollback segment to the transaction. Generally, large rollback segments are more useful for large batch jobs than for a large SQL query.

You can avoid many problems with rollback segments if you counsel your users to use frequent commits. A major problem with rollback segments is that of the "snapshot too old" error that occurs when a rollback segment wraps and writes over data needed for a read-consistent image. Generally, such errors can be greatly reduced by either making rollback segment extents larger or adding more rollback segments.

# Tuning Rollback Segments

Rollback segments are tuned through proper sizing and file placement. Several things can be monitored to determine whether your rollback segments meet the following criteria:

➤ Proper number of rollback segments

➤ Proper number of rollback segment extents

➤ Proper rollback segment size

➤ Proper rollback segment placement

## *Monitoring For Proper Number Of Rollback Segments*

To monitor the proper number of rollback segments, you need to monitor for rollback segment header contention (the undo header). This is accomplished by monitoring the **V$WAITSTAT** table using a **SELECT** command similar to

```
SELECT
        class,
        SUM(count) total_waits,
        SUM(time) total_time
FROM v$waitstat
```

```
GROUP BY
     Class;
```

with results similar to those shown in Table 6.1.

In the previous result set, you can see that we had 14 waits for undo headers. This indicates contention (though not at a very serious level) for rollback segments. If the waits become significant, you will need more rollback segments because transactions are contending for the rollback segments. Another source of information on too few rollback segments consists of the nonzero values in the **WAITS** column of the **V$ROLLSTAT** view. The undo (or rollback) header holds the rollback segment transaction table; if this table becomes full, contention occurs.

A common way to monitor is to combine results from the **V$ROLLSTAT**, **V$ROLLNAME**, and **DBA_ROLLBACK_SEGS** views into a set of two views. One view groups size-related data, whereas the other view groups rollback statistics.

 You need to be familiar with all three views: **V$ROLLSTAT**, **V$WAITSTAT**, and **DBA_ROLLBACK_SEGS**. Spend some time querying and familiarizing yourself with these views and the data they contain, and you will find the rollback questions easier to answer.

| Table 6.1 | Example output from a "waits" select. | |
|---|---|---|
| **Class** | **Total Waits** | **Total Time** |
| Data block | 27 | 23 |
| Free list | 0 | 0 |
| Save undo block | 0 | 0 |
| Save undo header | 0 | 0 |
| Segment header | 0 | 0 |
| Sort block | 0 | 0 |
| System undo block | 0 | 0 |
| System undo header | 0 | 0 |
| Undo block | 0 | 0 |
| Undo header | 14 | 4 |

## Monitoring For Proper Number Of Rollback Segment Extents

The proper number of rollback segment extents is shown by not finding values greater than zero in the **V$ROLLSTAT** view for the **WAITS** column. The proper balance between the number of rollback segments and the number of rollback segment extents is usually reached (according to Oracle sources) at a maximum of 20 allocated extents per rollback segment. Don't confuse allocated extents with **MAXEXTENTS**; allocated extents will usually be a fraction of the total allowed number of extents as expressed by the **MAXEXTENTS** storage clause value. **MAXEXTENTS** is usually set by determining the absolute largest transaction you expect and then setting **MAXEXTENTS** to accommodate this size of transaction.

## Monitoring For Proper Size Of Rollback Segment Extents

As discussed previously, rollback segment extent size should be determined by empirical methods. Some fairly complex methods for setting extent sizes for rollback segments have been put forth by various experts, but perhaps the simplest method is to monitor a test database that is executing representative transactions. The view to monitor is the **V$ROLLSTAT** dynamic performance view. You want to size **INITIAL** and **NEXT** storage clause values for extents on the basis of the average of the **AVEACTIVE** column. By adding a comfort factor (say, 10 percent) to the size, you can allow for most average transactions by setting the storage clause **OPTIMAL** value such that the size will accommodate up to the maximum size of the **HWMSIZE** column. All these should be adjusted to minimize **WRAPS** and **EXTENDS**, as indicated in the **V$ROLLSTAT** view.

Generally, depending on statement complexity, an **INSERT** statement generates the least amount of rollback activity, followed by the **DELETE** and then the **UPDATE** statement.

## Monitoring For Proper Placement Of Rollback Segments

To monitor for proper placement of rollback segments, the UTLBSTAT and UTLESTAT report output report.txt should be examined for the I/O report section. The rollback segment tablespace should be placed such that it doesn't contend with other tablespaces or with the redo logs. System monitors such as vmstat and iostat, as well as sar on Unix, should also be used to monitor I/O contention. Generally, write-intensive areas such as redo logs should not be placed on RAID 5 devices, but instead on dedicated RAID 0/1 disks.

Rollback segments should not be placed in tablespaces containing data or indexes, nor should they be placed in the temporary tablespace. Setting storage parameters such that all rollback segments in a single tablespace have the same-size extents eliminates problems with the fragmentation of rollback tablespaces.

# Redo Logs

Redo logs act as transaction journals by providing a detailed log of all transactions that affect data for a database. Redo logs are used for recovery caused by media or instance failure and are used to apply transaction data against the database during the roll-forward portion of recovery. If archive logging is initialized using the **LOG_ARCHIVE_START** initialization parameter, filled redo logs are copied through the ARCH process to the location specified by the **LOG_ARCHIVE_DEST** parameter named according to the convention specified by the **LOG_ARCHIVE_FORMAT** parameter. All the redo log parameters are specified in the initialization file (init<SID>.ora, or simply referred to as the init.ora file).

Periodically, Oracle writes system change number (SCN) and timestamp data to the headers of all datafiles. This process, called a *checkpoint*, can be tuned to be either more frequent than or simultaneous with logfile switches. Normally, you tune for log switches and checkpointing to happen simultaneously. The DBWR process performs the file header updates while LGWR performs the log switch. Using the **CHECKPOINT_PROCESS** initialization parameter allows the CKPT process to start to relieve DBWR of checkpoint responsibilities. If CKPT is not started and DBWR is creating a checkpoint in the file that LGWR needs, LGWR must pause until DBWR completes the checkpoint.

Oracle requires a minimum of two redo log groups and a minimum of one member for each group. For archive logging, three groups are suggested (but remember that the minimum requirement is still two). If more than one group member is specified, be sure that the second and subsequent members for a group are on separate disks or sets of disks. It does little good to use multiplexed redo logs (known as *mirroring*) if you place both copies on the same disk or on volume groups that share a disk. Chances are good that the disk shared by a volume group or the disk with two members of the same group will be the one to fail. Having multiplexed redo logs builds in redundancy, which you defeat if the logs are on the same disk or share a common disk in their volume groups.

Oracle writes to all members of a log group. When the log group fills, DBWR issues a checkpoint, and one member is selected to be archived if archive logging is enabled. If the member chosen for archival is corrupt, Oracle will choose another member of the group and attempt to archive that member. If all members of a redo group are corrupt, the instance will hang.

Redo logs and archive logging are very robust features of Oracle. The worst thing that can happen with redo logs and archive logging is that the archive log location fills up and the database hangs until space is available. Although the database hangs, no data is lost, and operations pick up where they left off before the archive destination filled.

# Sizing And Tuning Redo Logs

The proper sizing and tuning of redo logs is critical to database performance and recoverability. Too large a redo log might cause you to lose unacceptable amounts of data if an active (nonmultiplexed or improperly multiplexed) redo log is lost. Too small a redo log might require you to apply hundreds of thousands of the smaller redo logs to recover a database. To speed instance recovery, use smaller redo logs.

## Sizing Redo Logs

Sizing redo logs is an empirical art. You should size redo logs so that they switch at a frequency at which you don't lose a critical amount of data were you to lose the online redo log and, for some reason, the mirror copy as well. However, the smaller the redo log, the more checkpoints are generated.

Checkpoints are generated at each log switch if the initialization parameter **LOG_CHECKPOINT_INTERVAL** is set to a number larger than the number of blocks in a redo log and the **LOG_CHECKPOINT_TIMEOUT** parameter is set to zero; these are the recommended setpoints. A checkpoint forces DBWR to update all datafile headers, causing DBWR to stop doing dirty buffer writes. To help DBWR, the CKPT process should be started by setting the initialization parameter **CHECKPOINT_PROCESS** to **TRUE**. If present, the CKPT process takes over the header update responsibilities.

Indications that redo logs might be too small include checkpoint errors that show up in the alert log for the instance. If you start seeing frequent waits in the alert log (located in the location specified by the initialization parameter **BACKGROUND_DUMP_DEST**) while the checkpoint process completes, this shows either that your redo logs are too small or that you don't have enough redo log groups. What is shown by wait messages for the checkpoint process to complete is that the redo logs are filling so fast that the database fills the one it just switched to before either CKPT or DBWR can finish updating the datafile headers. If you are archiving and the alert log shows wait messages that logs are waiting for archival and this is causing a wait ("Cannot allocate log, archival required"), the logs need to be increased in number of groups, size, or both.

To reduce redo requirements, you can use several new options for Oracle (new to version 7.3). These new options include direct path loading of data in SQL*Loader, where blocks are prebuilt and fully inserted into the database. However, if the insert fails, it will need to be completely restarted because no redo is generated. Also, the use of the parallel and unrecoverable modes when creating objects such as tables and indexes reduces redo but results in having to reexecute the complete build if the process fails. In addition, **TRUNCATE** rather than **DELETE** should be used to remove all data from a table.

## Tuning Redo Logs

Redo logs are tuned using the following initialization parameters:

➤ **LOG_ARCHIVE_BUFFERS** Sets the number of archive buffer pools to use for archiving; 4 is the usual default.

➤ **LOG_ARCHIVE_BUFFER_SIZE** Sets the size of the archive buffer pools in logfile blocks; 64 is the usual default.

➤ **LOG_BUFFER** Sets the size of the redo circular log buffer in bytes. Default is operating system specific but usually around 8K. A larger value will reduce redo log I/O. LGWR reads this buffer to write redo log entries. The actual redo log buffers are contained within the SGA for the specific instance.

➤ **LOG_CHECKPOINT_INTERVAL** Set to the number of redo log blocks between checkpoints; normally a value larger than the size of a redo log so that checkpoints occur only at log switches. The blocks used in sizing this parameter are operating system blocks, not Oracle buffer blocks.

➤ **LOG_CHECKPOINT_TIMEOUT** Sets the time in seconds between checkpoints. Usually, this should be set to zero to force checkpoints at log switches only.

➤ **LOG_BLOCK_CHECKSUM** Set to **TRUE** only if you suspect redo write corruption problems. This forces each redo block to use a checksum to validate consistency. This parameter is very CPU intensive.

➤ **LOG_ARCHIVE_START** Set to **TRUE** if you want automatic archiving. This parameter is used with setting the database to **ARCHIVELOG** mode either at creation in the **CREATE DATA-BASE** command or after creation using the **ALTER DATABASE** command to turn on automatic archiving. If the database is set to **ARCHIVELOG** mode and this parameter is set to **FALSE,** you must archive the redo logs manually by using the **ARCHIVE LOG** command; otherwise, the database will halt when the last online redo log is filled. The default is **FALSE**.

➤ **LOG_SMALL_ENTRY_MAX_SIZE** Size in bytes of the largest copy to the redo log buffer that can be made under the redo allocation latch. A larger value than **LOG_SMALL_ENTRY_MAX_SIZE** uses a redo copy latch if available. Redo copy latches are available only if **LOG_SIMULTANEOUS_COPIES** is set to greater than zero.

➤ **LOG_SIMULTANEOUS_COPIES** Sets the number of redo copy latches, generally twice the number of CPUs for multiple-CPU machines or zero for single-CPU machines. Should be dynamically set based on the automatically set **CPU_COUNT** parameter.

➤ **LOG_CHECKPOINTS_TO_ALERT** This parameter, if set to **TRUE**, logs all checkpoint activity to the alert log. If you suspect that checkpoints are not occurring as expected, set this to **TRUE**. Normally, checkpoints will happen whenever there is a log switch and log switches are automatically logged. This parameter should be set to **FALSE**. This parameter can cause increased I/O to the alert log, so I/O monitoring might be indicated if this is set to **TRUE**.

 Some systems have problems with the automatic setting of **CPU_COUNT**. Always check that **CPU_COUNT**, and therefore **LOG_SIMULTANEOUS_COPIES**, is set properly. Always verify that **LOG_SIMULTANEOUS_COPIES** is set to twice the number of CPUs and that **CPU_COUNT** is set to the number of CPUs in your system. It is more efficient to have the proper number of redo copy latches as set by **LOG_SIMULTANEOUS_COPIES**.

Redo logs are monitored by keeping a close eye on the alert log and by monitoring the following dynamic performance views:

➤ V$LOG

➤ V$LOGFILE

➤ V$LOG_HISTORY

➤ V$ARCHIVED_LOG

➤ V$SYSTEM_EVENT

➤ V$LOGSTAT

➤ V$LATCH

➤ **V$LATCHNAME**

➤ **V$SYSSTAT**

The latches that deal with the redo logs are the redo allocation and redo copy latches, which are monitored using the **V$LATCH** and **V$LATCHNAME** views. Redo statistics are monitored using the **V$SYSSTAT** view with a select against the **NAME** and **VALUE** columns, where the name is like '%redo%'. Use the previously mentioned **V$LOGFILE** and **V$LOG_HISTORY** views to get information on log switches and logfile status.

The **V$LATCH** view is used to detect latch contention. If the values from the **V$LATCH** view for the redo copy or allocation latch for the ratio of misses to total gets exceeds 10 percent, contention is occurring and the parameters for the redo processes need adjusting. One caveat to redo copy latch tuning is that it is not possible to tune the redo copy latch on single-CPU machines. The latch statistics are also returned in the UTLESTAT.SQL report.txt file. The number of times a process has waited on a latch is indicated by the **SLEEPS** column of the **V$LATCH** view.

The **MISSES** and **GETS** column in the **V$LATCH** view contains statistics used to determine information about **WILLING_TO_WAIT** requests. Whereas a redo allocation latch might use a **WILLING_TO_WAIT** request, a redo copy latch will almost always issue an **IMMEDIATE** request. If you see a value greater than one percent for the ratio of misses to gets for a redo copy latch, increase the number of latches, if possible. On a single-CPU machine, the redo allocation latch is the only latch used; the redo allocation latch is released by a process only when the work in the latch is copied to the buffer.

The DBA only needs to worry about a few of the values that will be retrieved from the **V$SYSSTAT** view: "redo log space wait," "redo buffer allocation re-tries," and "redo size" (these values are also returned in the UTLESTAT.SQL report.txt file), which are discussed in detail here:

➤ **Redo log space wait** This statistic indicates the number of times that a process had to wait to get space in a redo log buffer. It should be as close to zero as possible. Increase the **LOG_BUFFER** parameter to correct excessive waits.

➤ **Redo allocation retries** This statistic indicates how many attempts were made to allocate space in the redo buffer. If this value is high compared to the "redo entries" parameter, your redo logs might be too small and should be increased. This can also result from redo logs that are small in comparison to the SGA size. Prior to version 7.3, Oracle had to flush all dirty blocks from the SGA on each log switch, possibly generating retries. Now Oracle uses a delayed block cleanout that reduces waits.

➤ **Redo size** This statistic is the total redo utilized since startup of the instance. Divide this value by the size of your redo logs in bytes to get the number of log switches since startup. If this ratio of redo size to logfile size exceeds 1 every 15 minutes, your redo logs might be sized too small (remember to adjust for low-use periods). On the other hand, if the ratio is too low, say, only one or two per day, your logs might be too large.

The **V$SYSTEM_EVENT** view is queried to determine whether the redo logs are experiencing I/O contention. An example is a query against this view indicating waits for the "log buffer space" event. In this case, a larger setting for the **LOG_BUFFER** parameter is indicated.

As with many other aspects of Oracle, tuning redo log sizing and tuning is very instance and application specific. You must tune each instance according to its usage and transaction cross-section.

# Tuning Archiving

Archiving is dependent on the mode of the database (it is either **ARCHIVELOG** or **NOARCHIVELOG**) and the setting of the initialization parameters **LOG_ARCHIVE_START**, **LOG_ARCHIVE_DEST**, and **LOG_ARCHIVE_FORMAT**. The frequency of archive logging is controlled by the size of the redo logs and the number, size, and frequency of transactions (usually DML, such as **INSERT**, **UPDATE**, or **DELETE**, although long-running **SELECT** statements with sorts also generate redo activity).

Archive logging can be monitored by using the alert log as well as the **V$LOG_HISTORY** view. Additional data on archive logging can be obtained by setting the **LOG_CHECKPOINTS_TO_ALERT** parameter to **TRUE** and then comparing archive log timing to checkpoint timing. However, most data on archive log problems comes from alert log warning and error messages. For example, an alert log message such as "Checkpoint not complete; unable to allocate log" indicates that LGWR has waited for DBWR or CKPT to complete a checkpoint.

Checkpoints can be reduced by setting the initialization parameters to force checkpoints to occur only when a log switch happens and making your redo logs relatively large. Previous sections of this chapter discussed how to force checkpoints to occur only at log switches.

Archive logging can be done to disk or tape (on certain systems). If archiving to disk, you must monitor disk space usage and periodically back up to tape or remove archive logs to prevent the archive log destination from filling. If the archive log destination fills, archive logging halts and the instance stops until the archive destination is changed or room is cleared on the current destination. You must always be sure that if the database mode is set to **ARCHIVELOG**, the initialization parameter **LOG_ARCHIVE_DEST** is set to a proper location or that archiving to tape is enabled.

# Practice Questions

## Question 1

When building applications, what can the developer do to avoid overextending the rollback segment?

○  a. Use **DELETE** rather than **TRUNCATE** statements

○  b. Avoid long-running queries

○  c. Do not use nested SQL statements

○  d. Avoid long transactions when possible

The correct answer is d. Long DML transactions cause large amounts of rollback to be generated. This is especially true of **INSERT, UPDATE,** and **DELETE.** Answer a is incorrect because it is actually **DELETE** you want to avoid, and **TRUNCATE** is a DDL statement and doesn't generate rollback. Answer b is incorrect because a **SELECT** statement, even a long-running one, doesn't generate rollback; however, it can cause problems with "snapshot too old" errors because of its need for a read-consistent image. Answer c is incorrect because, again, even nested SQLs don't generate that much rollback.

## Question 2

The size of the **INITIAL** storage parameter for your rollback segment is 2MB. To which value should you set the **NEXT** storage parameter?

○  a. 2MB

○  b. 4MB

○  c. 256K

○  d. 1MB

The correct answer is a. The **INITIAL** storage parameter should be based on transaction sizes for the average transaction. Because each user who is assigned a rollback segment gets a single extent, each extent should be the same size as the **INITIAL** value, so **INITIAL** and **NEXT** should be set the same.

# Question 3

> You view the alert_<SID>.log and see this error:
>
> ```
> 'Checkpoint not complete; unable to allocate
> file'
> ```
>
> What does this indicate?
>
> - ○ a. LGWR has waited for a checkpoint to finish
> - ○ b. DBWR has waited for LGWR to finish
> - ○ c. LGWR has waited for ARCH to finish

The correct answer is a. The error says it all: "Checkpoint not complete; unable to allocate file." It could be waiting on either DBWR or CKPT to finish, but in either case it's waiting on a checkpoint to finish and can't allocate a new logfile. Answer b is incorrect because DBWR would be the problem child if CKPT were not initialized and would be performing the checkpoint causing the wait, so it would not be waiting on LGWR. Answer c is incorrect because we are waiting on a checkpoint, not an archival. The ARCH process has nothing to do with checkpoints.

# Question 4

> You are evaluating rollback segments on your system. Which criteria should you use to determine the number of rollback segments you will need?
>
> - ○ a. Number of redo log buffers
> - ○ b. Number of concurrent users
> - ○ c. Number of concurrent DML transactions
> - ○ d. Number of datafiles in the tablespace

The correct answer is c. A user is not assigned to a rollback segment until something is done that might need rolling back. Only DML can be rolled back, so the number of concurrent DML transactions determines the needed number of rollback segments. Answer a is incorrect because redo log buffers have nothing to do with rollback segments. Answer b is incorrect because a user is not assigned to a rollback segment until a DML action is performed. Answer d is incorrect because, although the number of datafiles might determine whether you start a checkpoint process, it has nothing to do with rollback segments.

## Question 5

Which background process writes the data to the redo logfile?

O a. CKPT

O b. LGWR

O c. DBWR

O d. ARCH

The correct answer is b. The log writer process, otherwise known as LGWR, writes data from the log buffer to the redo log. Answer a is incorrect because all the CKPT (checkpoint) does is write the checkpoint information to the datafile headers. Answer c is incorrect because DBWR writes dirty buffers to the disk from the db buffer cache and, if no CKPT process is started, does checkpoints but never writes data to the logfiles. Answer d is incorrect because ARCH writes filled redo logs to the archive location, and that is its only function.

## Question 6

How many redo log groups must be created for a database running in **ARCHIVELOG** mode?

O a. Six

O b. Three

O c. Two

O d. One

You must read this question carefully. The correct answer is c. The question asks how many groups *must* be created, not *should* be created. Regardless of whether the database is in **ARCHIVELOG** or **NOARCHIVELOG**, you must have a minimum of two redo log groups. So, although a minimum of three or more groups is suggested in **ARCHIVELOG** mode, only two are required and must be present. Therefore, answer c is the correct choice.

# Question 7

> Which DML statement will generate the least amount of rollback
> on the database?
>
> ○  a. **DELETE**
>
> ○  b. **INSERT**
>
> ○  c. **UPDATE**

The correct answer is b. An **INSERT** statement has a simple one-place entry
in a rollback segment, and its inverse is a **DELETE** statement. Answer a is
incorrect because for read consistency, a **DELETE** requires a before-image
copy of the changed block. Answer c is incorrect because for an **UPDATE**, a
before-image copy of the block is also required for read consistency.

# Question 8

> In which situation would it be beneficial for you to use the **SET**
> **TRANSACTION USE ROLLBACK SEGMENT large_rbs;** command
> (assuming **large_rbs** is indeed a large rollback segment)?
>
> ○  a. Running a large PL/SQL package
>
> ○  b. Running a large SQL query
>
> ○  c. Running a large batch job

The correct answer is c. A large batch job more than likely involves a large
DML transaction, such as a large **INSERT, UPDATE,** or **DELETE**, all of
which require a large amount of rollback. Answer a is incorrect because generally a large PL/SQL package will have many small procedures and functions
that would not be run together, but would be done piecemeal so that only small
amounts of redo would be generated. Answer b is incorrect because SQL queries (**SELECT** statements) do not, as a rule, generate large amounts of rollback.

## Question 9

> For which three things are rollback segments used?
>
> ❏ a. Data entry
>
> ❏ b. Rollback
>
> ❏ c. Performance
>
> ❏ d. Recovery
>
> ❏ e. I/O
>
> ❏ f. Read consistency

The correct answers are b, d, and f. Rollback segments are used for rollback operations, to perform rollback operations during recovery, and to ensure that a read-consistent image of data being manipulated is readily available to other queries. Answer a is incorrect because rollback segments are not used for data entry. Answer c is incorrect because rollback segment usage decreases performance because of the additional write requirements. Answer e is incorrect because rollback segment usage increases I/O.

## Question 10

> What is the worst problem you are likely to encounter with redo mechanisms?
>
> ○ a. The archive destination fills and causes the database to hang
>
> ○ b. The archive destination fills and the PMON process hangs
>
> ○ c. The archive destination fills and the background processes halt

The correct answer is a. If the archive destination is full, then the archive process cannot write out any more archive logs to the destination. This means that once all online logs are filled, the LGWR process cannot switch to a new log and thus the database hangs. Answer b is incorrect because PMON has nothing to do with redo mechanisms. Answer c is incorrect because this causes a hang, not a halt.

# Need To Know More?

 Ault, Michael R.: *Oracle8 Administration and Management.* John Wiley & Sons, 1998. ISBN 0-471-18234-1. Although the title mentions only Oracle8, this book also covers Oracle7.3. Chapters 1, 2, and 13 discuss redo logs and rollback segments, from creation to monitoring and tuning.

 Corey, Michael, Michael Abbey, and Don Dechichio: *Tuning Oracle.* Oracle Press/Osborne, 1995. ISBN 0-07-881181-3. Chapters 1, 2, and 5 discuss rollback and redo issues as well as other aspects of tuning.

 Gurry, Mark and Peter Corrigan: *Oracle Performance Tuning, 2nd Edition.* O'Reilly & Associates, 1996. ISBN 1-56592-237-9. Chapters 4, 8, 9, 11, 12, and 14 and Appendix B discuss tuning, sizing, and the use of redo logs and rollback segments.

# Monitoring And Detecting Lock And Latch Contention

**7**

## Terms you'll need to understand:

✓ Deadlock

✓ Row-level lock

✓ Table-level lock

✓ Transaction-level lock

✓ Lock tree

✓ Spin

✓ Lock

✓ Latch

## Techniques you'll need to master:

✓ Detecting lock and latch problems

✓ Tuning locks

✓ Freeing locks

✓ Tuning latches

✓ Detecting latch contentions

Oracle uses latches (a form of low-level locking) and locks to protect both data structures and memory structures. Generally, a latch always protects a memory structure, and a lock always protects a data structure. Locks and latches are usually controlled automatically, although you can tune them for peak efficiency. Most locking problems can usually be traced to application-forced locking that is not properly applied. This chapter discusses locking and latching issues.

# Oracle Locks

Locks are used to protect data. Locks default to the row level, but they can be forced—through either initialization parameters or program statements—to occur at other levels as well. Oracle automatically assigns the lowest level of lock to achieve the statement's implicit goal. Therefore, as long as transactions are properly designed, Oracle should automatically invoke the proper locking strategy. Incorrect locking will result in deadlock situations. Locks consist of several types (for example, DML, DDL, table, and row) and can be either exclusive locks or share locks. Only one exclusive lock can be placed at any time on a given resource. Multiple share locks are possible against the same resource at the same time. Queries are always allowed, even on locked resources, but other activities are prohibited, depending on the type of lock.

Locks are held for the duration of the transaction. This prevents destructive interactions from other processes or transactions, therefore maintaining data integrity for the length of a specific transaction. A **COMMIT** or **ROLLBACK** will release all locks held by a transaction. Locks acquired from the time a **SAVEPOINT** is issued will be released when the transaction is rolled back to that **SAVEPOINT**; locks acquired before the **SAVEPOINT** are not affected. However, if a resource was locked in a **SAVEPOINT** and then the transaction rolled back to that **SAVEPOINT**, only transactions without current lock waits can acquire locks on those resources on which the locks were released. Transactions with active waits will still wait until the entire transaction is complete.

Lock conversion happens automatically in Oracle databases. A lower-level table lock will convert to a higher-level lock as required. Row-exclusive locks are the highest level of locks and therefore cannot be converted. Exclusive locks are held for rows participating in all **INSERT, UPDATE,** and **DELETE** transactions. A **SELECT FOR UPDATE** statement assigns row-exclusive locks to rows referenced by the **SELECT** and a row-share table lock. The row-share table lock is automatically updated to an exclusive lock once a row is updated.

Lock escalation is never done in Oracle because it increases the chance that a deadlock will occur. Oracle attempts to avoid deadlocks by using the highest granularity of locking possible for a transaction.

Even fine-grain locks can participate in what is known as a deadlock. Deadlocks happen when two processes compete for the same data resource. Oracle has provided several scripts and packages of procedures that should be used to monitor and control locks. The statement that detects a deadlock is the one that is rolled back automatically by Oracle. The rolled-back statement receives an error.

Locks are controlled by means of enqueue processes. Enqueue processes are controlled by setting the **ENQUEUE_RESOURCES** initialization parameter, which controls the size of the internal locking table. Therefore, the total number of locks is controlled by the total number of enqueues. Some forms of lock contention are resolved by increasing the **ENQUEUE_RESOURCES** initialization parameter.

# Types Of Locks

Oracle has several types of locks. Oracle automatically uses the proper type of lock for a transaction. Oracle locks are of one of the following categories:

➤ **DML (data) locks**  DML locks protect the data. Can be either table level or row level.

➤ **DDL (dictionary) locks**  DDL locks protect the structure of objects, such as a table's or view's definition.

➤ **Internal locks and latches**  Internal locks and latches protect internal structures such as datafiles. Entirely automatic.

➤ **Distributed locks**  Distributed locks ensure that structures are consistent across the different instances that participate in the parallel database (used in Oracle parallel server). Held at the instance level, not the transaction level.

➤ **Parallel cache management (PCM) locks**  PCM locks act to lock one or more data blocks in the system global areas (SGAs) participating in a shared-server configuration. A form of distributed lock. Held at the memory, data-block level and do not lock rows.

# DML Locks

DML locks guarantee the integrity of data accessed simultaneously by multiple transactions. They prevent destructive interference from transactions other than the one holding the lock. Oracle DML locks ensure that a row can be updated by only one transaction at a time and that a table cannot be dropped if an uncommitted transaction contains an insert into the table. DML locks are either row level or table level.

## Row-Level DML Locks (TX Locks)

Row-level locks represent the finest level of granularity for Oracle locking. These locks are the only DML locks acquired automatically. A transaction can have an unlimited number of row locks acquired. DML locks ensure that contention for rows occurs only when two transactions attempt to acquire a lock on the same row or rows at the same time. DML row locks are also known as TX or transaction locks. The following rules apply to DML row locks:

➤ Readers of data never wait for writers of the same data row.

➤ When automatic locking is used, writers never wait for readers, unless **SELECT...FOR UPDATE**, which is explicit locking, is used.

➤ Writers wait for other writers only if they are attempting to update the same data row.

➤ They are always accompanied by table-level share locks.

Notice that a row lock is always accompanied by a table share lock. A table share lock prevents other transactions from issuing a table-level lock against the table being updated until the transaction with the row lock completes. The table-level share lock also prevents DDL operations against tables participating in the transaction.

## Table-Level Locks (TM Locks)

Oracle uses a number of different levels of table locks to control read, write, and general access to tables. Table-level locks are usually indicated by "TM" in the lock-type column when queried by Server Manager. Table 7.1 shows which statements cause which types of locks and which types of locks are permitted against tables undergoing that transaction statement.

The following guides should be used in interpreting Table 7.1:

➤ **Row-share lock (RS)** Least restrictive of the table locks; also known as a subshare lock (SS). Allows other transactions to insert, update, delete, or lock other rows in the same table. Prevents a **LOCK TABLE...IN EXCLUSIVE MODE** operation by another transaction.

➤ **Row-exclusive lock (RX)** Almost identical to a row-share lock but further limits the types of lock operations that other transactions can use; also known as a subexclusive table lock (SX). Allows insert, update, delete, and lock of other rows. Prohibits **LOCK TABLE** commands with the following options: **IN SHARE MODE, IN SHARE EXCLUSIVE MODE,** and **IN EXCLUSIVE MODE.**

**Table 7.1    Summary of table locks.**

| SQL Statement | Mode Of Table Lock | Lock Modes Permitted? | | | | |
|---|---|---|---|---|---|---|
| | | **RS** | **RX** | **S** | **SRX** | **X** |
| INSERT | RX | Y | Y | N | N | N |
| UPDATE | RX | Y* | Y* | N | N | N |
| DELETE | RX | Y* | Y* | N | N | N |
| SELECT | None | Y | Y | Y | Y | Y |
| SELECT...UPDATE | RS | Y* | Y* | Y* | Y* | N |
| LOCK TABLE IN ROW SHARE MODE | RS | Y | Y | Y | Y | N |
| LOCK TABLE IN SHARE MODE | RX | Y | Y | N | N | N |
| LOCK TABLE IN SHARE MODE | S | Y | N | Y | N | N |
| LOCK TABLE IN SHARE ROW EXCLUSIVE MODE | SRX | Y | N | N | N | N |
| LOCK TABLE IN EXCLUSIVE MODE | X | N | N | N | N | N |

* Yes if no conflicting locks are held by another transaction; otherwise, waits occur.

➤ **Share lock (S)** Explicitly acquired through use of the **LOCK TABLE...IN SHARE MODE** command. Allows query, **SELECT...FOR UPDATE**, or other **LOCK TABLE...IN SHARE MODE** operations. However, it restricts updates from transactions other than the one holding the share lock. If multiple transactions hold the share lock, no transaction can update the table. The following are prohibited operations in tables that have a share lock:

➤ UPDATES

➤ LOCK TABLE...IN SHARE ROW EXCLUSIVE MODE

➤ IN EXCLUSIVE MODE

➤ IN ROW EXCLUSIVE MODE

➤ **Share-row-exclusive lock (SRX)** More restrictive than a share lock; also known as a share-subexclusive table lock (SSX). Explicitly acquired through the **LOCK TABLE...IN SHARE ROW EXCLUSIVE**

MODE command. Only one transaction can acquire an SRX lock on a specific table at any time. Other transactions can query the table or issue **SELECT...FOR UPDATE** commands, but cannot update data until the lock is released. Prohibits almost all other locking, specifically the following lock operations:

➤ LOCK TABLE...IN SHARE MODE

➤ IN SHARE ROW EXCLUSIVE MODE

➤ IN ROW EXCLUSIVE MODE

➤ IN EXCLUSIVE MODE

➤ **Exclusive lock (X)** The most restrictive of locks. Only a single transaction can lock a table in X mode. A table locked in X mode can be queried only by other transactions; all other operations are prohibited until the X lock is lifted.

Data manipulation language (DML) locks are automatically created by Oracle as they are needed. However, the database administrator can control the number of allowed DML locks with the **DML_LOCKS** initialization parameter. Queries (**SELECT**s) are the DML statements that are least likely to cause interference with other SQL statements because they only read data. A query acquires no data locks (as long as it does not have a **FOR UPDATE** clause). DML locks are always issued implicitly at the row level.

# DDL Locks

Data definition language (DDL) locks protect the definition of a schema object while the object is acted on or referred to by an ongoing DDL operation. For example, an index creation will prohibit other DDL operations against the indexed table until the index build is complete. DDL locks are always automatic, and no implicit creation of DDL locks occurs. DDL locks affect only individual data dictionary objects, and never the entire data dictionary. DDL locks are either share mode or exclusive mode; most are exclusive. Share DDL locks are used for operations such as **CREATE PROCEDURE**, which issues share DDL locks on all tables that the procedure references. The entire purpose of a share DDL lock is to ensure that the definition of the locked object does not change while the object is being defined. The following commands acquire a shared DDL lock:

➤ AUDIT

➤ NOAUDIT

- ➤ COMMENT

- ➤ GRANT

- ➤ CREATE (OR REPLACE) VIEW/PROCEDURE/PACKAGE/ PACKAGE BODY/FUNCTION/TRIGGER

- ➤ CREATE SYNONYM

- ➤ CREATE TABLE (when the **CLUSTER** parameter is not included)

An exclusive DDL lock is created when statements such as **ALTER** are issued. A DDL lock will not be issued against an object that has exclusive row locks issued against it. Therefore, exclusive DDL locks usually do not cause contention problems.

Another form of DDL lock is a breakable parse lock. Such a lock is held by any object in the shared pool on each object it references. Parse locks are held for as long as the SQL statement remains in the shared pool. As its name implies, a breakable parse lock is breakable, allowing conflicting DDL operations to acquire and modify the object on which the lock is set. Of all locks, DDL locks are the least likely to cause contention. A breakable parse lock is also called a PL/SQL user lock (UL).

## Oracle Latches

Latches are simple, low-level serialization mechanisms that are used to protect internal shared data structures in the SGA, including lists of currently used tables and users accessing the database. They are also used to protect the data structures that describe the contents of the data block buffers. Processes acquire latches when looking at or manipulating these internal structures. Latching is operating system-specific.

## Lock Utility Scripts And Packages

Oracle has provided several utility scripts and utility packages to help DBAs monitor locks. These scripts must be explicitly run by the DBA before their contents can be utilized. These scripts and packages are:

- ➤ catblock.sql This script builds tables and views used by the other lock utilities. The script creates the following tables and views: **DBA_KGLLOCK, DBA_LOCK, DBA_LOCK_INTERNAL, DBA_DML_LOCKS, DBA_DDL_LOCKS, DBA_WAITERS,** and **DBA_BLOCKERS**. This script must be run before utllockt.sql will execute.

➤ **dbmslock.sql** This script creates the capability for developers to create and maintain their own locks.

➤ **utllockt.sql** This script creates a simple wait-for lock tree display. You must have run catblock.sql before running this script for the first time. However, catblock.sql needs to be run only once.

The catblock.sql script is run first. It usually should be run right after running the catproc.sql script when building an instance. The catblock.sql script needs to be run only once for an instance, except when updating to a newer version of Oracle.

# Monitoring Locks

Locks have several internal sources of information. In addition to the tables created by the catblock.sql script, there is also lock information stored in several other tables and views. The trace files generated by Oracle processes are a great source of information about lock problems. In fact, the rowid for the row that causes a deadlock will be pinpointed in the session trace file for the session participating in the deadlock. The trace files for a session are located in the location specified by the **USER_DUMP_DEST** initialization parameter. If you suspect that lock contention is occurring in your instance, you can view the **V$SESSION** view to see which row in a table is causing the lock contention.

Of the locks discussed here, the TM, TX, and UL types of locks are usually obtained by user applications and should be monitored the most frequently.

If in your monitoring you discover that a user has locked a table or set of rows and has left for vacation or a user has simply left for the day with locks in place, you should kill that Oracle session using the **ALTER SYSTEM KILL SESSION** command. To use the kill command, you must obtain the **SERIAL#** and **SID** values from the **V$SESSION** view.

Latch contention can be caused by improperly setting the **SPIN_COUNT** initialization parameter. This parameter controls the number of times a process will loop (or spin) when trying to lock a busy latch before going to sleep and then trying again some time later. The **SPIN_COUNT** parameter is usually set to 2,000 on most computers. If you receive an indication of latch contention, increasing this parameter might improve overall performance because latches usually are not held for long.

# Parallel Server Locks

A parallel server requires that two or more Oracle instances share data between their SGAs. This sharing of data is accomplished through PCM locks.

These locks are used to maintain cache coherency and are explicitly configured by the DBA when the instances are configured. All PCM lock initialization parameters must match between all instances of an Oracle parallel server configuration.

The DBA can use the **GC_DB_LOCKS** and **GC_FILES_TO_LOCKS** parameters to set the total number of available PCM locks and the granularity of those locks. You can never have more PCM locks configured by the **GC_FILES_TO_LOCKS** parameter than are created by the **GC_DB_LOCKS** parameter. PCM locks require about 115 bytes of memory per lock specified. The granularity of PCM locks refers to the number of database file blocks covered per individual lock. The **GC_FILES_TO_LOCKS** parameter is used to specify granularity and whether PCM locks are assigned to contiguous blocks or whether a hashing algorithm is used to randomize the assignment of lock to blocks.

The granularity of PCM locks is based on how the data in the database is to be accessed. Online transaction processing (OLTP) systems generally require fine-grain locking, whereas decision support system (DSS) or data warehouse (DWH) applications generally require coarser grain locking. A mixed-mode environment (such as one that has OLTP action during the day and large batch reporting done at night) might require a compromise.

If improper granularity is specified, a condition can occur in which instance A has a lock on several blocks and instance B requires a record in one of A's locked blocks so that A must release the PCM lock to allow B to access the record. Instance B might not even be interested in the same block that A was using, but because A and B are covered by the same lock, the lock must be released. When a lock that covers more than one block is released because of interest by another instance in a nonactive block, this is called a *false ping*. If two instances swap locks over the same block, it is simply called a *ping*. The ultimate goal of a proper PCM lock configuration is to minimize all forms of pinging.

# Practice Questions

## Question 1

> How does Oracle7 server resolve deadlocks?
>
> ○ a. By rolling back the statement that detected the deadlock
>
> ○ b. By rolling back all statements causing the deadlock
>
> ○ c. By automatically killing the user process that detected the deadlock
>
> ○ d. By automatically killing all user processes involved in the deadlock

The correct answer is a. Oracle will roll back the statement that detects the deadlock. Usually, this means the second statement in a series. This is done because it was decided that a first-come, first-served model would be used for this resolution model; that is, the first statement to get a lock deserves to keep it. Answer b is incorrect because only the detecting statement is rolled back. However, if both a and b are part of a single transaction, it might result in the entire transaction rolling back, but usually only the detecting statement is affected. Answers c and d are incorrect because Oracle kills user sessions only during shutdowns.

## Question 2

> A PL/SQL procedure is executed within the application, and its objects are placed in the cache. Which type of lock will Oracle place on these objects?
>
> ○ a. An exclusive DML lock
>
> ○ b. An exclusive DDL lock
>
> ○ c. A shared DML lock
>
> ○ d. A breakable parse lock (UL)

The correct answer is d. Whenever a stored object is placed in the shared pool, a UL (breakable parse) lock is used for it and its objects. Answer a is incorrect because this type of lock is used for rows undergoing DML operations. Answer b is incorrect because this type of lock is used for objects undergoing DDL operations. Answer c is incorrect because this type of lock is used only for objects undergoing DML operations.

## Question 3

> How will a table lock be named when the lock-type column is queried in lock views using Server Manager?
>
> ○ a. TM
>
> ○ b. TX
>
> ○ c. SSX
>
> ○ d. RX

The correct answer is a. Answer b is incorrect because TX is used for a transaction lock. Answer c is incorrect because SSX is used to designate a lock mode, not a type of lock (lock mode share subexclusive table lock). Answer d is incorrect because RX (row-exclusive lock mode) is also used to indicate a lock mode, not a type of lock.

## Question 4

> Which view contains information giving the row participating in lock contention?
>
> ○ a. **V$LOCK**
>
> ○ b. **V$SYSSTAT**
>
> ○ c. **V$ROWCACHE**
>
> ○ d. **V$SESSION**

The correct answer is d. Using data contained in **V$SESSION**, a DBA can determine the row and table participating in lock contention. Answer b is incorrect because although **V$SYSSTAT** might contain information on contention, it contains no row information. Answer c is incorrect because **V$ROWCACHE** deals with data dictionary cache information, not locks.

## Question 5

Which script must be run before you can use the utllockt.sql script?

○ a. catexp.sql

○ b. catblock.sql

○ c. dbmsutil.sql

○ d. utlxplan.sql

The answer is b. The catblock.sql script must be run to set up the views used by the utllockt.sql script. Answer a is incorrect because the catexp.sql script sets up the tables used by export and import and has nothing to do with lock data. Answer c is incorrect because dbmsutil.sql sets up many useful packages and has none that deals with locks. Answer d is incorrect because utlxplan.sql builds the **EXPLAIN_PLAN** table and has nothing to do with locks.

## Question 6

Which Oracle mechanism maintains all locks in the database?

○ a. Data dictionary

○ b. Library cache

○ c. Enqueues

○ d. Dispatchers

The correct answer is c. The enqueue processes maintain all locks in the system and are configured using the **ENQUEUE_RESOURCES** initialization parameter. Answer a is incorrect because the data dictionary might use locks and store data about locks but does not maintain them. Answer b is incorrect because although the library cache might use locks, it does not maintain them. Answer d is incorrect because dispatchers are used in multithreaded servers and have nothing to do with locks and maintaining locks.

## Question 7

When are DML locks held by a transaction released?

○ a. After each DML statement completes

○ b. When the user commits the transaction

○ c. When the user enters a new DML statement

○ d. When the data entry screen in an application fills

The correct answer is b. Locks are released only after a commit, rollback, or abnormal transaction termination. Answers a and c are incorrect because a large transaction might include multiple DML statements, but no locks are released until a commit, rollback, or termination of the complete transaction. Answer d is incorrect because the simple act of filling a screen forces no database action unless the screen is coded to commit when all the screen is filled, which is not specified in this answer.

## Question 8

A deadlock is detected in statement B of a large transaction after statement A has started but not completed. What is the state of the transaction?

○ a. Statement A is rolled back and an error message is generated for statement B

○ b. Statements A and B are rolled back, and the transaction receives an error message

○ c. The entire transaction is rolled back

○ d. Statement B is rolled back and an error message is generated for the transaction

The correct answer is d. When a statement detects a deadlock, the detecting statement is rolled back and an error is generated. Answer a is incorrect because A is already active (and presumably holds the lock that B is deadlocking against) and is not rolled back. Answer b is incorrect because only B, the detecting statement, is rolled back. Answer c is incorrect because we do not have enough information about the transaction to make this call.

## Question 9

> Robyn has an active database connection and leaves for lunch. She did not commit her work, and the table she was accessing has a table-level lock on it. Which action should you take to release the locks so that other users can access this table?
>
> ○ a. Kill Robyn's session
> ○ b. Make the users wait until Robyn returns
> ○ c. Shut down the instance and restart
> ○ d. Kill Robyn's session with an operating system command
> ○ e. Commit Robyn's transactions using SQL*Plus

*Trick! question*

The correct answer is a. Because you do not know the state of Robyn's transaction, answer a is the only solution. Answer b is incorrect because what would happen were Robyn to decide to go home rather than return after lunch? Answer c is incorrect because although you can kill individual sessions, why shut down the entire database to fix one user's oversight? Answer d would also work, but what if you are using a multithreaded server or Robyn is coming in over a database link? You might not be able to recognize Robyn's process at the operating system level. So, although this will work, you might kill the wrong session. Answer e is incorrect because again you do not know whether the data being entered or changed by Robyn is correct or whether she would decide to roll it back after lunch; besides, she might be in an entirely different location than you!

## Question 10

> Which lock types are usually obtained by user applications? [Check all correct answers]
>
> ❏ a. TM
> ❏ b. UL
> ❏ c. SS
> ❏ d. TX
> ❏ e. RX

The correct answers are a, b, and d. Users usually obtain TM (table locks), UL (breakable parse locks), and TX (transaction locks). Answer c is the indication for a subshare table lock, otherwise known as a row-share table lock (RS lock) and is a lock mode, not a lock. Answer e is the indication for a row-exclusive lock mode and is a lock mode, not a lock.

# Need To Know More?

 *Oracle8 Server Concepts, Release 8, Volume 2.* Oracle Corporation, 1997. Part Number A54644-01. Do not let the title throw you. Chapter 22 contains excellent cross-release information about locks.

 Gurry, Mark and Peter Corrigan: *Oracle Performance Tuning, 2nd Edition.* O'Reilly & Associates, Inc., 1996. ISBN 1-56592-237-9. Chapters 8, 10, 12, and 18 and Appendix B on locking and latches are required reading for all DBAs.

# Tuning
# Oracle Sorts

. . . . . . . . . . . . . . . . . . . . . . . . .

### Terms you'll need to understand:

√ Disk sort

√ Memory sort

√ Distinct selects

√ Order by selects

√ Temporary tablespace

√ Sort extent pool (SEP)

√ Program global area (PGA)

√ User global area (UGA)

√ Shared pool

√ System global area (SGA)

√ Sort direct writes

### Techniques you'll need to master:

√ Using initialization parameters to control sorts

√ Using SELECT statements to control sorts

√ Configuring temporary tablespaces

√ Monitoring sort activity with V$SYSSTAT and V$SORT_SEGMENT

√ Tuning direct write sorts

Although data, by definition, is stored nonsorted in a relational database, result sets that are nonsorted are frustrating and difficult to deal with. To return an ordered set of values, Oracle performs sorts. Some operations, such as forced uniqueness or distinctiveness of returned data sets, will always cause a sort operation.

Sorts are of two general types: disk sorts, which are the most expensive in terms of resources, and memory sorts, which are the least expensive. You control the number of sorts done on disk and the number done in memory through the proper setting of several Oracle initialization file parameters. You can determine how efficiently sorts that must be done on disk are accomplished by a combination of temporary tablespace storage setup and special initialization parameter settings.

The tuning exam will contain several questions regarding sorts and the tuning and monitoring of sorts. After you study the material in this chapter, you should have no problem facing the questions on the exam that cover sorting.

# Types Of Oracle Sorts

As mentioned previously, Oracle uses disk sorts and memory sorts. Because disk accesses are usually an order of magnitude longer (or more) in duration than memory-based operations, any operations that require the reading, writing, and access of data on disk will be a major performance hit. Memory sorts are done entirely with the process memory area preallocated for sorting. Memory sorts are cheap in terms of resources, and they should be the target for tuning (making all sorts memory sorts).

## Disk Sorts

If a sort exceeds the size of the **SORT_AREA_SIZE** initialization parameter, it will require a disk sort. Disk sorts are always performed in the user's designated temporary tablespace. Because sorts are always performed in the temporary tablespace for a user, the database administrator (DBA) must be sure that no user has the **SYSTEM** tablespace assigned as a temporary tablespace. If the value of **SORT_AREA_SIZE** is greater than 10 times the size of **DB_BLOCK_SIZE**, memory area from the sort area is allocated to perform direct writes to disk if **SORT_DIRECT_WRITES** is set to **AUTO**. One exception is when sorts are being used during the creation of indexes. In this case, the sorts are done in the target tablespace for the index. You especially need to be aware of when index creations are performed on parallel tables. These types of index creations will involve multiple initial extents that are then consolidated into the final set of extents.

If, when a user is created, the default and temporary tablespaces are not explicitly assigned, the assignment will default to the **SYSTEM** tablespace. Always explicitly assign users their default and temporary tablespaces. Fragmentation and excessive **SYSTEM** tablespace I/O are prime indicators that a user's temporary tablespace assignment has been set to **SYSTEM**.

In environments rich in memory and disk space, you might want to do disk sorts rather than tie up memory resources. Forced disk sorting is accomplished by setting the **SORT_DIRECT_WRITES, SORT_WRITE_BUFFERS, SORT_BUFFER_SIZE, SORT_SPACEMAP_SIZE,** and **SORT_READ_FAC** initialization parameters correctly. Some general guidelines for setting these parameters are:

➤ **SORT_DIRECT_WRITES** Turns on forced disk sorts when this parameter is set to **TRUE**; its default setting is **AUTO**. This controls whether sort writes pass through the buffer caches. Bypassing the buffer caches means that sort speed can be increased by a factor of 6 or more.

➤ **SORT_WRITE_BUFFERS** The number of sort direct write buffers; set at 2 as a default and increase as needed to a maximum of 8 to improve sort speeds. Each process has its own set of sort write buffers.

➤ **SORT_BUFFER_SIZE** The size of each sort write buffer, initially set at 32,768 bytes; increase as needed up to 65,536 bytes to improve sort speed.

➤ **SORT_SPACEMAP_SIZE** The size of the disk map used to map disk areas used for sorting; defaults to 512 bytes, which is usually enough, unless you have extremely large sorts, such as during index builds. Suggested setpoint is

```
(total sort bytes / (SORT_AREA_SIZE) + 64
```

where total sort bytes is equal to (number of records) * (sum of column sizes + (2 * number of columns)).

➤ **SORT_READ_FAC** The number of blocks read from disk in a single operation for a sort; defaults to 20, which is usually enough but can be increased if you do numerous large sorts. The calculation for this parameter is:

```
(avg_seek_time + avg_latency + blk_transfer_time) /
blk_transfer_time
```

Therefore, if you have abundant memory and temporary disk space on your system, using **SORT_DIRECT_WRITES** to bypass the buffer cache and to write directly to disk for large sorts (through sort buffers defined for each process) can increase the speed of large sorts by up to six times. Because we are talking about increasing disk I/O load by using **SORT_DIRECT_WRITES**, I/O should be properly tuned for your system as well.

## Memory Sorts

Ideally, all sorts should be done in memory because memory provides the fastest data sorting and access capabilities. Doing all sorts in memory, except for a few small databases, is not a very realistic possibility. However, we can tune sorts using the **SORT_AREA_SIZE** and **SORT_AREA_RETAINED_SIZE** initialization parameters to minimize disk sorts and to reduce memory requirements for sorts.

By monitoring the **V$SYSSTAT** table through use of a query similar to

```
SELECT name, value FROM v$sysstat WHERE name like '%sort%' ;
```

we can determine how many sorts are being done to disk and how many sorts are being done in memory. For example, running the previous query against a 20GB production that mixed online transaction processing (OLTP) and batch system with a 3MB **SORT_AREA_SIZE** and a 2MB **SORT_AREA_RETAINED_SIZE** produced the following results:

```
SQL> SELECT name,value FROM v$sysstat WHERE name LIKE '%sort%';

NAME                                                        VALUE
---------------------------------------------------------- ---------
sorts (memory)                                             234126
sorts (disk)                                               30
sorts (rows)                                               75234036
```

Therefore, in this system, we are seeing 0.013 percent of sorts going to disk (not a bad ratio). The 0.013 percent ratio is especially good when you realize that several large batch jobs (for example, snapshot builds and table analysis operations) were run since the last time this database was restarted. Your goal should be to reduce disk sorts to less than 10 percent, and generally less than 1 percent is attainable. Some general guidelines for setting **SORT_AREA_SIZE** and **SORT_AREA_RETAINED_SIZE** follow:

➤ For **SORT_AREA_SIZE**, the default setting usually is insufficient, except in the most minimal of OLTP environments. If you can quantify the average sort done on your system, set this parameter to that value or a multiple of that value; otherwise, monitor the sort statistics in **V$SYSSTAT** and adjust this parameter up until disk sorts are less than 10 percent of total sorts as a minimum. For non-multithreaded server (non-MTS) systems, this memory is taken from the user's process global area (PGA). For systems using MTS, this memory is taken from the shared pool area of the system global area (SGA), which is referred to as the user global area (UGA). If a sort is larger than **SORT_AREA_SIZE**, it is broken into **SORT_AREA_SIZE** chunks and done on disk.

➤ The **SORT_AREA_RETAINED_SIZE** parameter sets the initial size of the sort area allocated per user. In memory-poor environments, set this parameter to a fraction of the value of **SORT_AREA_SIZE**. Users will be allocated **SORT_AREA_RETAINED_SIZE** for initial sorting and will grow to **SORT_AREA_SIZE**. Any memory in addition to the **SORT_AREA_RETAINED_SIZE** that is allocated for a large sort will be returned to the user's UGA after the sort.

Whenever possible, sorting should be done in memory rather than disk. By properly analyzing your sort activities, you can reduce the number and size of sorts such that most if not all are done in memory.

# Sorts And The Temporary Tablespace

All disk sorts are done in the user's assigned temporary tablespace. If users are not assigned default and temporary tablespaces when they are created, these items will default to the **SYSTEM** tablespace. All users, including SYS and SYSTEM, should have their temporary tablespace reassigned to one other than **SYSTEM**. Sorts that are allowed to occur in the **SYSTEM** tablespace can cause excessive fragmentation of the **SYSTEM** tablespace. In addition, allowing large sorts in the **SYSTEM** tablespace could result in the database hanging if the **SYSTEM** tablespace runs out of space. Another consideration is that the default storage parameters are not optimized for sorting in the **SYS-TEM** tablespace, and this will result in inefficient sorting operations.

## *Temporary Tablespace Storage Considerations*

Temporary tablespaces exist entirely to support sorting operations. The temporary tablespace default storage clause must be based directly on how you have designated sorting to be done on your system.

In all systems, even where direct writes are being done, the **INITIAL** and **NEXT** values for the temporary tablespace default storage clause should be the same and should equal the value of the **SORT_AREA_SIZE** initialization parameter. The **PCTINCREASE** default storage parameter for a temporary tablespace should always be set to zero. Setting **PCTINCREASE** to zero for a temporary tablespace does two things. First, it prevents automatic coalescing of unused extents. Second, it ensures that the extent size always matches **SORT_AREA_SIZE** and therefore wastes little space.

Why don't we want automatic coalescing of the unused extents in a temporary tablespace? Because **INITIAL** is equal to **NEXT** and **PCTINCREASE** is equal to zero, all extents in a temporary tablespace will be of equal size. If all extents in a temporary tablespace are of equal size, any used extent that is returned to the free extent pool will be the proper size for the next sort operation that requires an extent. Having unused extents already available in the temporary tablespace by setting **PCTINCREASE** to zero and not allowing automatic coalescing reduces the time required to reallocate extents.

If your system is using Oracle7.3.x, use the **TEMPORARY** clause for creating temporary tablespace. A tablespace designated as **TEMPORARY** will not allow the creation of nontemporary segments (such as tables, indexes, and clusters) and is optimized for sorting. Remember that the **COMPATIBLE** initialization parameter must be set to your Oracle release (such as 7.3.3) to make full use of new features and capabilities. The actual sort segment in a tablespace designated as **TEMPORARY** is not created until the first sort request is issued.

The extents in a temporary tablespace are mapped into a sort extent pool (SEP) when the first sort operation occurs against that temporary table. Once a tablespace is mapped into a SEP, subsequent sorts will use the SEP to locate available sort extents. The **V$SORT_SEGMENT** dynamic performance view is used to view information about sort extents in the SEP. The **V$SORT_SEGMENT** view is new in version 7.3 and is not present in earlier Oracle releases. The contents of the **V$SORT_SEGMENT** view are shown in Table 8.1.

The use of **SORT_DIRECT_WRITES** can increase the required temporary tablespace disk space. Therefore, when going from a system where **SORT_DIRECT_WRITES** is not configured to one where it is used, be sure to allow for more temporary tablespace storage space.

# Controlling Sorts
By properly tuning SQL statements and understanding which type of operations produce which sorts, you can reduce the number and size of sort operations

### Table 8.1    Contents of the V$SORT_SEGMENT view.

| Column | Description |
| --- | --- |
| TABLESPACE_NAME | Name of the temporary tablespace |
| SEGMENT_FILE | Number of the datafile that contains the segment |
| SEGMENT_BLOCK | Number of the block in the datafile where the segment begins |
| EXTENT_SIZE | Size of the temporary segment extent |
| CURRENT_USERS | Number of users using the tablespace |
| TOTAL_EXTENTS | Total number of extents available in this tablespace |
| TOTAL_BLOCKS | Total number of blocks available in this tablespace |
| USED_EXTENTS | Total number of extents being used in this tablespace |
| USED_BLOCKS | Total number of blocks being used in this tablespace |
| FREE_EXTENTS | Total number of free extents in this tablespace |
| FREE_BLOCKS | Total number of free blocks in this tablespace |
| ADDED_EXTENTS | Total number of extents added to this tablespace |
| EXTENT_HITS | Total times this unused extent has been found in the SEP |
| FREED_EXTENTS | Number of extents released to the SEP |
| FREE_REQUESTS | Number of times a request was made for a free extent |
| MAX_SIZE | Maximum size available for a segment to use |
| MAX_BLOCKS | Maximum blocks available for a segment to use |
| MAX_USED_SIZE | Maximum size area currently used by a segment |
| MAX_USED_BLOCKS | Maximum number of blocks currently used by a segment |
| MAX_SORT_SIZE | Largest sort done to date in bytes |
| MAX_SORT_BLOCKS | Largest sort done to date in blocks |

and therefore allow more sorts to be performed in memory. The following operations always require a sort:

➤ SELECT DISTINCT

➤ SELECT UNIQUE

➤ SELECT...GROUP BY...

➤ CREATE INDEX

➤ **CREATE TABLE...AS SELECT** with primary key specification

➤ **INTERSECT, MINUS,** and **UNION** set operators

➤ Unindexed table joins

➤ Some correlated subqueries

Proper indexing often can reduce sorts. If a **SELECT** uses an index, it will normally return the values in indexed order. By creating an index on the column by which you want the query to be ordered, you can eliminate the need for an **ORDER BY** clause. Avoid using **SELECT DISTINCT** or **SELECT UNIQUE** unless absolutely necessary. An example of an unneeded **DISTINCT** or **UNIQUE** might be a **SELECT** that includes the primary key value as, by definition, a row including a primary key will always be distinct or unique.

# Practice Questions

## Question 1

> Which initialization file parameter can you set to prevent sort writes
> to the buffer cache?
>
> ○ a. **SORT_AREA_SIZE**
>
> ○ b. **SORT_DIRECT_WRITES**
>
> ○ c. **SORT_WRITE_BUFFERS**
>
> ○ d. **SORT_WRITE_BUFFER_SIZE**

The correct answer is b. **SORT_DIRECT_WRITES** can be set to **TRUE,
FALSE,** or **AUTO. TRUE** sets all sorts to bypass the buffer cache and write
through the **SORT_WRITE_BUFFERS. FALSE** turns off direct writes, and
all sorts go through the buffer cache. A setting of **AUTO** for the
**SORT_DIRECT_WRITES** parameter decides on the basis of SGA and
**DB_BLOCK_SIZE** settings. Answer a is incorrect because **SORT_
AREA_SIZE** determines the size of the normal sort area but has nothing to
do with direct writes; in fact, it can be reduced in size if direct writes are enabled. Answer c is incorrect because, although **SORT_WRITE_BUFFERS**
sets the number of sort write buffers, it does not turn on or off the direct writes
option. Answer d is incorrect because, although **SORT_WRITE_
BUFFER_SIZE** controls the size of sort write buffers, it does not turn on or
off the direct writes option.

## Question 2

> Which SQL clauses will cause a sort operation? [Check all correct
> answers]
>
> ☐ a. **INTO**
>
> ☐ b. **WHERE**
>
> ☐ c. **ORDER BY**
>
> ☐ d. **DISTINCT**

The correct answers are c and d. **ORDER BY, DISTINCT, UNIQUE,** and
**GROUP BY** clauses will always result in sorts. Answer a is incorrect because
**INTO** is used in embedded SQL to place a value into a variable. Answer b is
incorrect because **WHERE** simply shows the beginning of a restriction clause.

# Question 3

> Which dynamic performance view can you query to see whether sorts are being done in memory or on disk?
>
> O a. **V$ROWCACHE**
> O b. **V$SESSION**
> O c. **V$SYSSTAT**
> O d. **V$SQLAREA**

The correct answer is c. The **V$SYSSTAT** view contains entries for the sorts (disk) and sorts (memory) statistics, which give the total number of those types of sorts since the database was started. Answer a is incorrect because the **V$ROWCACHE** view contains statistics about the data dictionary caches but not about sorts. Answer b is incorrect because **V$SESSION** contains statistics about user sessions but not about sorts. Answer d is incorrect because **V$SQLAREA** contains information about SQL statements that have been placed in the shared pool but not about sorts.

# Question 4

> Where will a process look for sort space if needed?
>
> O a. UGA
> O b. PGA
> O c. SEP

The correct answer is c. The SEP (sort extent pool) tracks available sort extents. Answer a is incorrect because the UGA (user global area) might contain sort data but does not track free sort extent areas. Answer b is incorrect because the PGA (process global area) might again be used for sorting but does not track free sort extents.

# Question 5

> What is one purpose of the **SORT_AREA_SIZE** initialization parameter?
>
> ○ a. Gives the size that a sort area will shrink to when not needed
>
> ○ b. Determines whether a sort can be done in memory or must be done in sort sets on disk
>
> ○ c. Forces sorts to bypass the buffer cache
>
> ○ d. Sets the size of direct sort buffers

The correct answer is b. **SORT_AREA_SIZE** sets the size of the memory sort area for a process; if a sort exceeds the **SORT_AREA_SIZE**, it is done in **SORT_AREA_SIZE** sections on disk. Answer b is incorrect because this is a function of the **SORT_AREA_RETAINED_SIZE** parameter. Answer c is incorrect because this is a function of the **SORT_DIRECT_WRITES** parameter. Answer d is incorrect because this is a function of the **SORT_WRITE_BUFFER_SIZE** parameter.

# Question 6

> In Oracle7.3, which dynamic performance view can be queried to determine the value of **TOTAL_EXTENTS** for the temporary tablespaces?
>
> ○ a. **V$TYPE_SIZE**
>
> ○ b. **V$SQLTEXT**
>
> ○ c. **V$SORT_SEGMENT**
>
> ○ d. **V$DB_OBJECT_CACHE**

The correct answer is c. The **V$SORT_SEGMENT** view contains statistics on all temporary tablespace used for sorting. Answer a is incorrect because **V$TYPE_SIZE** contains information on the sizes of various datatype sizing parameters. Answer b is incorrect because **V$SQLTEXT** contains information about SQL that has been placed in the shared pool. Answer d is incorrect because **V$DB_OBJECT_CACHE** contains data about stored objects in the shared pool.

## Question 7

> What is the purpose of the **EXTENT_HITS** column in the
> **V$SORT_SEGMENT** dynamic performance view?
>
> ○ a. Shows the maximum number of blocks available for
> sorting in the tablespace
>
> ○ b. Shows the number of extents currently used in the
> tablespace for sorting
>
> ○ c. Shows the number of times an unused extent was found
> in the SEP (sort extent pool)
>
> ○ d. Shows the total extents in the tablespace

The correct answer is c. The **EXTENT_HITS** column shows the number of
times an unused extent was found in the SEP. Answer a is incorrect because
this is the description of the **MAX_SORT_BLOCKS** column. Answer b is
incorrect because this is the description of the **USED_EXTENTS** column.
Answer d is incorrect because this is the description of the **TOTAL_EXTENTS**
column.

## Question 8

> To which value should you set the value of **PCTINCREASE** for a
> temporary tablespace?
>
> ○ a. 10
>
> ○ b. 0
>
> ○ c. 50
>
> ○ d. 20

The answer is b. You should set **PCTINCREASE** to zero for a temporary
tablespace. Setting **PCTINCREASE** to zero when **INITIAL** and **NEXT** are
set correctly in a temporary tablespace prevents fragmentation and limits the
need for coalescing the temporary tablespace by ensuring that each extent in
the tablespace is of uniform size.

# Question 9

When should you consider setting **SORT_DIRECT_WRITES** to **TRUE**?

○ a. When you have little memory or disk space available for sorting

○ b. When you have a lot of disk space and low memory

○ c. When you have a lot of temporary disk space and a lot of memory

○ d. When you have a lot of memory and little temporary disk space for sorting

The correct answer is c. When **SORT_DIRECT_WRITES** is set to **TRUE**, each user receives **SORT_WRITE_BUFFERS** * **SORT_BUFFER_SIZE** memory allocation to write through sort data to disk, bypassing the buffer cache. In addition, because of the way in which **SORT_DIRECT_WRITES** is allocated disk area, it will require more disk space than standard sorting.

# Question 10

When will a sort be separated into sort runs and written to disk?

○ a. When the sort data exceeds **SORT_AREA_RETAINED_SIZE** in size

○ b. When **SORT_DIRECT_WRITES** is set to **FALSE**

○ c. When the sort data exceeds **SORT_AREA_SIZE** in size

○ d. With every sort

The correct answer is c. Answer a is incorrect because this only results in more memory being allocated to **SORT_AREA_SIZE**. Answer b is incorrect because this turns direct writes off. Answer d is incorrect because if the size of the sort is less than **SORT_AREA_SIZE**, it is performed in memory.

# Need To Know More?

 Gurry, Mark and Peter Corrigan: *Oracle Performance Tuning, 2nd Edition*. O'Reilly & Associates, 1996. ISBN 1-56592-237-9. This book contains the best discussions we've have seen on sorting and on tuning sorts. Chapters 9, 11, and 15 are especially helpful.

 *Oracle8 Server Concepts, Release 8, Volume 1*. Oracle Corporation, June 1997. Part Number A54646-01. Although this is an Oracle8 release of the manual, it has an excellent section on sorts that pertains to both Oracle7 and Oracle8.

# Sample Test: Performance Tuning

The following sections provide tips for developing a successful exam-taking strategy, including how to choose proper answers, how to decode ambiguity, how to work within the Oracle framework, how to decide what to memorize, and how to prepare for the exam. This chapter also provides 65 questions that cover the subject matter that likely will appear on the exam. Good luck!

# Questions, Questions, Questions

Each exam in the database administrator (DBA) exam series comprises 60-70 questions. You are allotted 90 minutes for each of the DBA exams. The questions on the exam are of two types:

➤ Multiple choice with a single answer

➤ Multiple choice with multiple answers

Always take the time to read the question twice before selecting an answer. If an exhibit button is provided, always review the exhibit, as it would not be there if it were not needed to answer the question. You will find it tough, if not impossible, to answer an exhibit question if you have not looked at the exhibit.

Some questions will have multiple answers. The questions will clearly state how many answers you are expected to select. No partial credit is given for incomplete answers. If the question asks for two answers, you must select two answers, or the entire question will be counted as incorrect.

Finally, always read all the answers and never assume that a question cannot be as easy as it looks. Second-guessing the question is one of the biggest problems encountered in these kinds of exams.

# Selecting Proper Answers

The only way to pass any exam is to select the proper answers. Unfortunately, exams are written by human beings. Exams such as the SAT and the GRE have been run through batteries of test experts and have been standardized; the OCP exams have not. Although a question might make perfect sense to the person who wrote it, the wording can be ambiguous, diabolical, or convoluted to just about everyone else. In other cases, the question can be so poorly written or, worse, contain simply an opinion rather than a hard fact that, unless you have an inside track, you cannot divine the correct answer from your knowledge base. When you do not know the answer to a question, remember that one answer or more out of the set of answers can almost always be eliminated because:

➤ The answer does not apply to the situation

➤ The answer describes a nonexistent issue

➤ The answer is already eliminated by the text of the question

After you have eliminated obviously wrong answers, you must rely on your retained knowledge to eliminate further answers. Look for what are called distracters, which are answers that sound perfectly plausible but that refer to actions, commands, or features not present or not available in the described situation.

If you have eliminated all the answers that you can through logic and your knowledge and are left with more than one choice, try using question inversion. Question inversion is the process by which you rephrase the question in terms of each remaining answer, seeking the premise of the existing question as the answer. For example:

---

The color of a clear daytime sky is blue because:

○  a. Dust particles in the atmosphere scatter the blue
       components of light

○  b. The sun puts out a great deal of the blue spectrum

○  c. Oxygen absorbs most of the other spectral elements

○  d. The Van Allen belt absorbs much of the ultraviolet
       spectrum, therefore allowing only the blue components
       to reach us

---

Say that you have reduced the possible answers to answers a and c. Try rephrasing the question

The dust in the atmosphere scattering the blue components of light causes the daytime sky to be _____ in color.

or:

Oxygen absorbing other spectral elements causes the daytime sky to be _____ in color.

Sometimes, this rephrasing will jog your memory to produce the correct answer. (By the way, the correct answer is a.) Answer d is an example of a distracter. It sounds logical on the surface, unless you know that the Van Allen belt absorbs and deflects charged particle radiation but that light passes straight through (the ozone layer takes care of the ultraviolet radiation).

Finally, if you just cannot decide between two (or more) answers, guess. An unanswered question is always wrong, but with an educated guess you have at least some chance of answering the question correctly.

# Decoding Ambiguity

Exams are not designed to ensure that everyone passes. They are designed to test knowledge on a given topic, and a properly designed test will have a normal (bell-shaped) distribution for the target audience, of whom a certain number will fail. A problem with this exam is that it has been tailored to Oracle's training materials even though some of the material in the training is hearsay, some is old DBA tales, and some is just incorrect. Where obvious errors in the exam questions exist, the previous chapters have attempted to point them out to you. If you select the highest answer for a numeric response, you will generally be correct if the highest answer is the most conservative way to go, lowest if that is the most conservative. For example, the exam insists that the percentage increase for a temporary tablespace should be 50 percent and that a rollback segment, to be properly tuned, should have a minimum of 20 extents.

The only way to overcome some of the exam's limitations is to be prepared. You will discover that many of the questions test your knowledge of something that is not directly related to the issue raised by the questions. This means that the answers offered to you, even the incorrect ones, are as much a part of the skill assessment as are the questions. If you do not know all the aspects of an exam topic (in this case, database administration) cold, you will not be able to eliminate answers that are obviously wrong because they relate to a different aspect of the topic than the one addressed by the question itself.

Questions can reveal answers, especially when dealing with commands and data dictionary topics. Read a question and then evaluate the answers in light of common terms, names, and structure.

Another problem is that Oracle uses some terminology in its training materials that is found nowhere else in its documentation sets. Whether this was a deliberate attempt to force you to take its classes to pass the exam or simply sloppy documentation is not known.

# Working Within The Framework

The questions will be presented to you randomly. A question on tuning applications might follow one on tuning rollback segments, followed by one on using the utlestat and utlbstat scripts. However, this can work to your advantage in that a future question might unwittingly answer the question you are puzzling over. You might find that an incorrect answer to this question will be the correct answer to a question later in the exam. Take the time to read all the answers for each question, even (or especially) if you spot the right one immediately. Also, the exam format allows you to mark questions that you want to revisit. Mark those questions that you feel might give you insight into other questions, even if you know that you have answered them correctly.

## Deciding What To Memorize

The amount of memorization you will need to do depends on whether you are a visual learner. If you can see the command structure diagrams in your head, you will not need to memorize as much as if you cannot. The exam will stretch your recollection skills through command syntax and operational command sequences used within the Oracle environment, testing not only when you should use a feature but also when you should not.

The important types of information to memorize are:

➤ Commonly used **V$** views

➤ Tuning scripts and their uses

➤ The use of initialization parameters for sort and system global area (SGA) tuning

➤ Restrictions on command use (such as with joins in **SELECT**)

➤ The use of SQL*Plus in tables related to query performance

➤ Tuning rollback segments and redo logs

If you work your way through this book while sitting in front of an Oracle database that you have access to and try out commands and exam answers and play with unfamiliar features, you should have no problem understanding the questions on the exam.

# Preparing For The Test

To excel in any endeavor, one must practice. The perfect musical performance looks easy because you do not see the hours, days, and weeks of practice that were required to make it look easy. Passing exams is the same. Without having practiced and discovered your areas of weakness, you will walk into the exam with blinders on and can be easily broadsided.

Give yourself 90 uninterrupted minutes to complete the practice exam in this chapter. Use the honor system, as you will gain no benefit from cheating. The idea is to see where you are weak and require further study, not to answer all the questions correctly by looking up the answers. When your time is up or when you finish, you can check your answers in the following chapter. It might even be easier to make copies of the next section and take the exam multiple times.

If you want additional practice, sample exams are available from Oracle's education and certification site (http://education.oracle.com/certification) or from SelfTest Software's site (http://www.stsware.com).

# Taking The Exam

Once you are sitting in front of the exam computer, you can do nothing more to increase your knowledge or preparation, so *relax!* Take a deep breath, stretch, and attack the first question.

Do not rush. You will have plenty of time to complete each question and to return to the ones you skipped or marked. If you have read a question twice and are still clueless, mark it to revisit it, then move on. Questions that are both easy and difficult are randomly distributed, so do not take too long on the difficult ones, or you might cheat yourself of the chance to answer some easy ones near the end of the exam. Both kinds of questions count the same number of points, so take care of the easy ones first and revisit the difficult ones after answering all that you can.

As you answer each question that you have marked to revisit, remove the mark and continue. If a question is still impossible to answer, go to the next one that you marked. On your final pass (just before time is called), guess on those that you are completely clueless about. Again, a question that you do not answer is always counted wrong, but a guess just might be correct.

# Sample Test: Performance Tuning

## Question 1

Which information is contained in the **V$CACHE** view?

○ a. Objects currently being cached

○ b. Objects cached since the database was started

○ c. Objects waiting to be cached

○ d. Objects too small to be cached

## Question 2

You have a high-volume OLTP system with numerous inserts and updates. For what should you monitor tables with high levels of inserts?

○ a. Monitor for freelist contention

○ b. Monitor for row chaining

○ c. Monitor for block fragmentation

○ d. Monitor for index fragmentation

## Question 3

When will the proper addition of indexes improve performance?

○ a. When you have excessive redo header waits

○ b. When you have a shortage of memory

○ c. When SQL statements are performing poorly

○ d. When you have excessive undo header waits

## Question 4

If you have latch contention and query the **V$LATCH** view, what will the **SLEEPS** column tell you?

- ○ a. The number of times that a process missed getting a lock
- ○ b. The number of times that a process got a latch immediately
- ○ c. The number of times that a process missed getting an immediate latch
- ○ d. The number of times that a process waited on a latch

## Question 5

When would you allocate extents of a table explicitly to separate datafiles?

- ○ a. When following OFA guidelines
- ○ b. When optimizing file placement
- ○ c. When striping tables by hand
- ○ d. When you are absolutely sure that your sizing estimates are correct

## Question 6

What exactly is a TM lock?

- ○ a. The identifier given to an exclusive table lock in the lock-type column of the Server Manager
- ○ b. The identifier given to a share table lock in the lock-type column of the Server Manager
- ○ c. The identifier given to a table lock in the lock-type column of the Server Manager
- ○ d. The identifier given to an row-exclusive lock in the lock-type column of the Server Manager

# Question 7

Which columns contain statistics concerning **WILLING_TO_WAIT** requests in the **V$LATCH** view? [Check all correct answers]

☐  a. **HITS**

☐  b. **WAITS**

☐  c. **SLEEPS**

☐  d. **MISSES**

☐  e. **GETS**

# Question 8

What can you instruct developers to do to ensure that low-level database tuning is possible?

○  a. Be sure that all SQL statements are well written

○  b. Use only ANSI SQL92 standard statements

○  c. Nothing; well-written applications do not require low-level tuning

# Question 9

You query the **V$WAITSTAT** view and see a value of 215 in the **UNDO HEADER** column. Which problem does this indicate?

○  a. An extent shortage for rollback segments

○  b. LRU latch contention

○  c. Contention for rollback segment header blocks

○  d. An excessive number of rollback segment header blocks

# Question 10

What is the purpose of the library cache area of the shared pool?

○  a. Store data on data dictionary caches

○  b. Store data retrieved from data files

○  c. Store shared SQL and PL/SQL

○  d. Provide for sort areas

## Question 11

What is the purpose of the report.txt file?

○ a. Contains information about database errors and alerts

○ b. Contains information you would use to tune your database

○ c. Preloads temporary tables with database statistics

○ d. Calculates the delta values of database statistics for tuning

## Question 12

Assuming that your initialization parameters are set correctly, what can be done to minimize the number of checkpoints that happen?

○ a. Use fewer redo log groups

○ b. Use smaller redo log group members

○ c. Use more redo log groups

○ d. Use larger redo log group members

## Question 13

At which level will Oracle resolve deadlocks?

○ a. Transaction

○ b. Statement

○ c. Row

○ d. Table

## Question 14

What are the only objects that should be stored with rollback segments?

○ a. User-created objects

○ b. Database triggers

○ c. Temporary segments

○ d. Other rollback segments

# Question 15

The chemical application has tables that undergo numerous deletes. Which of the following values for **PCTUSED** would be the best for these tables?

○ a. 20

○ b. 10

○ c. 50

○ d. 0

# Question 16

What would sizing the shared pool too small cause?

○ a. Heavy I/O in the system tablespace

○ b. Excessive checkpointing

○ c. Undo header contention

○ d. Latch contention

# Question 17

You are creating the database for a decision support system (DSS). To what value should you set the **DB_BLOCK_SIZE** initialization parameter?

○ a. 10K

○ b. The maximum value for the platform

○ c. 4K

○ d. The minimum value for the platform

○ e. Oracle automatically sets the right size when the database is created

## Question 18

Which script would you run to enable the **DBMS_APPLI-CATION_INFO** package?

- ○ a. utlestat.sql
- ○ b. utlbstat.sql
- ○ c. dbmsutil.sql
- ○ d. catalog.sql

## Question 19

Which criteria should you use when determining the number of rollback segments you will need?

- ○ a. The value of the **DB_BLOCK_BUFFERS** parameter
- ○ b. The number of concurrent processes on the system
- ○ c. The number of concurrent DML processes on the system
- ○ d. The number of indexes in the application

## Question 20

The document management system was installed several years ago. When installed, the system had several large tables manually striped across several disks. The application was very well tuned and performed excellently. Since installation, datafiles for the striped tables and other tablespaces have been placed haphazardly around the disk farm in whatever space was large enough to hold them. Which tuning issue should you look at first if the users complain of poor performance?

- ○ a. Retune the application
- ○ b. Check memory tuning
- ○ c. Tune I/O to ensure that the load is balanced evenly across the disk farm
- ○ d. Tune for latch contention
- ○ e. Redesign the entire application

# Question 21

You run utlbstat and utlestat. After reviewing the output, you find an indication of a high **GET_MISS/GET_REQ** ratio for the library cache. What can you do to correct this problem?

- ○ a. Increase the shared pool size
- ○ b. Decrease the shared pool size
- ○ c. Pin all the objects in the library cache
- ○ d. Increase redo log buffers

# Question 22

Which view do you query to get the value of **TOTAL_EXTENTS** for the temporary tablespace?

- ○ a. **V$SQLTEXT**
- ○ b. **V$DB_OBJECT_CACHE**
- ○ c. **V$TYPE_SIZE**
- ○ d. **V$SORT_SEGMENT**

# Question 23

When developing a tuning strategy, which area is usually considered most important?

- ○ a. I/O
- ○ b. Design
- ○ c. Application
- ○ d. Memory
- ○ e. Contention

## Question 24

Which change would you make if you wanted to decrease the number of disk sorts?

○ a. Increase **SORT_AREA_RETAINED_SIZE**

○ b. Decrease **SORT_AREA_SIZE**

○ c. Increase **SORT_AREA_SIZE**

○ d. Decrease **SORT_AREA_RETAINED_SIZE**

## Question 25

Which SQL statement would require a sort?

○ a.
```
SELECT * FROM nuclides;
```

○ b.
```
SELECT nuclide, atomic_no FROM nuclides;
```

○ c.
```
SELECT nuclide, atomic_no FROM nuclides
    WHERE atomic_no<80;
```

○ d.
```
SELECT DISTINCT result FROM samples;
```

## Question 26

Users have complained that they experience delays when getting results back from ad hoc queries to the document control application. As the DBA, which area should you examine first when troubleshooting the problem?

○ a. PGA

○ b. SQL statements

○ c. I/O

○ d. SGA

## Question 27

When you increase the number of dispatchers using the **ALTER SYSTEM** command in a system using a multithreaded server (MTS), when are the new dispatchers activated?

○ a. After the **ALTER SYSTEM** command is issued

○ b. As soon as new connections are made to the database

○ c. After the database is shut down and restarted

○ d. After the listener process is stopped and restarted

## Question 28

Which SQL statement will not require a sort?

○ a.
```
SELECT name, atomic_wt, atomic_mass
FROM nuclides
    WHERE group = 'I' ORDER BY atomic_wt;
```

○ b.
```
SELECT * FROM nuclides;
```

○ c.
```
SELECT name, atomic_wt, atomic_mass
FROM nuclides
    ORDER BY atomic_wt;
```

○ d.
```
SELECT DISTINCT(atomic_mass) FROM nuclides
    WHERE atomic_wt>53;
```

## Question 29

What is one of the purposes of the **DBMS_SHARED_POOL** package?

○ a. To create functions needed for PL/SQL

○ b. To create procedures and packages needed to create other procedures and packages

○ c. To create utilities used by the DIANA routines

○ d. To pin large or frequently used packages in the library cache

## Question 30

What is the purpose of the SQL Trace facility?

- ○ a. To generate a set of delta reports for database tuning
- ○ b. To generate a human-readable-format report from a trace file
- ○ c. To generate an execution plan for a SQL statement
- ○ d. To identify SQL areas that might be causing performance problems

## Question 31

What is the common characteristic of the TM, UL, and TX lock types?

- ○ a. They are table-level locks
- ○ b. They are share locks
- ○ c. They are lock types obtained usually by user applications
- ○ d. They are lock types used only by Oracle7 internal processes

## Question 32

You have tuned the application, and your manager still wants an extra bit of performance. What should you tune next?

- ○ a. Memory
- ○ b. I/O
- ○ c. Contention
- ○ d. Design

# Question 33

What is the purpose of the Oracle Expert tool?

- ○ a. To configure the Oracle database
- ○ b. To monitor Oracle performance
- ○ c. To monitor tablespaces
- ○ d. To monitor the user sessions that are using the most resources

# Question 34

Which Enterprise Manager tool can you use to collect data about application events?

- ○ a. Oracle Trace
- ○ b. Oracle Expert
- ○ c. Oracle Tablespace Manager
- ○ d. Oracle Performance Manager

# Question 35

When tuning the shared pool, which structure should be your main concern?

- ○ a. Overall shared pool size
- ○ b. Library cache
- ○ c. Data dictionary cache

# Question 36

When is freelist contention likely to occur?

- ○ a. When applications explicitly lock tables
- ○ b. When there is insufficient space in the shared pool
- ○ c. When an application has many inserts and deletes performed on tables

## Question 37

A deadlock is detected in statement B of a large transaction containing statements A and B. What is the state of the transaction?

- ○ a. Statement A is rolled back and an error message is generated for statement B
- ○ b. Statements A and B are rolled back, and an error message is generated for the transaction
- ○ c. The transaction is rolled back
- ○ d. Statement B is rolled back and an error message is generated for the transaction

## Question 38

You issue the command:

```
ANALYZE TABLE nuclides ESTIMATE STATISTICS
        SAMPLE 30 PERCENT;
```

Which column of the **DBA_TABLES** view can you query to see the number of migrated rows in the **NUCLIDES** table?

- ○ a. **CHAIN_CNT**
- ○ b. **BLOCKS**
- ○ c. **AVG_ROW_LEN**
- ○ d. **NUM_ROWS**

## Question 39

If there is sufficient space in the shared pool, what does Oracle use to manage the SQL and PL/SQL in the library cache?

- ○ a. LRU algorithm
- ○ b. Clusters
- ○ c. User global area (UGA)
- ○ d. Database buffer cache
- ○ e. Program global area (PGA)

# Question 40

Which view is used to detect the actual row that is causing lock contention?

- ○ a. **V$ROWCACHE**
- ○ b. **V$LOCK**
- ○ c. **V$SYSSTAT**
- ○ d. **V$SESSION**

# Question 41

What is one characteristic of a DDL lock?

- ○ a. It allows other processes to access the object being locked
- ○ b. It allows other processes to access the row being locked
- ○ c. It probably will not cause contention
- ○ d. It can cause contention if used carelessly

# Question 42

What is the purpose of the **SHARED_POOL_RESERVED_SIZE** initialization parameter?

- ○ a. To set the size of the shared pool
- ○ b. To set the minimum size of a reserved section of the shared pool
- ○ c. To set reserved areas of the shared pool for large packages
- ○ d. To prevent the release of cursor areas from the shared pool

## Question 43

What happens when the work being done is copied to the buffer on a single-CPU computer?

○ a. The latch times out

○ b. The redo allocation latch is released

○ c. Nothing; work is not copied to the buffer on single-CPU computers

○ d. Nothing; work is not copied to the buffer cache until another process requests the latch

## Question 44

Which latch statistics column in the report.txt file shows that tuning is required if it displays a high percentage?

○ a. **SLEEPS**

○ b. **HIT_RATIO**

○ c. **GETS**

○ d. **SLEEPS/MISS**

## Question 45

Which initialization parameter determines whether Oracle will bypass the buffer cache when sorting?

○ a. **SORT_AREA_RETAINED_SIZE**

○ b. **SORT_AREA_SIZE**

○ c. **SORT_DIRECT_WRITES**

○ d. **SORT_WRITE_BUFFER_SIZE**

# Question 46

You have an OLTP system and notice that your **DATA** tablespace keeps becoming fragmented. What is the probable cause?

○ a. Rollback segments were placed in the **DATA** tablespace

○ b. Your **DATA** tablespace is too small for the load it is carrying

○ c. This is nothing to worry about because it is normal for Oracle

○ d. Tables are automatically shrinking as data is deleted from them

# Question 47

When a redo copy latch is needed, which type of request is made?

○ a. **WILLING_TO_WAIT**

○ b. **BUFFER**

○ c. **IMMEDIATE**

○ d. **ALLOCATION**

# Question 48

Which process is responsible for placing blocks in the database buffer cache?

○ a. SMON

○ b. PMON

○ c. DBWR

○ d. User-server processes

## Question 49

What is the purpose of the database buffer cache in the SGA?

- ○ a. To store shared SQL and PL/SQL
- ○ b. To store data dictionary information
- ○ c. To store copies of data blocks that can be shared by all users
- ○ d. To store transaction data before it is copied to the redo logs

## Question 50

You query the **V$LIBRARYCACHE** view. Which column contains the executions of an item stored in the library cache?

- ○ a. **RELOADS**
- ○ b. **PINS**
- ○ c. **INVALIDATIONS**
- ○ d. **GETS**

## Question 51

Which views can you query to evaluate the effect of an increase or a decrease in the size of the database buffer cache? [Check all correct answers]

- ❑ a. **V$CACHE**
- ❑ b. **V$FILESTAT**
- ❑ c. **X$STATS**
- ❑ d. **X$KCBRBH**
- ❑ e. **V$SYSSTAT**

# Question 52

If you are using parallel query mode, what can you do to improve performance when querying large tables?

○ a. Manually stripe tables across the system

○ b. Increase sort area size

○ c. Increase redo log size

○ d. Decrease the degree setting for the tables

# Question 53

If you query the **X$KCBRBH** virtual table, which value will the **COUNT** column display?

○ a. The number of blocks in the database buffer cache

○ b. The number of additional cache hits gained by adding additional buffer cache blocks

○ c. The number of reads in the database buffer cache

○ d. The number of buffers added to the database buffer cache

# Question 54

Your SQL statements are properly tuned, yet performance is still slow. What might improve performance?

○ a. Increasing the redo log size

○ b. Increasing the sort area size

○ c. Increasing the number of database block buffers

○ d. Decreasing the sort area size

## Question 55

In which state should the operating system be when using sort direct writes?

○ a. Optional background processes cannot be running

○ b. I/O should be well tuned

○ c. The system should have adequate disk and memory resources

○ d. Datafiles must be sized appropriately

## Question 56

What is one characteristic of the **MTS_LISTENER_ADDRESS** initialization parameter?

○ a. Configures the number of dispatchers used in the database

○ b. Must contain the same value as its counterpart in listener.ora

○ c. Configures the number of servers used in the database

○ d. Creates the name for the MTS service process

## Question 57

What is one purpose of the **SET TRANSACTION** command?

○ a. To control redo for a large transaction

○ b. To create a transaction

○ c. To modify a transaction

○ d. To change a system parameter

# Question 58

Which copies of a single database block can be found in the database buffer cache at all times? [Check all correct answers]

- ❏ a. Deleted copy
- ❏ b. Read-consistent copy
- ❏ c. Backup copy
- ❏ d. Current copy

# Question 59

You run the utlbstat.sql script, then shut down and restart the instance. What will you need to do next to generate a tuning report?

- ○ a. Rerun utlbstat.sql
- ○ b. Run utlestat.sql
- ○ c. Run utlbstat.sql and utlestat.sql
- ○ d. Run utlestat.sql and utlbstat.sql

# Question 60

What is one benefit of using bitmapped indexes in a decision support system (DSS)?

- ○ a. They use very little space
- ○ b. They must be ordered
- ○ c. They are great for small tables
- ○ d. They work great on columns of high cardinality

# Question 61

What is one purpose of the alert_<SID>.log file?

- ○ a. To store information about a process's SQL statement
- ○ b. To track alerts issued by Oracle about your release
- ○ c. To provide information about database events
- ○ d. To track user login attempts

## Question 62

Why should you be sure that the **DB_BLOCK_SIZE** parameter is set correctly when creating the database?

- ○ a. If it is too large, database performance will suffer
- ○ b. If it is set too low, excessive amounts of memory might be used
- ○ c. It requires a rebuild of the database to change
- ○ d. This is set automatically, so you do not need to worry about it

## Question 63

Where are only before images of data blocks stored?

- ○ a. In rollback segments
- ○ b. In redo logs
- ○ c. In datafiles
- ○ d. In indexes

## Question 64

When should sorts be done in memory?

- ○ a. Whenever possible
- ○ b. When there is insufficient temporary tablespace room
- ○ c. When **SORT_DIRECT_WRITES** is set to **TRUE**

## Question 65

Which parameter should be set prior to running the utlbstat.sql script?

- ○ a. **AUDIT_TRAIL**
- ○ b. **INIT_SQL_FILES**
- ○ c. **SQL_TRACE**
- ○ d. **TIMED_STATISTICS**

# Answer Key To Performance Tuning Sample Test

**10**

| | | |
|---|---|---|
| 1. a | 23. c | 45. c |
| 2. a | 24. c | 46. a |
| 3. c | 25. d | 47. c |
| 4. d | 26. b | 48. d |
| 5. c | 27. b | 49. c |
| 6. c | 28. b | 50. b |
| 7. d, e | 29. d | 51. d, e |
| 8. a | 30. d | 52. a |
| 9. c | 31. c | 53. b |
| 10. c | 32. a | 54. c |
| 11. b | 33. a | 55. c |
| 12. d | 34. a | 56. b |
| 13. b | 35. b | 57. a |
| 14. d | 36. c | 58. b, d |
| 15. c | 37. d | 59. c |
| 16. a | 38. a | 60. a |
| 17. b | 39. a | 61. c |
| 18. c | 40. d | 62. c |
| 19. c | 41. c | 63. a |
| 20. c | 42. c | 64. a |
| 21. a | 43. b | 65. d |
| 22. d | 44. d | |

Here are the answers to the questions presented in Chapter 9.

## Question 1

The correct answer is a. The **V$CACHE** view is created when the catparr.sql script is run to install required support objects for Oracle parallel server. The **V$CACHE** view tracks currently cached objects. Answer b is incorrect because **V$CACHE** tracks only currently cached objects, not historical data on cached objects. Answer c is incorrect because **V$CACHE** tracks cached objects, not objects waiting to be cached. Answer d is incorrect because the smaller the object, the more likely it is to be cached; no objects are too small to be cached.

## Question 2

The correct answer is a. Because objects are created with a specific number of freelists and freelist groups, if an insufficient number is specified, processes might contend for these objects during periods of high insert activity. Note that the question states during periods of high insert activity. Answer b is incorrect because the question specified insert activity; if the second half of the question had mentioned update activity as well, row chaining would be an issue, but because the question restricts the answer to insert activity, row chaining is not an issue. Answer c is incorrect because blocks cannot fragment. Answer d is incorrect because again we are asked about periods of high insert activity. Insert activity can result in unbalanced B-tree structures but not in index fragmentation.

## Question 3

The correct answer is c. Adding a proper index can dramatically increase the performance of SQL statements. Answer a is incorrect because redo header waits deal with the redo logs and their size and availability and have nothing to do with indexes. Answer b is incorrect because even with proper indexes, if the memory shortage is causing performance problems, adding indexes will not help. Answer d is incorrect because undo header waits involve rollback segment problems, not indexes.

## Question 4

The correct answer is d. A **SLEEPS** indication means that a wait occurred; the latch has not been missed until the process times out while waiting. Answer a is incorrect because this is indicated by the **MISSES** column, not the **SLEEPS** column. Answer b is incorrect because this is indicated by the

IMMEDIATE_GETS column, not the **SLEEPS** column. Answer c is incorrect because this is shown by the **IMMEDIATE_MISSES** column, not the **SLEEPS** column.

## Question 5

The correct answer is c. One thing to watch on the exam is that this question, in its various forms, seems to confuse tables and tablespaces. Because most datafile placement is done by hand for tablespaces, it makes little sense to say "striping tablespaces by hand." The process of striping a table in Oracle7 involves creating a tablespace with several datafiles on separate drives and then creating a table with multiple extents in which each extent is either deliberately placed or sized to force placement into the multiple datafiles. Answer a is incorrect because the striping of tables is not covered in the OFA (Optimal Flexible Architecture) documentation. Answer b is incorrect because optimizing file placement deals with balancing I/O across the disk farm and does not involve table striping. Answer d is incorrect because, although absolutely correct sizing estimates are good to have, they would not lead you to allocate extents by hand.

## Question 6

The correct answer is c. TM always stands for table lock. Answer a is incorrect because exclusive locks have X somewhere in their names. Answer b is incorrect because share locks have S somewhere in their names. Answer d is incorrect because row locks have R somewhere in their names.

## Question 7

The correct answers are d and e. The **MISSES** and **GETS** columns are the only columns in the **V$LATCH** view that apply to **WILLING_TO_WAIT** requests.

## Question 8

The correct answer is a. If SQL statements are not well written, low-level application tuning might not be able to be performed. The use of functions in joins on the right-hand side of the condition, the use of unneeded distincts or uniques, and so on can prohibit proper low-level tuning. Answer b is incorrect because Oracle SQL provides a richer set of functionality in most cases than SQL92. Answer c is incorrect because even the best-written applications can have their performance improved by low-level tuning.

## Question 9

The correct answer is c. Any time you see the term **UNDO**, think rollback segment. Because the indication is **UNDO HEADER**, it is showing contention for header blocks. Therefore, it is actually saying that rollback header block contention is occurring. Answer a is incorrect because this is indicated by **UNDO SEGMENT** waits and would also be signaled by failure-to-extend errors involving the rollback segments. Answer b is incorrect because this is indicated by LRU latch, not **UNDO**, indications. Answer d is incorrect because if there were an excessive number of undo header blocks, you would not have waits for them.

## Question 10

The correct answer is c. Answer a is incorrect because this is the function of the data dictionary cache, which is a separate section of the shared pool from the library cache. Answer b is incorrect because this the function of the database buffer pool, which is a separate section of the SGA from the shared pool, which contains the library cache. Answer d is incorrect because this is the function of the sort areas provided as a separate section of the shared pool (in multithreaded servers) or as a part of the user's memory area in exclusive-mode databases.

## Question 11

The correct answer is b. The utlbstat and utlestat utility scripts are run, and the result is the report.txt file. This file gives the delta numbers between the initial statistics gathered and stored by utlbstat.sql and the final set gathered by utlbstat.sql. The utlbstat.sql script actually writes the report. Answer a is incorrect because this describes the alert_<SID>.log file. Answer c is incorrect because this describes the purpose of the utlbstat.sql script. Answer d is incorrect because this describes the purpose of the utlestat.sql script.

## Question 12

The correct answer is d. If your initialization parameters are set so that checkpoints occur only on log switches, increasing the size of your redo log group members will decrease the number of checkpoints performed. Answer a is incorrect because using fewer groups of the same size will result only in more redo log contention, not in fewer checkpoints. Answer b is incorrect because smaller redo log group members will result in more frequent checkpoints. Answer c is incorrect because simply adding redo log groups might reduce log contention, but if they are the same size as previous groups, the frequency of log switches will remain the same.

## Question 13

The correct answer is b. The first statement to detect a deadlock is rolled back. Answer a is incorrect because a transaction can have multiple statements, and a statement is what triggers a deadlock condition and causes itself to be rolled back. Answer c is incorrect because a deadlock is resolved by rolling back, and only statements and transactions, not rows, are rolled back. Answer d is incorrect because again the resolution occurs at the statement (logical) level, not at a table or a row (physical) level.

## Question 14

The correct answer is d. Because of the dynamic way in which rollback segments grow and shrink (if **OPTIMAL** is set), their tablespace tends to become fragmented. As long as all the rollback segments have identical values for **NEXT**, this is not a problem because any rollback segment can then use any released segment from any other rollback segment. Answer a is incorrect because tables, indexes, and clusters are user-created objects, and you should store rollback segments only with other rollback segments. Answer b is incorrect because all triggers are stored in tables in the data dictionary; therefore, they cannot be stored with other objects because they are a part of an object. Answer c is incorrect because storing temporary segments with rollback segments could result in space problems as both extend and contract dynamically. Temporary segments should be stored away from all other objects, including rollback segments.

## Question 15

The correct answer is c. Because of the answers provided and because you are given no other criteria to judge against, select the highest value.

## Question 16

The correct answer is a. Heavy I/O in the system tablespace as object definitions were constantly being reread from the data dictionary tables. Answer b is incorrect because excessive checkpointing is caused by either having improper initialization file values or having redo log group members that are too small. Answer c is incorrect because undo header contention is caused by having too few rollback segments. Answer d is incorrect because latch contention is caused by processes contending for latches, not by having too small a shared pool.

## Question 17

The correct answer is b. DSSs use many full table scans to produce their rollups and reports, and large block sizes facilitate full table scans. Answer a is incorrect because a block size must be a multiple of the operating system block size and in the range of 2K, 4K, 8K, 16K, and so on. Answer c is incorrect because 4K is not the maximum value for any platform that Oracle is ported to. Answer d is incorrect because the minimum value for a platform would be insufficient to support full table scans and therefore would produce excessive disk I/O. Answer e is incorrect because this parameter is set manually or will default to a low value, not a maximum value.

## Question 18

The correct answer is c. The dbmsutil.sql script creates the **DBMS_ APPLICATION_INFO** package and several others in Oracle7. Answer a is incorrect because the utlestat.sql script is used for tuning, not for creating packages. Answer b is incorrect because the utlbstat.sql script is used for tuning, not for creating packages. Answer d is incorrect because catalog.sql is used to create views, not packages.

## Question 19

The correct answer is c. Only transactions using DML statements use rollback segments; therefore, only **INSERT, UPDATE, DELETE,** and some forms of **SELECT** generate rollback. Because only DML generates rollback, only processes using DML will be assigned rollback segments. Answer a is incorrect because the value of the **DB_BLOCK_BUFFERS** parameter determines the size of the database buffer cache but has nothing to do with rollback segments. Answer b is incorrect because only processes using DML use rollbacks. Answer d is incorrect because the number of indexes has nothing to do with the number of rollback segments.

## Question 20

The correct answer is c. In the scenario here, I/O has most likely become unbalanced because the datafiles have been carelessly placed on the system. Answer a is incorrect because we have stated that the application is already well tuned, and adding datafiles does not affect application tuning. Answer b is incorrect because we can assume that memory was tuned when the application was tuned, and as long as our sorts and data-use patterns have not changed, our memory tuning should not change; besides, everything in the question points to a physical tuning issue. Answer d is incorrect because the question does not discuss excessive waits, which is the only indication that latches need tuning. Answer e is incorrect because we have stated that we have a properly tuned application, and all we have done is add datafiles.

## Question 21

The correct answer is a. A high **GET_MISS/GET_REQ** ratio indicates that the shared pool is aging objects out when they are still being requested. This indicates that the shared pool size is too small. Answer b is incorrect because a larger, not a smaller, shared pool is indicated. Answer c is incorrect because pinning objects will not affect the aging of objects because of too small a shared pool size. Answer d is incorrect because redo log buffers have nothing to do with a high **GET_MISS/GET_REQ** ratio.

## Question 22

The correct answer is d. The **V$SORT_SEGMENT** view is the only view that shows information on temporary tablespaces and their relationship to sort extents. Answer a is incorrect because **V$SQLTEXT** shows the text of currently active SQL and PL/SQL objects. Answer b is incorrect because **V$DB_OBJECT_CACHE** has information on the shared pool but not on the temporary tablespace. Answer c is incorrect because **V$TYPE_SIZE** shows the size information for different type structures used in Oracle7.

## Question 23

The correct answer is c. Application tuning is where you get most of the gain in all your tuning effort. From 70 to 90 percent of all tuning gains come from tuning the application and its SQL. Answer a is incorrect because I/O tuning might contribute 10 percent of performance gains during tuning, assuming that even a minimal attempt has been made to place files correctly. Answer b is incorrect because design, although important, can contribute only so much to tuning if the SQL and other aspects are not properly implemented. Answer d is incorrect because although proper tuning of memory structures is the second-largest area for performance gains, application tuning is still number one. Only 20 to 30 percent of performance gains come through memory tuning in most systems, assuming that even a minimal attempt has been made to size memory structures. Answer e is incorrect because most contention issues are resolved internally with Oracle, and tuning contention accounts for only 5 to 10 percent of performance gains.

## Question 24

The correct answer is c. Increasing the **SORT_AREA_SIZE** value allows larger sorts to occur in memory. The more sorts that happen in memory, the fewer that are sent to disk. Answer a is incorrect because **SORT_AREA_RETAINED_SIZE** sets the size of a process's retained sort area size, not the size of sort that can be done. Answer b is incorrect because decreasing **SORT_AREA_SIZE** increases the number of disk sorts. Answer d is incorrect because **SORT_AREA_RETAINED_SIZE** does not govern the size sort that can be done in memory.

## Question 25

The correct answer is d. Any **SELECT** that uses a **DISTINCT** requires a sort. The other statements shown do not require sorts.

## Question 26

The correct answer is b. Improperly written SQL statements are the number one cause of poor performance. The question states that users are having problems with ad hoc queries, which are notorious for being poorly written. Answer a is incorrect because, other than a few database and initialization parameters, you have little control over the PGA size. Answer c is incorrect because generally I/O is one of the last things you need to tune and is usually one of the last things you need to check in a tuning problem. Answer d is incorrect because further adjusting a properly sized SGA (memory) accounts for very little performance gain for ad hoc queries. The question states that ad hoc queries are their source of complaint, not general application performance, so further tuning of the SGA is not warranted.

## Question 27

The correct answer is b. Answer a is incorrect because Oracle will start new dispatchers only as they are needed. Answer c is incorrect because the starting and killing of dispatcher processes is dynamic up to the maximum allowed number, as specified by the **MTS_MAX_DISPATCHERS** initialization parameter, and down to the value of the **MTS_DISPATCHERS** parameter. Answer d is incorrect because the starting and stopping of dispatcher processes is database controlled, not SQL*Net controlled.

## Question 28

The correct answer is b. Any use of **SORT BY, ORDER BY,** or **DISTINCT** will cause a sort in a **SELECT** statement, and answer b is the only answer that has none of these.

## Question 29

The correct answer is d. The **DBMS_SHARED_POOL** package was created specifically to help DBAs manage the shared pool by providing packages that allow monitoring shared pool usage and pinning objects in the shared pool. Answer a is incorrect because this is one function of the standard.sql script. Answer b is incorrect because this is the function of the dbmsstdx.sql script. Answer c is incorrect because this is a function of the diutil.sql script.

## Question 30

The correct answer is d. The SQL Trace facility of the Oracle Enterprise Manager is used to generate traces of user sessions that can be analyzed to pinpoint performance problems with SQL statements. Answer a is incorrect because this is the purpose of the utlbstat.sql and utlestat.sql scripts. Answer b is incorrect because this is the purpose of the TKPROF utility. Answer c is incorrect because this is the purpose of the Explain Plan utility.

## Question 31

The correct answer is c. A TM lock is a general table lock, a UL is a breakable parse lock, and a TX is an exclusive table lock, all of which are most generally obtained by user applications. Answer a is incorrect because a UL lock is a lock on an object involved in a SQL statement, not a table. Answer b is incorrect because TX is an exclusive lock. Answer d is incorrect because these are not internal lock types.

## Question 32

The correct answer is a. Tuning memory will give the next-largest jump in performance next to application tuning. Answer b is incorrect because I/O tuning generally contributes only half the performance gains of memory tuning. Answer c is incorrect because only minimal performance gains are realized through contention tuning, and it is usually the very last thing tuned. Answer d is incorrect because changing the application design will negate nearly all previous tuning efforts, and you will need to restart your tuning effort. By the time you do application tuning, the design is usually fixed, and it will be difficult, if not impossible, to change.

## Question 33

The correct answer is a. Oracle Expert uses internal Oracle tools to examine tables, indexes, and tablespaces and to provide you with a set of steps and suggestions to improve the configuration of your database. Answer b is incorrect because performance monitoring is the job of the Oracle Performance Pack. Answer c is incorrect because monitoring tablespaces is the job of the Oracle Tablespace Manager. Answer d is incorrect because monitoring user sessions that are using the most resources is the job of the Oracle Top Sessions monitor.

## Question 34

The correct answer is a. The Oracle Trace tool allows you to trace sessions of the entire database to monitor for events that occur inside the application. Answer b is incorrect because Oracle Expert is used for tuning and configuration suggestions. Answer c is incorrect because Oracle Tablespace Manager is used to monitor tablespaces. Answer d is incorrect because Oracle Performance Manager is used to monitor Oracle performance, not events.

## Question 35

The correct answer is b. The main concern with sizing the shared pool is ensuring that you have an adequately sized library cache. A library cache miss is an expensive performance hit because it involves reading from disk and reparsing SQL or PL/SQL. Answer a is incorrect because a shared pool that is made too large can adversely affect other memory structures while not appreciably improving library cache hit ratios past a certain point. Answer c is incorrect because the data dictionary cache is a small part of the overall shared pool, and a data dictionary miss is not a big performance hit.

## Question 36

The correct answer is c. Freelists maintain a list of blocks that can have inserts performed to them. If an insufficient number of freelists exists, contention will occur on systems in which multiple processes perform inserts and deletes against the same data block. Answer a is incorrect because explicit table locking can result in deadlocks but not in freelist contention. Answer b is incorrect because although too small a shared pool can result in shared pool thrashing and library and dictionary cache misses, it cannot cause freelist contention.

## Question 37

The correct answer is d. Remember that deadlocks are resolved at the statement level by having the statement that detects the deadlock rollback. Answer a is incorrect because statement A did not detect the deadlock. Answer b is incorrect because this might occur, but we cannot determine this from the information given; all we can say for sure is that statement B will be rolled back and an error generated. Answer c is incorrect because only statement B is rolled back; this might cause the entire transaction to roll back, but we do not have enough data to determine this.

## Question 38

The correct answer is a. The **CHAIN_CNT** column is loaded with the number of chained rows when an analysis is done on the table. Answer b is incorrect because **BLOCKS** gives only the size of the table in blocks. Answer c is incorrect because **AVG_ROW_LEN** contains information only on average row length. Answer d is incorrect because **NUM_ROWS** gives only the count of rows in the table.

## Question 39

The correct answer is a. Assuming that enough memory is available, the shared pool is managed by an LRU algorithm that ages old SQL and PL/SQL out of the pool. If the pool is sized too small and is filled to nearly 100 percent of its volume, a LIFO algorithm is used to thrash the top few percent of the pool by shuffling out the last SQL or PL/SQL entered to make room for new PL/SQL. Answer b is incorrect because clusters constitute a physical structure and have nothing to do with the shared pool. Answer c is incorrect because the UGA is a structure, not a management tool. Answer d is incorrect because the database buffer pool is another structure in the SGA and is not used in shared pool management. Answer e is incorrect because the PGA is a memory structure and is not used to manage the shared pool.

## Question 40

The correct answer is d. The **V$SESSION** view has statistics that are used to show not only that lock contention is occurring but also which row is causing the problem. Answer a is incorrect because the **V$ROWCACHE** view is used to monitor the data dictionary cache and has nothing to do with locks. Answer b is incorrect because although **V$LOCK** is used to monitor locks, it contains only object-level, not row-level, identification. Answer c is incorrect because **V$SYSSTAT** monitors system statistics but has few statistics on locking.

## Question 41

The correct answer is c. Answer a is incorrect because this is a property of a share lock, not a DDL lock. Answer b is incorrect because this is a characteristic of a row-share lock, not a DDL lock. Answer d is incorrect because a DDL lock is controlled internally, and users do not control its use.

## Question 42

The correct answer is c. Answer a is incorrect because this is the purpose of the **SHARED_POOL_SIZE** parameter. Answer b is incorrect because this is the purpose of the **SHARED_POOL_RESERVED_MIN_ALLOC** parameter. Answer d is incorrect because this is the purpose of the **CURSOR_SPACE_FOR_TIME** parameter.

## Question 43

The correct answer is b. Answer a is incorrect because latch timeouts happen to processes waiting for the latch. Answer c is incorrect because work is copied to the buffer on all computers. Answer d is incorrect because the work is copied as soon as it is done and the latch freed.

## Question 44

The correct answer is d. The **SLEEPS/MISS** column showing a high percentage indicates that a large number of timeouts is occurring and that tuning is required. Answer a is incorrect because **SLEEPS** does not show a percentage value. Answer b is incorrect because **HIT_RATIO** should be as high a percentage as possible. Answer c is incorrect because **GETS** is not reported as a percentage.

## Question 45

The correct answer is c. If **SORT_DIRECT_WRITES** is set to **TRUE**, any sort requiring a disk sort will bypass the buffer cache and use sort buffers assigned to each process to write directly to disk. This requires more memory and more disk space than normal writes through buffer cache sorting. Answer a is incorrect because **SORT_AREA_RETAINED_SIZE** is used to specify the size of retained sort area in memory for a process. Answer b is incorrect because **SORT_AREA_SIZE** is used to size the overall sort area assigned to each process. Answer d is incorrect because **SORT_WRITE_BUFFER_SIZE** is used only to size the sort write buffers and is not used if **SORT_DIRECT_WRITES** is not set to **AUTO** or **TRUE**.

## Question 46

The correct answer is a. If rollback segments are placed in the same tablespace as data, their dynamic growth and shrinkage can cause fragmentation of the data tablespace. Another possible cause is the use of a data tablespace as a temporary tablespace for users. Answer b is incorrect because too small a data tablespace will result in application errors of the unable-to-allocate-extent type, not fragmentation. Answer c is incorrect because this is not normal for Oracle. Answer d is incorrect because although tables will grow automatically, they do not shrink automatically.

## Question 47

The correct answer is c. A request for a redo copy latch is always an **IMMEDIATE** type request. Answer a is incorrect because a redo copy latch is always an **IMMEDIATE** request, not a **WILLING_TO_WAIT** request. Answer b is incorrect because we are requesting a latch, which might cause a buffer request when the work is done, but first we must get the latch. Answer d is incorrect because an **IMMEDIATE** request, not an **ALLOCATION** request, is made for a redo copy latch.

## Question 48

The correct answer is d. The only process in Oracle that reads disk blocks into the buffer is the user-server process. Answer a is incorrect because SMON is responsible for system monitoring and instance cleanup as well as coalescing freespace in tablespaces; however, it does not place data in the buffer cache. Answer b is incorrect because PMON is responsible for process monitoring and cleanup but does not write disk data into the buffer cache. Answer c is incorrect because DBWR writes dirty buffers to disk and performs checkpointing activities but never reads data into the buffers.

## Question 49

The correct answer is c. All data that comes from or goes to Oracle databases flows through the buffer cache. Answer a is incorrect because this is the purpose of the shared pool. Answer b is incorrect because this is the purpose of the data dictionary cache. Answer d is incorrect because this is the purpose of the redo log buffers.

## Question 50

The correct answer is b. The **PINS** column of the **V$LIBRARYCACHE** view shows the number of times an item in the shared pool was executed. Answer a is incorrect because **RELOADS** shows the number of times a requested item had to be reloaded after being aged out by the LRU; excessive **RELOADS** shows a need to increase the size of the shared pool. Answer c is incorrect because **INVALIDATIONS** shows how many times an item in the shared pool was marked invalid because of changes in the objects that the item refers to. Answer d is incorrect because **GETS** shows the number of times requests were made for the object; in an ideal setup, **GETS** and **PINS** should be nearly identical.

## Question 51

The answers are d and e. The **X$KCBRBH** view is created when **DB_BLOCK_LRU-STATISTICS** is set to **TRUE** and **DB_BLOCK_LRU_EXTENDED_STATISTICS** is set to a positive number. The view stores the number of hits gained by adding buffers up to the number specified. The **V$SYSSTAT** table contains the statistics used to calculate hit ratio, which tells how effectively the cache area is utilized. Answer a is incorrect because **V$CACHE** stores data about currently cached objects. Answer b is incorrect because **V$FILESTAT** contains I/O statistics about database files, not buffer cache areas. Answer c is incorrect because **X$STATS** probably does not exist.

## Question 52

The correct answer is a. By manually striping the tables, you improve the efficiency of a parallel query by reducing I/O contention. Answer b is incorrect because an increase of the shared pool will not affect query speed in this situation. Answer c is incorrect because an increase in redo log size will not affect query speed in this situation. Answer d is incorrect because a decrease in the degree of parallel will reduce, not increase, performance.

## Question 53

The correct answer is b. Answer a is incorrect because no column in **X$KCBRBH** shows this value. Answer c is incorrect because no column in **X$KCBRBH** shows this value. Answer d is incorrect because no column in **X$KCBRBH** shows this value. If you issue a count against the entire table, not specifying a summation (for example, **SELECT COUNT(*) FROM X$KCBRBH**), you can find out how many additional buffers it is projecting hits for, but that is all.

## Question 54

The correct answer is c. Many default items, such as the maximum size of cached tables and whether direct sort writes are performed (if **SORT_DIRECT_WRITES** is set to **AUTO**), are based on the size of the data buffer area, which, of course, is based on the number of database block buffers (**DB_BLOCK_BUFFERS**) and the size of the database blocks (**DB_BLOCK_SIZE**). In addition, the more buffers in the database buffer cache, the less contention and the higher the hit ratio, all of which translate into better performance. Answer a is incorrect because the need for increasing the redo log size is indicated by excessive log switches causing excessive checkpointing activity; because this has not been indicated in the question, we must assume that this is not occurring. Answer b is incorrect because a need for increasing the sort area size is indicated by a large number of disk sorts; again, because the question did not mention this, we must assume that this is not occurring. Answer d is incorrect because generally a decrease in sort area size will result in less, not more, performance.

## Question 55

The correct answer is c. Sort direct writes bypass the database base buffer caches when doing disk sorts. To bypass the data buffers, each user is given his own set of sort write buffers to use when writing to disk. Giving each user their own buffers will usually result in more memory being required for Oracle usage overall. In addition, depending on how the sort direct write option uses the disk, more temporary space will be required. Answer a is incorrect because sort direct writes do not care which background processes are running. Answer b is incorrect because the only prerequisite for using sort direct writes is the one mentioned in answer c. However, be careful if this question appears on the exam because the original version of the exam considered this the correct answer (though the powers that be now know that it is incorrect). Answer d is incorrect because sort direct writes do not depend on datafile sizing.

## Question 56

The correct answer is b. If the addresses listed in listener.ora and init<SID>.ora files do not match, the users will receive dedicated rather than shared connections. The entries must be identical. For example, if the actual IP address is used in one and the host name as used by your domain name server is used in the other, connections will be dedicated. Answer a is incorrect because this describes the **MTS_DISPATCHERS** and **MTS_MAX_DISPATCHERS** initialization parameters. Answer c is incorrect because this describes the **MTS_SERVERS** and **MTS_MAX_SERVERS** initialization parameters. Answer d is incorrect because this describes the **MTS_SERVER** parameter.

## Question 57

The correct answer is a. Using **SET TRANSACTION USER ROLLBACK SEGMENT seg_**, you can force a transaction to use any rollback segment you desire. Remember that you must issue a **COMMIT** command before issuing **SET TRANSACTION** to set rollback segment usage to force any previous transaction to close and that the command must be the first command in the transaction. Answer b is incorrect because transactions are created automatically or by using the **BEGIN** and **END** commands or the **COMMIT** command. Answer c is incorrect because a transaction cannot really be modified—it either is or is not. Answer d is incorrect because any session-related system parameters are changed with the **ALTER SESSION** command, not the **SET TRANSACTION** command.

## Question 58

The correct answers are b and d. The read-consistent and current copies of a database block are maintained in memory at all times. When a block is read into memory and subsequently modified, a second copy of the block with the original data is maintained until the data is committed back to the database. This ensures that a read-consistent version of the data is always available to other transactions. Answer a is incorrect because once a delete action is committed, there is no need for the deleted blocks information; before a delete is committed, you have the current and read-consistent copies in the buffers. Answer c is incorrect because there is no such thing as a backup copy of a block.

## Question 59

The correct answer is c. If a restart of the database occurs between the time you run utlbstat.sql and the time you run utlestat.sql, the statistical data contained in the report.txt output will be bad. To get a proper tuning report in the case of a database restart, you must run both utlbstat.sql and utlestat.sql, in that order. Remember that the report generated by utlestat.sql calculates a delta set of statistics and that the statistics in the base tables are always from the startup of the instance. Answer a is incorrect because simply rerunning utlbstat.sql will not generate a tuning report. Answer b is incorrect because although running utlestat.sql will generate a tuning report, the information contained in the report will be invalid. Answer d is incorrect because the scripts are in the incorrect order; you must always run utlbstat.sql before you run utlestat.sql.

## Question 60

The correct answer is a. Because bitmapped indexes map values in the column to bits and store only the bit values, storage is reduced by several orders when using bitmapped indexes. This is the only one of the answers given that is a benefit of using bitmapped indexes. Answer b is incorrect because bitmapped indexes do not need to be ordered; in fact, because they are used for columns of low cardinality, ordering would not make much sense. Answer b is incorrect because they are actually great for large tables, which are prevalent in DSSs. Answer d is incorrect because they work great on columns of low, not high, cardinality.

## Question 61

The correct answer is c. The alert_<SID>.log file stores information about errors and events (for example, startup, shutdown, and log switches and DDLs issued against the database) that occur against the database. Answer a is incorrect because process SQL statements are tracked through trace files, not the alert log. Answer b is incorrect because no file tracks alerts issued by Oracle Corporation. Answer d is incorrect because this is accomplished with the internal audit tables in Oracle, not through the alert log.

## Question 62

The correct answer is c. **DB_BLOCK_SIZE** is used to initialize all datafiles in the system. If the block size is changed, the database files will not be readable, so to change the block size you need to export all data, drop and rebuild the database, and import the data back into the datafiles. Answer a is incorrect because Oracle recommends setting it large, and this usually improves performance. Answer b is incorrect because setting it too low results in less, not more, memory being used. Answer d is incorrect because Oracle does not automatically set it. The standard default value for block size is 2048, which is too small for most applications.

## Question 63

The correct answer is a. The purpose of the rollback segment is to allow for rollback of transactions. Rollback of transactions is possible only if before images of database blocks are stored in the rollback segments. Answer b is incorrect because redo logs store transaction information for redoing transactions, not information on how to roll them back. Answer c is incorrect because datafiles are the source of data, not repositories of transient data. Answer d is incorrect because indexes store current fixed values, not transient values.

## Question 64

The correct answer is a. Memory sorts are performed using reads and writes of microseconds, whereas disk sorts are done at millisecond read-write speeds at best. Memory sorts are always faster than disk sorts, so they are the preferred sorting mechanism. Answer b is incorrect because disk sorts, being slower, are not the preferred method of sorting, so doing sorts in memory is always a good idea regardless of the amount of space in your temporary tablespace. Answer c is incorrect because **SORT_DIRECT_WRITES** determines how large sorts are written to disk, not whether they should be done in memory.

## Question 65

The correct answer is d. If the **TIMED_STATISTICS** parameter is not set prior to running utlbstat.sql, time-based statistics will not be properly collected. Answer a is incorrect because **AUDIT_TRAIL** only turns on auditing, which is not used by utlbstat.sql. Answer b is incorrect because **INIT_SQL_FILES** tells Oracle which files to run on startup and has nothing to do with utlbstat.sql. Answer c is incorrect because **SQL_TRACE** turns on tracing across the entire database and has nothing to do with utlbstat.sql.

# Backup And Recovery Strategies And Motivation

**11**

**Terms you'll need to understand:**

√ Restore

√ Recover

√ Roll forward

√ Control file

√ System Change Number (SCN)

√ Rollback segments

√ Redo logs

√ Backup

√ Checkpoint

√ ARCHIVELOG mode

√ Standby database

**Techniques you'll need to master:**

√ Understanding what an Oracle backup is

√ Understanding why backups are important

√ Understanding when to perform backups

√ Understanding types of failures

Backup and recovery is one of the most important duties of the database administrator (DBA). A complete understanding of how the Oracle backup and recovery operations work is essential to success on the OCP exams. This chapter explains backup strategies and the motivations for using them.

# When Should You Perform Backups?

An Oracle backup is a copy of data that can be used to restore the original data if it is lost. The backup might include the control file, archive logs, and datafiles. Without a proper backup strategy, recovering the database because of a failure might not be possible. You should tailor your backup strategy to the business requirements of the data.

If you are charged with developing a backup strategy for a development database that is refreshed often from a consistent set of test data, you might not need to perform frequent backups. On the other hand, if your database is a 24×7 catalog sales database, you will want to perform frequent backups to minimize downtime. One of the first steps in developing a backup strategy is understanding the types of database failures that can occur.

## Types Of Failures

Every database is subject to failure. Understanding the different types of failures is key to developing an adequate backup strategy and being successful on the backup and recovery exam.

### Statement Failure

Statement failure happens when a SQL statement fails. This can be caused by incorrect syntax or incompatible middleware between the client and the server databases. Oracle handles statement failures automatically and returns control to the user with an error message. Recovery is not necessary when a statement fails.

### Process Failure

Process failure occurs when a user process that is connected to Oracle ends abnormally. This can happen because of a network or client-side power failure or simply because the user killed the client process, causing an abnormal end. Process failure is recovered automatically by Oracle's PMON process, which wakes up periodically, then cleans up the cache and frees resources that a failed user process was using.

### Instance Failure

Instance failure occurs when the Oracle instance fails. This can happen when there is a power outage or an operating system crash or when one or more of the Oracle processes fail, causing the instance to stop. When an instance fails, buffers in the system global area (SGA) are not written to disk. Oracle automatically recovers from instance failure when the instance is restarted. The SMON process is responsible for instance recovery at startup. SMON uses the online redo logfiles for instance recovery. In a parallel server environment, the SMON of one instance can also recover other instances that have failed.

### User Or Application Error

User or application errors occur when a user or application has an error. For example, an error occurs when deleting data from a table in error or dropping a table that is still needed. To recover from this type of failure, Oracle provides an exact point-in-time recovery. Point-in-time recovery can recover the database to the point in time just before the error occurred.

### Media Or Disk Failure

Media failure occurs when files needed by the database can no longer be accessed, normally when a disk drive fails. Oracle provides several ways to recover from media failure, depending on the situation and the business needs of the data. Which backup strategy is chosen determines the media recovery options.

# Backup Plans

This section will help you decide when to perform database backups and which parts of a database need to be backed up. Before you create any database, you should design a backup and recovery plan on the basis of the business need for the data. If this step is not completed, there is no guarantee that the data can be recovered as required.

## What Is Backed Up?

The physical database structure of an Oracle database that is included in a backup is important to understand. You need to understand each part of the database and its importance in backup and recovery.

### Control Files

Control files contain information on all physical database files (the database physical structure) and their current transaction states. Control files are read to mount and open the database, and transaction numbers are recorded for each datafile. If the control files and datafiles are out of sync, the database will not start up and will report either that recovery is needed or that the datafiles are out of sync with the control files. Control files are required for database startup and recovery. The database is required to have one control file to start up. Because of the importance of the control file, it is recommended to let Oracle write mirror copies of the control file to several locations on different disk drives. In addition to the normal backup schedule, control files should be backed up any time structural changes are made to the database.

## Online Redo Logfiles

Redo logfiles are set up at instance creation. A minimum of two one-member groups in a single thread is required for instance startup. Redo logs hold records used for recovery purposes and contain information on all data-modifying transactions that occur in the database, unless these transactions have been run as nonrecoverable. The LGWR process writes data on changes from the redo log buffers to the redo logs. A **COMMIT** is not considered complete until the LGWR signals that all redo log entries have been written to disk. Remember that the redo log buffer is a part of the SGA. Because of the importance of redo logfiles, it is recommended to let Oracle write mirror copies of the redo logfiles to several locations on different disk drives.

You need not back up the online redo logfiles as part of the normal backup strategy. If the database crashes and all copies of the online redo logfiles are lost, recovery depends on whether your database is in **ARCHIVELOG** mode.

In **ARCHIVELOG** mode, you should recover the database to the last archive log. Once recovery is complete, open the database with the **RESETLOGS** option.

In **NOARCHIVELOG** mode, the last consistent whole backup is restored and the database opened with the **RESETLOGS** options. No recovery is done because the database is at a consistent state. All changes made since the last backup are lost.

In performing disk maintenance or moving a database from one computer to another, you can back up the redo logfiles and use them so that the database can be opened without the **RESETLOGS** option. This allows you to use for recovery the backup that was taken before the move, saving you the time of doing another whole backup of the database.

## Database Datafiles

The Oracle system uses logical and physical storage. Logical storage uses the concept of tablespaces. A tablespace is physically implemented through one or more datafiles. Datafiles are subdivided into segments, which are subdivided into extents, which can be of several types, depending on what they store or on their usage. The following list shows the types of segments:

➤ Table segment

➤ Index segment

➤ Rollback segment

➤ Temporary segment

A single segment extent cannot span multiple datafiles, and it must be contiguous. Datafiles should be included in any backup strategy.

## Rollback Segments

Rollback segments contain records of changes for multiple transactions. Each transaction is assigned to a single rollback segment extent. Rollback segments are used to provide read consistency and rollback transactions and to put the database in a transaction-consistent state as part of recovery. During recovery, the rollback segments are used to undo any uncommitted changes applied from the redo logs to the datafiles. Rollback segments are included in the backup of datafiles.

## Archive Logfiles

Archive logfiles are redo logfiles that have been filled with redo information and copied to a backup location as an archive file. Archive logs are created only when the database is in **ARCHIVELOG** mode. In **NOARCHIVELOG** mode, redo files are simply overwritten without being archived.

Archive logfiles, if kept on disk, should be backed up to tape before deleting them to make room for more archive logfiles. You should keep archive logfiles until they are older than the latest database backup you want to use to for recovery. For example, if you back up your tablespaces once a week and keep four weeks' worth of tablespace backups, archive logfiles older than four weeks are no longer needed.

## Frequency

Whole database and tablespace backups are part of all backup strategies. The frequency of performing backups should be based on the amount of changes made to the data and, as stated earlier, the business needs of the data. If the data has changed a lot through insertions, deletions, or updates, you should perform backups more frequently. On the other hand, if downtime is not an issue and the loss of some data is acceptable, you can perform backups less frequently. If the database is read-only and refreshed monthly, you need to perform backups only monthly after the scheduled refresh.

When structural changes are made to your database, you should perform a backup both before and after the change. Structural changes include:

➤ Adding a datafile to an existing tablespace

➤ Renaming an existing datafile or moving it to a new location

➤ Adding or dropping an online redo log group or member

➤ Renaming an existing redo log group or moving it to a new location

➤ Creating or dropping a tablespace

If the database is in **ARCHIVELOG** mode, you need to back up only the control file with an **ALTER DATABASE BACKUP CONTROLFILE** command. If the database is in **NOARCHIVELOG** mode, you need to perform a consistent whole database backup before and after structural changes are made.

If your database is in **ARCHIVELOG** mode, you can back up tablespaces individually by backing up the datafiles associated with them. This can be very useful if parts of your database change often and other parts do not. You can have a more frequent backup schedule for the more active parts of your database and a less frequent backup schedule for the less active parts. This kind of strategy can reduce both recovery time and the time spent performing backups.

When you perform database operations using the unrecoverable option, you should perform backups after the objects are created. When you use the unrecoverable option to create tables or indexes, no redo information is recorded, and the objects cannot be recovered until the tablespaces they are in are backed up. The same holds true for direct path loads with SQL*Loader.

You should back up read-only tablespaces immediately after making the tablespace read-only. As long as the tablespace is read-only, it does not need to be backed up again. When backing up a read-only tablespace, you do not need to use the **BEGIN BACKUP** and **END BACKUP** commands; in fact, these commands will cause errors if used on a read-only tablespace. Once the tablespace is made read-write again, you should resume backing up the tablespace.

## History

How long you keep database backups depends on the needs of the data. If there is a possibility that the database will need to be recovered to a previous point in time, a backup from before that point in time will be used in the recovery. In **NOARCHIVELOG** mode, this means keeping consistent whole database backups. In **ARCHIVELOG** mode, you will need to perform a whole database backup with the control file and the archive logs from the point in time that the recovery is needed.

## Strategy

To develop a proper backup strategy, you must answer three questions:

➤ **If a media failure happens, is it acceptable to lose any transactions performed between the last backup and the time of failure?** If the answer is yes, you can run the database in **NOARCHIVELOG** mode. If the answer is no, you must run the database in **ARCHIVELOG** mode.

➤ **Does the database need to be available 24 hours a day, 7 days a week?** If the answer is yes, you must run the database in **ARCHIVELOG** mode. In addition, if any downtime for recovery must be minimized, you can use the standby database feature. If the answer is no, you can run the database in **NOARCHIVELOG** mode and perform consistent whole database backups, which require that the database be shut down.

➤ **Will the database ever need to be recovered to a past point in time other than the time a backup was taken?** If the answer is yes, you must run the database in **ARCHIVELOG** mode. If the answer is no, you could run the database in **NOARCHIVELOG** mode.

## NOARCHIVELOG Mode

When the database is operated in **NOARCHIVELOG** mode, redo logfiles are not copied and saved as archive logfiles. This means that the only recovery option for media failure is to restore the last consistent whole database backup. Consistent whole database backups are taken while the database is shut down. You should perform backups on a schedule according to the amount of work that it is acceptable to lose. If losing one day's worth of work is acceptable, shut down the database nightly and perform a full backup. If losing five days worth of work is acceptable, shut down the database once every five days and back it up.

Remember that whenever the physical structure of the database is changed in **NOARCHIVELOG** mode, the database should be shut down and backed up immediately before and after the change is made.

## ARCHIVELOG Mode

When the database is operated in **ARCHIVELOG** mode, redo logfiles are being copied and saved as archive logfiles. This means that the archive log, redo logs, and datafile backups can be used for complete recovery to the point of failure or any previous point in time.

Once a database is created, put it in **ARCHIVELOG** mode, then shut it down and perform a complete backup. Now the database can be restarted and run continuously without doing a consistent whole backup again. From this point, you can perform open or closed tablespace backups to keep the backups current and to reduce recovery time. Remember that all tablespaces do not need to be backed up with the same frequency. The backup schedule should be determined by the rate at which the data changes and by the desired recovery time.

When structural changes are made in **ARCHIVELOG** mode, the control file should be backed up using the **ALTER DATABASE BACKUP CONTROLFILE** command. Do not use the operating system to back up the control file unless the database is shut down.

### Standby Database

Oracle7.3 has a standby database feature that can be used when recovery time must be at an absolute minimum. This feature uses a primary database and the standby database. The primary database operates in **ARCHIVELOG** mode, whereas the standby database operates on duplicate hardware in a constant state of recovery, applying the archive logfiles from the primary database. When the primary database goes down, the standby database applies the last archive from the primary database. The DBA can now cancel the recovery and open the standby database as the new primary database. Normally, the standby database resides on a different computer and possibly even at a different location, although not necessarily. When a standby database is used to recover the primary database, any transaction that are not archived will be lost.

## Multilevel Backup Schemes

The Oracle Export utility can be used to add flexibility to your backup strategy. It is not a substitute for operating system backups because it is a logical backup and cannot give the same level of recovery as other Oracle backup scenarios. The Export and Import utilities can back up and restore database objects selectively. This type of backup can be used for a set of tables that never change. If user error causes the data in one of these tables to be lost, the whole tablespace need not be taken offline for recovery. The Import utility can simply reimport the data for the table, and no other recovery is needed.

# Recovery Plans

This section discusses the concepts involved in choosing a recovery strategy. To develop a recovery strategy, you should understand the meanings of the following terms:

➤ **System Change Number (SCN)** The SCN is like a timestamp that Oracle uses to control concurrency and redo record ordering. This is the mechanism that allows Oracle to keep transaction consistency.

➤ **Restored files** Files are restored from a backup made by using an operating system utility.

➤ **Recovered files** Files are recovered by first restoring the file from a backup and then applying archive log information to roll forward the file until it is recovered to the desired point in time.

➤ **Checkpoint** A checkpoint establishes a consistent point of the database across redo log threads. This mechanism tells Oracle where to start reading the log threads for recovery.

## Testing

The time to test your recovery plans is not when your database has failed and your phone is ringing off the hook with irate users. Go through the motions of causing the types of failures that you want to be able to recover from and make sure that your backup strategy works. Answering the following questions might help you decide which scenarios to test:

➤ Is the database in **ARCHIVELOG** mode?

➤ Are database files lost or damaged? If so, which files?

➤ Is the data loss due to user error?

If the database is not in **ARCHIVELOG** mode, you have only one option: Restore the database from the last consistent backup. All changes made from that point are lost. If the database is in **ARCHIVELOG** mode and files were lost, you should perform a tablespace recovery while the database is still open. The damaged files should be taken offline (if they are not already) and restored from the last backup and then recovered and put online. Other tablespaces in the database remain available during the recovery. If the database was not open, it can still be recovered, but the other tablespaces will not be available during the recovery.

If an archive log or a redo log that is needed for recovery is lost, you will need to perform a point-in-time recovery. If user error caused the data loss, you will need to perform a recovery to a point in time before the user error. All changes beyond that point are lost.

# Media Recovery Options

Media recovery restores datafiles to a point in time before failure. The following is a list of media recovery options:

➤ **Complete media recovery** Complete media recovery recovers all damaged or missing database files and the application of all redo information. The database might need to be opened with the **RESETLOGS** option if a backup control file or new control file was created for the recovery. The three types of complete media recovery are:

  ➤ Closed database recovery

  ➤ Open database, offline tablespace recovery

  ➤ Open database, offline tablespace datafile recovery

➤ **Incomplete media recovery** Incomplete media recovery is also called point-in-time recovery. Point-in-time recovery that is not continued to a complete recovery must be terminated by the **OPEN RESETLOGS** option. The database must be closed during incomplete recovery operations. The three types of incomplete media recovery are:

  ➤ Cancel-based recovery

  ➤ Time-based recovery

  ➤ Change-based recovery

# Practice Questions

## Question 1

> Your company has a relatively static database because changes are seldom and sporadic. The time it takes to recover is not an issue with the business users. Which backup strategy should you follow?
>
> ○ a. Back up less frequently than a company with a high volume of change
>
> ○ b. Back up more frequently than a company with a high volume of change
>
> ○ c. Back up each time the data is changed
>
> ○ d. Do not back up because the data does not change frequently enough

The correct answer is a. The less frequent the changes to the database, the less frequently backups need to be performed, depending on the required recovery time.

## Question 2

> How does the backup strategy affect recoverability?
>
> ○ a. It will determine whether a complete or an incomplete recovery can be performed
>
> ○ b. It will determine whether rollback segments are required
>
> ○ c. It will not affect recoverability
>
> ○ d. It will help you get funding for your recovery from management

The correct answer is a. The two basic concepts in backup and recovery are **ARCHIVELOG** mode and **NOARCHIVELOG** mode. The decision to run in **ARCHIVELOG** mode or in **NOARCHIVELOG** mode will determine whether an incomplete or a complete recovery can be performed.

## Question 3

> Your have been hired as the DBA for an Internet store selling merchandise around the world 24 hours a day, 7 days a week. What do the business requirements for a system like this indicate when developing your backup and recovery strategy?
>
> ○ a. Backup and recovery are critical to this business
>
> ○ b. Backup and recovery is not important because the database never shuts down
>
> ○ c. Backup and recovery is of little importance for this type of business

The correct answer is a. Because sales are conducted around the clock, any downtime could result in lost sales.

## Question 4

> What is the DBA's most important responsibility?
>
> ○ a. Keeping the database organized
>
> ○ b. Keeping up-to-date backups
>
> ○ c. Keeping the database available to users
>
> ○ d. Keeping users from corrupting the database

The correct answer is c. The database is useless to the enterprise if it is not available for use.

## Question 5

> Why is it important to understand the business requirements of data when developing a backup strategy?
>
> ○ a. The size of the company will determine the type of backups needed
>
> ○ b. The type of business will determine the type of backups needed
>
> ○ c. The nature of the data will determine the type of backups needed
>
> ○ d. The number of users will determine the type of backups needed

The correct answer is c. The rate of change to, and the requirements for, the data will determine the type of backups needed.

## Question 6

> You have just been hired as the new DBA for a paper supply company. The previous DBA left a copy of the backup and recovery plan being used for the database. What should you do to test the plan?
>
> ○ a. Rely on the documentation in the plan if it looks like it should work
>
> ○ b. Throw away the current plan and write your own
>
> ○ c. Test the backup and recovery to make sure that a complete recovery can be performed
>
> ○ d. Make sure that the documentation is correct

The correct answer is c. All backup and recovery plans should be tested to make sure that recovery can be performed.

## Question 7

> What is the main objective of backup and recovery?
>
> ○ a. Performing backups only when absolutely necessary
>
> ○ b. Backing up all files
>
> ○ c. Keeping backed up files off-site
>
> ○ d. Minimizing data loss and downtime

The correct answer is d. A proper backup and recovery strategy will minimize data loss and downtime, depending on the requirements of the data.

## Question 8

> Which two factors determine the frequency with which backups should be performed? [Check all correct answers]
>
> ❏ a. The size of the database
>
> ❏ b. The frequency of structural changes made to the database
>
> ❏ c. The type of operating system
>
> ❏ d. The nature of the data

The correct answers are b and d. Backups should always be taken after a structural change is made to the database. The nature of the data (that is, the rate at which data changes) will also determine the frequency of backups.

## Question 9

You are hired as a new DBA for a company and are asked to develop a backup and recovery plan. What are the four most important factors that will help you develop a plan to meet the needs of the company? [Check all correct answers]

❑ a. The frequency of database structural changes

❑ b. The type of tape drives used for backup

❑ c. The frequency of data changes

❑ d. The business requirements of the data

❑ e. The size of the disk drives

❑ f. The activity level of the database

The correct answers are a, c, d, and f. Any time there is a structural change to the database, a backup should be done as soon as possible. The frequency of data changes will play a major role in your decisions to operate in **ARCHIVELOG** mode or **NOARCHIVELOG** mode. Business requirements are always a factor in any database system. Finally, a very active system will affect your decision on how often a backup should be done.

## Question 10

What is the responsibility of the DBA when a media failure occurs?

○ a. Restoring the file system

○ b. Restoring the operating system

○ c. Restoring the database

○ d. Re-creating the Oracle account

The correct answer is c. The DBA is responsible for restoring the database.

# Question 11

What is an important consideration in a data warehouse environment in which the database cannot be re-created easily?

○ a. Data concurrency

○ b. Fault tolerance

○ c. Logical backups

○ d. The number of tapes available for backup

The correct answer is b. Fault tolerance is one reason to have a standby database.

# Question 12

How would you back up an order-processing database that is critical to the cash flow of your company?

○ a. Back up the database daily

○ b. Back up the database monthly

○ c. Back up the database during inventory

○ d. Back up the database weekly

The correct answer is a. Daily backups will minimize recovery time, therefore enabling orders to be placed and the cash flow from operations to continue.

# Question 13

You are creating a new database that will be updated monthly. Which backup plan should you use?

○ a. Back up the database daily

○ b. Back up the database monthly

○ c. Back up the database after the updates are made

○ d. Back up the database weekly

The correct answer is c. Because the data changes only once a month, it should be backed up immediately after the updates are applied.

# Need To Know More?

 Backup and recovery is covered in the *Oracle Server Concepts Book* and the *Server Administrators' Guide*.

 Loney, Kevin: *DBA Handbook, 7.3 Edition*. Oracle Press, 1996. ISBN 0-07882-289-0.

 Velpuri, Rama: *Oracle Backup and Recovery Handbook*. Oracle Press, 1995. ISBN 0-07882-106-1.

# Backup
# Methods

**Terms you'll need to understand:**

√ Physical backup

√ Logical backup

√ Table mode export

√ User mode export

√ Full database export

√ Read-only tablespace

**Techniques you'll need to master:**

√ Exporting databases

√ Performing online (cold) backups

√ Performing offline (hot) backups

√ Supporting 24-hour operations

√ Creating a standby database

√ Speeding up recovery time

The method used in backing up a database is very important because it affects the recovery options available to the database administrator (DBA) when a failure occurs. All databases can fail for one reason or another. It is your job as the DBA to protect the data in the database with the proper backup methods.

This chapter explains how to perform physical and logical backups of a database and how to use different methods to protect your database from data loss or excessive downtime due to failure.

# Export

An export is a logical backup of a database. The Export utility copies the data and database definitions to a binary operating system file. Export can be used only against an open database. Because Export copies one table at a time, it can guarantee read consistency only for individual tables. Read consistency between tables is not guaranteed. For a read-consistent export of the entire database, changes to the database must stop during the export. This can be enforced by closing the database and then reopening it in restrict mode. Exports can be used to supplement operating system backups and have several advantages:

➤ Unlike an operating system backup, Export reads each Oracle data block and will list an error if it discovers a bad block. This warns you so that you can try to correct the problem before users try to access the bad data.

➤ Export backups can be used to move databases between computers. Because exports are contained in a binary file, they can be sent to tape or disk and moved by hand or through an FTP (File Transfer Protocol) on a network. Exports can also move a database from one operating system to another, such as from Unix to NT.

➤ It is much easier to replace a table that was dropped by accident with an import than by performing an incomplete recovery.

➤ Exports can provide much more granularity to your backup scheme by backing up individual tables, schemas, or entire databases.

➤ The Export utility can perform a complete, an incremental, or a cumulative export.

Remember that exports are not alternatives to operating system backups. Physical operating system backups should be performed, and exports should be used as well, to add flexibility to recovery. For example, a lost datafile should be recovered using the operating system backup. In the case of a dropped table, importing the table will be quicker than a point-in-time recovery. Multiple exports can be run simultaneously to improve performance. For example, multiple user mode exports could be done at the same time instead of performing one long-running full database export. The **DIRECT** parameter can also be used to significantly speed up exports.

# Export Modes

Three export modes determine which parts of the database can be exported. A full database export can be done only by a user who has been given the EXP_FULL_DATABASE role. This role is included in the DBA role and need not be granted to DBA users.

## Table Mode

In table mode, a list of tables is exported. The table definitions, data, grants, indexes, constraints, and triggers are exported with the table. Cluster definitions are not included in the export. Import can therefore be used to uncluster tables. DBAs can export tables belonging to any schema.

## User Mode

In user mode, all the objects belonging to a schema are exported. These include clusters, database links, views, private synonyms, sequences, snapshots, snapshot logs, and stored procedures. DBAs can export any schema in the database.

## Full Database Mode

Only users with the EXP_FULL_DATABASE role can export using the FULL=Y option. In full database mode, all objects in the database are exported, except the ones owned by SYS. Included in a full export are roles, all synonyms, system privileges, tablespace definitions, tablespace quotas, rollback segment definitions, system audit options, all triggers, and profiles. A full database export can be complete, cumulative, or incremental, as explained here:

➤ **Complete** Establishes the starting point for cumulative and incremental exports. A complete export will export all objects and update the data dictionary tables that record incremental and cumulative exports. A complete export is done when the **INCTYPE=COMPLETE** parameter is used. Now, incremental exports or cumulative exports can be taken by using the **INCTYPE=INCREMENTAL** and **INCTYPE= CUMULATIVE** parameters, respectively.

➤ **Incremental** Exports all the tables changed or created since the last incremental, cumulative, or complete export. Because incremental exports back up only the new or changed tables, they perform much faster and create smaller files.

➤ **Cumulative** Backs up tables that have changed since the last cumulative or complete export. Cumulative exports are a way to roll up many incremental exports into one file. Once the cumulative export is done, the incrementals done between the last cumulative or complete export and the current cumulative export can be removed.

The following is an example of a full database export schedule using incremental and cumulative exports:

➤ Full complete exports every four weeks on Sunday

➤ Cumulative exports every seven days on Sunday

➤ Incremental exports every night

To restore the data on Wednesday of the third week, restore the system information from the last incremental, then import the data from the last complete export. Next, import the second- and third-week cumulative exports. Finally, import the incremental data from Monday, Tuesday, and Wednesday.

Oracle keeps track of complete, incremental, and cumulative exports by updating the following SYS tables:

➤ **INCFIL** Tracks the incremental and cumulative exports and assigns a unique identifier to each.

➤ **INCEXP** Maintains which objects were exported in specific exports.

➤ **INCVID** Contains one column for the **EXPID** of the last valid export. This information determines the **EXPID** of the next export.

When an incremental or cumulative export is done, a row is also added to the SYS.INCFIL to identify the export file and the user doing the export. When a complete export is done, all the previous entries are deleted from the SYS.INCFIL, and a new row is added, specifying an *x* in the **EXPTYPE** column.

# Export Parameters

This sections that follow describe the Export utility parameters and how to use them to write data from an Oracle database into an operating system file in binary format.

## BUFFER

BUFFER is the number of bytes used to fetch data rows. This will determine the number of rows fetched at a time. The formula for **BUFFER** is buffer size = (rows in array) * (maximum row size). The default is operating system-dependent.

## COMPRESS

COMPRESS will cause Export to resize the initial extents for all tables so that they will import into one initial extent. The default value is **YES**.

## CONSISTENT

If **CONSISTENT** is set to **YES**, Export will make the export consistent to a single point in time. A rollback segment will be retained for the duration of the export. The default value is **NO**. Setting this value to **YES** could cause rollback segments to grow very large if many changes are occurring to the database.

## CONSTRAINTS

If **CONSTRAINTS** is set to **YES**, constraints will be exported. The default value is **YES**.

## DIRECT

Setting **DIRECT=Y** will cause Export to read data directly without using the public buffer cache or the SQL command processing layer. The default value is **NO**.

## FEEDBACK

When **FEEDBACK** is set to a nonzero number, Export will display a dot every time that many rows are exported. The default value is zero, which gives no feedback.

## FILE

The **FILE** parameter is the name of the export file you want to create. The default value is EXPDAT.DMP.

## FULL

If **FULL** is set to **YES**, a full database export is performed. The default value is **NO**. Only users with the EXP_FULL_DATABASE role enabled can use this parameter.

## GRANTS

If **GRANTS** is set to **YES**, grants will be exported with database objects. The default value is **YES**.

## HELP

**HELP=Y** will display the export parameters on screen with a brief explanation. The default value is **NO**.

## INCTYPE

INCTYPE determines whether the export is a complete, cumulative, or incremental. There is no default value for **INCTYPE**. If **INCTYPE** is left blank, the export cannot be used as part of an incremental backup scheme.

## INDEXES

INDEXES specifies whether indexes are exported with the tables. The default value is **YES**.

## LOG

LOG specifies the file name to which to record the screen output and error messages. By default, no logfile is created.

## OWNER

The **OWNER** parameter specifies one or more usernames whose objects will be exported in user mode. There is no default value.

## RECORD

If **RECORD** is set to **YES**, an incremental or cumulative export updates the SYS.INCVID, SYS.INCFIL, and SYS.INCEXP tables.

## ROWS

The **ROWS** parameter determines whether rows of data or only the object definitions are exported. The default value is **YES**.

## STATISTICS

The **STATISTICS** parameter can be set to **ESTIMATE, COMPUTE,** or **NONE**. The default value is **NONE**, which will not generate any statistics for the optimizer. The other parameters work the same as in the **ANALYZE** command.

## TABLES

TABLES specifies a list of tables to export in table mode. There is no default value.

## USERID

To connect with the database and use the Export utility, you must use a valid username and password. The correct usage of **USERID** is **USERID**=*username/ password.*

# Export Examples

Following are some examples of how to export:

➤ To execute an incremental, a cumulative, or a complete export:

```
exp username/password inctype=incremental file=export_file_name
             Cumulative
             Complete
```

➤ To execute a table mode export:

```
exp username/password tables=table1,table2,table3 ...
file=export_file_name
```

➤ To execute a user mode export:

```
exp username/password owner=schema_name file=export_file_name
```

➤ To export only the data definitions without the data:

```
exp username/password owner=schema_name rows=n
file=export_file_name
```

➤ To export a user's objects but not the grants to those objects:

```
exp username/password owner=schema_name grants=n
file=export_file_name
```

# Things To Remember About Exports

If the database continues to be updated during exports, sequence numbers can be skipped. Also, because sequence numbers are normally cached, the exported value for the sequence is the next number after the last cached value. Sequence numbers that are in cache but not used are lost when the sequence is imported.

LONG datatypes require contiguous memory when exporting and importing. This can cause problems because an Oracle LONG can be 2GB in length. Export can export LONG datatypes, but system resources could restrict this function.

Direct path exports cannot be used with previous versions of Import. If you want to import into an Oracle7.2 or earlier release, use a conventional path export.

# Offline (Cold) Backups

An offline (cold) backup is a physical backup of the database after it has been shut down using the **SHUTDOWN NORMAL** command. A database that is shut down with the **IMMEDIATE** or the **ABORT** option should be restarted in restrict mode and then shut down with the **NORMAL** option. An operating system utility is used to perform the backup. For example, in Unix you could use cpio, tar, dd, fbackup, or some third-party utility. For a complete cold backup, the following files must be backed up:

➤ All datafiles

➤ All control files

➤ All online redo logfiles (optional)

➤ The init.ora file (can be re-created manually)

The location of all database files can be found in the **DBA_DATA_FILES**, **V$DATAFILE, V$LOGFILE,** and **V$CONTROLFILE** data dictionary views. These views can be queried even when the database is mounted and not open.

A cold backup of the database is an image copy of the database at a point in time. The database is in a consistent state and is restorable. This image copy can be used to move the database to another computer, provided that the same operating system is being used. If the database is in **ARCHIVELOG** mode, the cold backup would be the starting point of a point-in-time recovery. All necessary archive logfiles would be applied to the database once the database is restored from the cold backup. Cold backups are useful if your business requirements allow for a shut-down window to back up the database. If your database is very large or you perform processing 24 hours a day, cold backups are not an option, and you must use online (hot) backups.

# Online (Hot) Backups

When databases must remain operational 24 hours a day, 7 days a week, or have become so large that a cold backup would take too long, Oracle provides for online (hot) backups to be made while the database is open and being used. To perform a hot backup, the database must be in **ARCHIVELOG** mode. Unlike a cold backup, in which the whole database is usually backed up at the same time, tablespaces in a hot backup can be backed up on different schedules. The other main difference between a hot and a cold backup is that before a tablespace can be backed up, the database must be informed when a backup is starting and when it is complete. This is done by executing two commands in Server Manager:

```
SVRMGR>Alter tablespace tablespace_name begin backup;

.... Perform Operating System Backup of tablespace_name datafiles

SVRMGR>Alter tablespace tablespace_name end backup;
```

Whenever a hot backup is performed in addition to the datafiles, at the conclusion the redo logs should be forced to switch, and all archived redo logfiles and the control file should be backed up as well. The control file cannot be backed up with a backup utility. It must be backed up with the following Oracle command in Server Manager:

```
SVRMGR>Alter database backup controlfile to 'file_name';
```

# Hot Backup, Step By Step

This example assumes that the database is in **ARCHIVELOG** mode and is open. The following sequence is the correct way to perform a hot backup:

1. Find the oldest online log sequence number with the following command:

   ```
   SVRMGR>Archive log list
   ```

2. In Server Manager, put the tablespace you want to back up in **BEGIN BACKUP** mode as follows:

   ```
   SVRMGR>alter tablespace tablespace_name begin backup;
   ```

3. Back up all the database files associated with the tablespace using an operating system utility.

4. Set the tablespace in **END BACKUP** mode by using the following command:

   ```
   SVRMGR>alter tablespace tablespace_name end backup;
   ```

   Repeat Steps 2, 3, and 4 for each tablespace that you want to back up.

5. In Server Manager, execute the **ARCHIVE LOG LIST** command to get the current log sequence number. This is the last logfile that you will

keep as part of the hot backup. Next, force a log switch so that Oracle will archive the current redo logfile:

```
SVRMGR>Alter system switch logfile;
```

6. Back up all the archived logfiles, beginning with the log sequence in Step 1 and progressing to the log sequence in Step 5.

7. Back up the control file using the following command:

```
SVRMGR> alter database backup controlfile to 'file_name';
```

Remember that the control file should always be backed up after any structural change to the database is made.

## Hot Backup Scenario

The following is a typical backup scenario for a large database that must operate 24 hours a day, 7 days a week, and is too large to back up all at once. The business requirements do not require fault tolerance, but management wants recovery time to be minimized. The database is laid out in 12 tablespaces across 24 disk drives. All the tablespaces are between 6GB and 9GB. The heaviest time for batch programs is on Saturday, making that a bad day to perform backups. The following hot backup schedule would support these business requirements:

➤ Sunday: Perform hot backup on tablespaces 1 and 2

➤ Monday: Perform hot backup on tablespaces 3 and 4

➤ Tuesday: Perform hot backup on tablespaces 5 and 6

➤ Wednesday: Perform hot backup on tablespaces 7 and 8

➤ Thursday: Perform hot backup on tablespaces 9 and 10

➤ Friday: Perform hot backup on tablespaces 11 and 12

➤ Saturday: Perform no backups

With this schedule, you have a complete backup of the database once a week, although not all tablespaces are backed up at the same time. With this schedule, the worst case in a recovery would be a media failure on a drive that was going to be backed up that night. In this case, the datafiles on the failed drive would be restored to a new drive, and seven days' worth of archive logs applied to the tablespaces affected by the failure.

## Read-Only Tablespaces

Read-only tablespaces should be backed up immediately after making the tablespace read-only. As long as the tablespace is read-only, it does not need to be backed up again. When backing up a read-only tablespace, it is not necessary to use the **BEGIN BACKUP** and **END BACKUP** commands; in fact, they will cause an error if used on a read-only tablespace. Once the tablespace is made read-write again, backups of the tablespace should resume. Bringing read-only tablespaces online or offline have no effect on backup procedures because it does not make the tablespaces read-write again.

## Things To Remember About Hot Backups

Once a hot backup is started, the database cannot be shut down with the **NORMAL** or **IMMEDIATE** option. An error message will indicate that the database is in backup mode. If the database is aborted or crashes when it is restarted, the database will think that it needs to be recovered. If this happens from Server Manager, use the following command:

```
SVRMGR>alter database datafile 'file_name' end backup;
```

This will change the file status from backup mode to no backup mode.

# Supporting 24-Hour Operations

Hot backups with archive logging (described in the preceding section) will support 24-hour operations. It will also give you the option of recovering individual tablespaces while other parts of the database stay online. In addition to the hot backup scenario, Oracle has a fault-tolerant feature that allows you to have a standby database in case the primary database fails.

A standby database is a duplicate of the primary database and is intended to be used if a disaster occurs. A standby database is in a constant state of recovery. If the primary database is lost, the standby database can finish recovering the last archive logs from the primary site and be opened for use. While a database is in standby mode, it cannot be opened or used for querying. Once a standby database is opened, it becomes the primary database and cannot go back into standby mode. Follow the steps below to create a standby database:

1. Make an online or offline backup of the datafiles from the primary database.

2. Create the control file for your standby database by using the **ALTER DATABASE CREATE STANDBY CONTROLFILE AS** '*file_name*'

command. This creates a modified copy of the primary database's control file.

3. Use the **ALTER SYSTEM ARCHIVE LOG CURRENT** command to archive all the current online redo logfiles.

4. Use operating system copy utilities such as FTP to move the standby control file, archived logfiles, and backed-up datafiles to the computer on which the standby database will reside.

5. Start the standby Oracle instance with the **NOMOUNT** option.

6. Execute the **ALTER DATABASE MOUNT EXCLUSIVE STANDBY DATBASE** command.

7. Copy archived redo logfiles as they are created to the standby database archive directory.

8. Issue the **RECOVER FROM** '*location*' **STANDBY DATABASE** command.

The standby database is now in a constant state of recovery and will continue to apply the archive logfiles as they are copied from the primary site.

To activate a standby database, perform the following tasks:

1. Execute the **ALTER DATABASE ACTIVATE STANDBY DATABASE** command.

2. Shut down the standby database.

3. Start up the new primary database.

Once a standby database is activated, it is not recoverable until it is backed up because the logs are reset. Depending on how fast the recovery must be, this step can happen before or after the new primary database is started. Once a standby database is made, the primary database can no longer be reset to standby. A new standby database must be created.

# Things To Remember About Standby Databases

When datafiles are added to the primary database, they will automatically be created at the standby site when the logs are applied. The standby database will attempt to create the datafile in the location it was at on the primary site. If the standby database is unable to create the datafile, recovery on the standby database will stop.

If you rename a datafile on the primary site, the change will not be made on the standby database. If you want the names to stay in sync, perform the re-name operation at the standby site as well.

You can add or drop logfile groups at the primary site without affecting the standby database. Although not required, a good practice is to keep the log groups the same on the primary and standby databases. The standby database can become invalid if you use the **ALTER DATABASE CLEAR UNARCHIVED LOGFILE** command or open the primary database with the **RESETLOGS** option. Likewise, the standby database becomes invalid if you use the **CREATE CONTROLFILE** command to change the maximum number of redo log groups or members, change the maximum number of data-files, or change the maximum number of instances.

Unrecoverable operations do not propagate to the standby database because no redo information is generated. To get the changes from your primary database to the standby database, re-create the standby database from a new database backup or back up the affected tablespaces and current logs in the primary database, copy them to the standby database, and resume recovery.

# Practice Questions

## Question 1

> You are the DBA for an Internet company that takes orders 24
> hours a day. Which type of backup should you perform?
>
> ○ a. Offline backup in **ARCHIVELOG** mode
>
> ○ b. Online backup in **NOARCHIVELOG** mode
>
> ○ c. Offline backup in **NOARCHIVELOG** mode
>
> ○ d. Online backup in **ARCHIVELOG** mode

The correct answer is d. This is the only backup mode that supports continuous database operations. Answer a is incorrect because, by definition, an offline backup is performed with the database shut down and therefore is unavailable. Answer b is incorrect because you cannot perform an online backup with the database in **NOARCHIVELOG** mode. Answer c is incorrect because an offline backup means that the database is shut down.

## Question 2

> Which type of backup is performed with online backups?
>
> ○ a. Database-level backup
>
> ○ b. Tablespace-level backup
>
> ○ c. Table-level backup

The correct answer is b. Online backups are performed one tablespace at a time by putting the tablespace in begin backup mode; after the datafiles are backed up, the tablespace is put in no backup mode. Answer a is incorrect because this is the mode for offline backups, not online backups. Answer c is incorrect because a table-level backup is an export.

## Question 3

> When a read-only tablespace is put in read-write mode, what should you do?
>
> ○  a. Nothing; read-only tablespaces cannot be put in read-write mode
>
> ○  b. Perform a full offline database backup
>
> ○  c. Resume normal backup procedures for the tablespace

The correct answer is c. Once the tablespace is made read-write, it should be included in the backup scheme, just like any other tablespace is. Answer a is incorrect because tablespaces can be altered in and out of read-only mode virtually at will. Answer b is incorrect because, although this might be a good idea, it is not a requirement.

## Question 4

> You have altered one of your tablespaces to be read-only. What should you do immediately after this is done?
>
> ○  a. Edit the init.ora file
>
> ○  b. Perform a full offline database backup
>
> ○  c. Back up the datafiles belonging to the read-only tablespace
>
> ○  d. Put the database in **ARCHIVELOG** mode

The correct answer is c. Once a tablespace is altered to read-only, its datafiles should be backed up immediately. The **BEGIN BACKUP** and **END BACKUP** commands are not necessary, and this tablespace can then be taken out of the regular backup scheme because it will not change. Answer a is incorrect because nothing in the init.ora file pertains to read-only tablespaces. Answer b is incorrect because a full database backup is not required at this time, only a backup of the read-only tablespace datafiles. Answer d is incorrect because redo is not generated by read-only tablespace actions; therefore, whether the database is in **ARCHIVELOG** mode is irrelevant.

## Question 5

When you perform an export of your database, what type of backup is it?

- ○ a. Physical database backup
- ○ b. Logical database backup
- ○ c. It is not a backup

The correct answer is b. Export does not back up the physical structure of the database; it backs up the data and definitions of all objects only so that they can be re-created.

## Question 6

A media failure has occurred. Which backup method would allow you to recover only to the point of the last backup?

- ○ a. Operating system backup with archiving
- ○ b. Export of the disk that failed
- ○ c. Operating system backup without archiving

The correct answer is c. When the database is in **NOARCHIVELOG** mode, it can be recovered only to the point of the last backup. Answer a is incorrect because although it also will allow recovery to the last backup, it also will allow point-in-time recovery up to the point of failure. Answer b is incorrect because exports, although allowing recovery only to the time they were taken, are not disk-level backups but database-, user-, or table-level backups; there is no disk-level export.

## Question 7

Once a backup is taken of a read-only tablespace, how often should you back up the datafiles for this tablespace?

- ○ a. During online backups only
- ○ b. During offline backups only
- ○ c. Never
- ○ d. Whenever the tablespace in taken offline and then put back online

The answer is c. Read-only tablespaces do not change and therefore need not be backed up more than once.

# Question 8

If you perform an operating system backup while the database is in **NOARCHIVELOG** mode, which type of backup have you done?

○ a. Physical backup

○ b. Logical backup

The correct answer is a. An operating system backup backs up the physical structure of the database. Answer b is incorrect because the only logical backup is an export.

# Question 9

Your database has suffered a media failure. Which backup method will allow you to recover to the point of media failure?

○ a. Database exports

○ b. Operating system backup with archiving

○ c. Operating system backup without archiving

The correct answer is b. Point-in-time recovery can be done only with operating system backups and the database in **ARCHIVELOG** mode. Both database exports and operating system backups without archiving allow recovery only to the time of backup.

# Question 10

Which backup method requires the tablespaces to be online and the database to be in **ARCHIVELOG** mode?

○ a. Full online database backup

○ b. Datafile backup

○ c. Database export

○ d. Incremental backup

The correct answer is a. A full online backup requires that the database and all tablespaces be online. Answer b is incorrect because datafile backups can be taken in backup mode with the tablespace datafiles online or in normal mode with the database shut down. Answer c is incorrect because a table-level export requires only that table's datafile be online, and a user export requires that user's tablespaces be online. Answer d is incorrect because, until Oracle8, there is no incremental backup, only incremental export.

## Question 11

> For which type of backup should you shut down the database?
>
> ○  a. Datafile backup
>
> ○  b. Read-only tablespace backup
>
> ○  c. Full offline database backup
>
> ○  d. Full online database backup
>
> ○  e. Full database export
>
> ○  f. Physical backup

The correct answer is c. The database should be shut down with the normal option. Answer a is incorrect because a datafile backup can be taken with the database either shut down or online. Answer b is incorrect because a read-only tablespace backup is done with the tablespace either online or offline with the database either shut down or operating. Answer d is incorrect because it specifies an online backup. Answer e is incorrect because an export cannot be performed on a shutdown database. Answer f is incorrect because both hot (online) and cold (shutdown) backups are physical backups.

# Need To Know More?

 Backup and recovery are covered in the *Oracle Server Concepts Book* and the *Server Administrator's Guide*.

 Loney, Kevin: *DBA Handbook, 7.3 Edition*. Oracle Press, 1996. ISBN 0-07882-289-0.

 Velpuri, Rama: *Oracle Backup and Recovery Handbook*. Oracle Press, 1995. ISBN 0-07882-106-1.

# Recovery
# Scenarios

· · · · · · · · · · · · · · · · · · · · · · · · · · · · · · · · · · · · · · · ·

### Terms you'll need to understand:

√  Statement failure

√  Process failure

√  Instance failure

√  User or application error

√  Media or disk failure

√  Complete media recovery

√  Incomplete media recovery

√  Parallel recovery

### Techniques you'll need to master:

√  Performing recovery without archive logging

√  Performing closed database recovery

√  Performing open database offline tablespace recovery

√  Performing open database offline tablespace datafile
   recovery

√  Performing cancel-based recovery

√  Performing time-based recovery

√  Performing change-based recovery

√  Performing distributed recovery

All database systems are subject to failure. As the database administrator (DBA), you must recover the database as quickly as possible and with as little effect on users as possible.

This chapter explains how to perform both complete and incomplete recoveries and how archiving affects your recovery choices. The emphasis is on media recovery because media recovery requires action from the DBA and is the most complicated form of recovery. This chapter also provides recovery scenarios and explains how questions constructed on the basis of those scenarios can be answered.

# Failure Modes

Recovery methods depend on the type of failure that occurs and the parts of the database that are affected. If no files are lost or damaged, recovery may be automatic and just require restarting an instance. If data has been lost, recovery may require additional steps. The following section describes the types of failure that can occur and how the database recovers them.

## Statement Failure

Statement failure occurs when a SQL statement fails. This can be caused by incorrect syntax or incompatible middleware between the client and the server database. Oracle handles statement failures automatically and returns control to the user with an error message. There is no need for recovery when a statement fails.

## Process Failure

Process failure occurs when a user process that is connected to Oracle ends abnormally. This can occur because of a network failure or a client-side power failure or simply because the user killed the client process on his or her PC. Process failure is recovered automatically by Oracle's PMON process. PMON wakes up periodically, cleans up the cache, and frees resources that a failed user process was using.

## Instance Failure

Instance failure occurs when an Oracle instance fails. This can be caused by power outages and operating system crashes or when one or more of the Oracle processes fail, causing the instance to stop. When an instance fails, buffers in the system global area (SGA) are not written to disk. Oracle recovers from instance failure automatically when the instance is restarted. The SMON process is responsible for instance recovery at startup. SMON uses the online redo logfiles for instance recovery. In a parallel server environment, the SMON of one instance also can recover other instances that have failed.

## User Or Application Error

User or application error occurs when a user makes a mistake. This can occur when a user deletes data from a table in error or drops a table that is still needed. To recover from this type of failure, Oracle provides an exact point-in-time recovery, which can recover the database to the point in time just before the error occurred.

## Media Or Disk Failure

Media failure occurs when files needed by the database can no longer be accessed. This normally occurs when a disk drive fails. Oracle provides several ways to recover from media failure, depending on the situation and business needs. Which backup strategy is chosen will determine the recovery options available for media recovery.

# The RECOVER Command

The **RECOVER** command can be issued in two ways: in Server Manager or as part of the **ALTER DATABASE** command. The **RECOVER** command in Server Manager is easier to use and is the preferred method for starting a recovery.

Here are the parameters used in the **RECOVER** clause of an **ALTER DATABASE** command:

➤ AUTOMATIC  Allows Oracle to generate the names of the redo logfiles needed during media recovery. If you do not use this option, you must use the **LOGFILE** clause to specify the names of the redo logfiles.

➤ CANCEL  Stops cancel-based recovery.

➤ CONTINUE  Restarts multi-instance recovery after it has been interrupted.

➤ DATABASE  Starts recovery of the entire database. This is the default recovery option.

➤ DATAFILE  Starts a datafile recovery of one or more datafiles. The datafiles being recovered must be offline.

➤ FROM  Must be used if the archived redo logfiles that are needed for recovery were not restored to the location specified by the

**LOG_ARCHIVE_DEST** initialization parameter. The full pathname where the logfiles are located must be given.

➤ **LOGFILE** Applies an archive logfile that is requested for recovery.

➤ **PARALLEL** Sets the degree of parallelism used in recovery.

➤ **STANDBY** Starts recovery of a standby database after the control file and archive logfiles have been copied from the primary database.

➤ **TABLESPACE** Starts a tablespace recovery of one or more tablespaces. The tablespaces being recovered must be offline.

➤ **UNTIL CANCEL** Starts a cancel-based recovery. To stop recovery, you must issue the **ALTER DATABASE RECOVER** command.

➤ **UNTIL CHANGE** Starts a change-based recovery. Recovery will continue until the database reaches a specified System Change Number (SCN). Note that the SCN should be one number higher than the transaction you want to recover. For example, if the transaction you want to recover has an SCN of 22, you set the **UNTIL CHANGE** to 23.

➤ **UNTIL TIME** Starts a time-based recovery. Recovery will continue until the time specified by the date, which is specified in the '*YYYY-MM-DD:HH24:MI:SS*' format.

➤ **USING BACKUP CONTROLFILE** Causes recovery to be done using a backup control file; the current control file is ignored.

The following are examples of the **ALTER DATABASE RECOVER** command.

➤ To recover the entire database and automatically generate the archive log names needed for recovery, use the following:

```
SVRMGR>ALTER DATABASE RECOVER AUTOMATIC DATABASE;
```

➤ To recover a tablespace, use the following:

```
SVRMGR>ALTER DATABASE RECOVER TABLESPACE tools;
```

Here are the parameters used in the **RECOVER** command of Server Manager:

➤ **CONTROL FILE** Specifies a control file other than the current control file.

➤ **DATABASE** Starts recovery of the entire database.

➤ **DATAFILE**  Starts a datafile recovery of one or more datafiles. These datafiles must be offline.

➤ **NOPARALLEL**  Starts a serial recovery.

➤ **PARALLEL**  Sets the degree of parallelism used in recovery. **PARALLEL DEGREE DEFAULT** will set the number of recovery processes to twice the number of datafiles being recovered. **INSTANCES** is used only for Oracle parallel server recovery. **INSTANCES** sets the number of instances to use in recovery.

➤ **TABLESPACE**  Starts a tablespace recovery of one or more tablespaces. These tablespaces must be offline.

➤ **UNTIL CANCEL**  Starts a cancel-based recovery. To stop recovery, enter "CANCEL" instead of the requested archive logfile.

➤ **UNTIL CHANGE**  Starts a change-based recovery. Recovery will continue until the database reaches a specified SCN. Note that the SCN should be one number higher than the transaction you want to recover. For example, if the transaction you want to recover has an SCN of 22, set the **UNTIL CHANGE** to 23.

➤ **UNTIL TIME**  Starts a time-based recovery. Recovery will continue until the time specified by the date, which is specified in the '*YYYY-MM-DD:HH24:MI:SS*' format.

➤ **USING BACKUP**  Causes recovery to be done using a backup control file; the current control file is ignored.

Here are some examples of the **RECOVER** command in Server Manager:

➤ The recover the entire database, perform the following. Archive log files are applied automatically if **AUTORECOVERY** is set to **ON** in Server Manager.

```
SVRMGR>RECOVER DATABASE
```

➤ To recover a tablespace, use the following:

```
SVRMGR>RECOVER TABLESPACE tools
```

➤ To recover a datafile, use the following:

```
SVRMGR>RECOVER DATAFILE 'file_name'
```

# Recovery Without Archive Logging

If you are operating your database in **NOARCHIVELOG** mode, your recovery options are very limited. In the case of a media failure in which one or more of the database files are lost or damaged, your only option is to restore the last full backup of the database. All changes made since that backup will need to be redone manually. If you are also taking regular exports of the database, an import could be used to recover the database if it is more recent than the last backup. To restore a full backup, follow these steps:

1. Make sure that the database is shut down.

2. You now have two options. If the media failure has been fixed and the backup files can be put back to their original locations, proceed to restore all the backup files so that the database is in a consistent state. If the files cannot be restored to their original locations, follow these steps:

   ➤ If the control file was damaged, edit the init<SID>.org or config <SID>.ora file to change the location of the control file.

   ➤ Start the instance and mount the database.

   ➤ If datafiles were damaged, rename the datafiles. If the logfiles were damaged or lost, use the **ALTER DATABASE** command with the **RENAME FILE** clause to rename the database's online redo logfiles.

3. Use the **ALTER DATABASE OPEN RESETLOGS** command.

The database is now recovered to the point of the full backup. The logfile sequence is reset to 1, and all changes made since the time of the backup are lost.

# Recovery With Archive Logging

If you are operating in **ARCHIVELOG** mode, you have many options for recovery, depending of the type of failure. The two types of media recovery are complete media recovery and incomplete media recovery. This section explains how to perform both types of recovery and the circumstances under which to do so.

## Complete Media Recovery

A complete media recovery will recover all lost changes to the database. Complete media recovery can be accomplished only if all online and archived redo logfiles are available. The three types of complete media recovery are closed database recovery, open database offline tablespace recovery, and open database offline tablespace datafile recovery.

## Closed Database Recovery

Follow these steps to execute a closed database recovery:

1. Make sure that the database is shut down.

2. Correct the media problem if possible.

3. Restore the most recent backup of only those datafiles that were damaged by the media failure. You need not restore any undamaged datafiles or any online redo logfiles. If the hardware problem has been repaired and damaged datafiles can be restored to their original locations, do so. If the hardware problem still exists, restore the datafiles to another location. This location will need to be recorded in the control file later in this procedure.

4. Start Server Manager and connect to Oracle as SYS or INTERNAL.

5. Start the instance and mount it, but do not open the database.

6. If you restored lost files to alternate locations in Step 3, the new location of these files must be recorded in the control file. Follow these three steps to relocate the datafile:

   ➤ Make sure that the tablespace that contains the datafiles is offline.

   ➤ Make sure that the new, fully specified file names are different from the old file names.

   ➤ Use the **ALTER TABLESPACE** SQL command with the **RENAME DATAFILE** option to change the file names within the database.

7. Query the **V$DATAFILE** view and make sure that all the datafiles you want to recover are online. If a datafile is offline, issue the **ALTER DATABASE** command with the **DATAFILE ONLINE** option. For example:

```
ALTER DATABASE DATAFILE 'users01.dbf' ONLINE;
```

8. To start closed database recovery, use the appropriate **RECOVER** command in Server Manager.

Oracle will now start the roll forward by applying the archived redo logfiles and the online redo logfile. If **AUTORECOVERY** is set to **ON** in Server Manager, applying the logfiles is automatic. If it is not set to **ON**, you will be prompted for each logfile.

When recovery is complete, open the database with the **ALTER DATABASE OPEN** command.

## Open Database Offline Tablespace Recovery

If your system suffers a media failure but the database stays up, you can perform an open database recovery and recover only the tablespaces that are damaged. Users can continue to access the online tablespaces and datafiles that were not damaged by the failure. Oracle will take damaged datafiles offline automatically. Follow these steps to execute an open database recovery with offline tablespaces:

1. The database should be started and open.

2. Take all tablespaces containing damaged datafiles offline. You can query the **V$DATAFILE** view to see which datafiles are offline. Use the **ALTER TABLESPACE** *tablespace_name* **OFFLINE** command.

3. Correct the problem that caused the media failure. If the problem cannot be corrected in a reasonable amount of time, your other option is to restore the damaged files to another location. Follow these three steps to relocate the datafile:

   ➤ Make sure that the tablespace that contains the datafiles is offline.

   ➤ Make sure that the new, fully specified file names are different from the old file names.

   ➤ Use the **ALTER DATABASE** SQL command with the **RENAME FILE** option to change the file names within the database.

   If the media problem can be corrected, restore the most recent backup files of only the datafiles damaged by the media failure. Remember that the database is open. Do not try to restore undamaged datafiles, logfiles, or control files.

4. Use the **RECOVER TABLESPACE** command in Server Manager to start offline tablespace recovery of all damaged datafiles in one or more offline tablespaces.

   Oracle will now start the roll forward by applying the archived redo logfiles and the online redo logfile. If **AUTORECOVERY** is set to **ON** in Server Manager, applying the logfiles is automatic. If it is not set to **ON**, you will be prompted for each logfile.

5. The damaged tablespaces of the open database are now recovered up to the point of failure. You can bring the offline tablespaces online using the **ALTER TABLESPACE** command with the **ONLINE** option.

## Open Database Offline Tablespace Datafile Recovery

If your system suffers a media failure but the database stays up, you can perform an open database recovery and recover only the datafiles that are damaged. Users can continue to access the online tablespaces and datafiles that were not damaged by the failure. Oracle will automatically take damaged datafiles offline. Follow these steps to execute an open database recovery with offline tablespaces:

1. The database should be started and open.

2. Take all tablespaces containing damaged datafiles offline. You can query the **V$DATAFILE** view to see which datafiles are offline. Use the **ALTER TABLESPACE** *tablespace_name* **OFFLINE** command.

3. Correct the problem that caused the media failure. If the problem cannot be corrected in a reasonable amount of time, your other option is to restore the damaged files to another location. Follow these three steps to relocate the datafile:

   ➤ Make sure that the tablespace that contains the datafiles is offline.

   ➤ Make sure that the new, fully specified file names are different from the old file names.

   ➤ Use the **ALTER DATABASE** SQL command with the **RENAME FILE** option to change the file names within the database.

   If the media problem can be corrected, restore the most recent backup files of only the datafiles damaged by the media failure. Remember that the database is open. Do not try to restore undamaged datafiles, logfiles, or control files.

4. Use the **RECOVER DATAFILE** command in Server Manager to start offline datafile recovery of all damaged datafiles in one or more offline tablespaces.

   Oracle will now start the roll forward by applying the archived redo logfiles and the online redo logfile. If **AUTORECOVERY** is set to **ON** in Server Manager, applying the logfiles is automatic. If it is not set to **ON**, you will be prompted for each logfile.

5. The damaged datafiles of the open database are now recovered up to the point of failure. You can bring the offline tablespaces online using the **ALTER TABLESPACE** command with the **ONLINE** option.

# Incomplete Media Recovery

In some situations, complete media recovery might not be possible or desired. This can happen because all the files needed for a complete recovery are not available (for example, all online redo logfiles are lost and you were not duplexing your log groups). You might want to perform an incomplete recovery if a user drops a table and you want to recover to the point before the table was dropped.

The three types of incomplete media recovery are cancel based, time based, and change based.

## Cancel-Based Recovery

Cancel-based recovery allows the DBA to cancel recovery at a desired point. This situation is most likely to occur when archive logfiles or redo logfiles that are needed for recovery are lost or damaged and cannot be restored. In this situation, you would apply all logs until you reached the missing files and then cancel the recovery. Follow these steps to execute a cancel-based recovery:

1. If the database is still open, shut down the database using the **SHUTDOWN** command with the **ABORT** option.

2. Make a full backup of the database, including all datafiles, a control file, and the parameter files in case an error is made during the recovery.

3. Correct the problem that caused the media failure. If the problem cannot be corrected, the datafiles must be restored to an alternate location. If this is the case, the **ALTER TABLESPACE RENAME DATAFILE** command must be used to change the location of the datafile in the control file.

4. If the current control files do not match the physical structure of the database at the time you want to recover to, restore a backup of the control file that matches the database's physical file structure at the point in time you want to recover to. Replace all current control files of the database with the one you want to use for recovery. If you do not have a backup copy of the control file, you can create a new one.

5. Restore backups of all datafiles. Make sure that the backups were taken before the point in time you want to recover to. Any datafiles added after the point in time you are recovering to should not be restored. They will not be used in the recovery and will need to be re-created after recovery is complete. Any data in the datafiles created after the point of recovery will be lost.

Make sure that read-only tablespaces are offline before you start recovery so that recovery does not try to update the datafile headers.

6. Start Server Manager and connect to Oracle as SYS or INTERNAL.

7. Start the instance and mount the database using the **STARTUP** command with the **MOUNT** option.

8. If you restored files to an alternate location, change the location now in the control file by using the **ALTER TABLESPACE RENAME DATAFILE** command.

9. Use the **RECOVER DATABASE UNTIL CANCEL** statement to begin cancel-based recovery. If a backup of the control file is being used, make sure to specify the **USING BACKUP** parameter.

   Oracle will now start the roll forward by applying the archived redo logfiles and the online redo logfile. Oracle will prompt you for each logfile. If you used a backup control file, you must enter the names of the online redo logfiles.

10. Continue applying redo logfiles until the most recent, undamaged logfile has been applied.

    Enter "CANCEL" instead of the logfile name to cancel the recovery. Oracle will respond with a message that recovery was successful.

11. Use the **ALTER DATABASE OPEN** command with the **RESETLOGS** or **NORESETLOGS** option. You should use the **RESETLOGS** option if you used a backup of the control file in recovery or if the recovery was incomplete. Use the **NORESETLOGS** option if the recovery was complete. If you are using a standby database and must reset the logs, the standby database will need to be re-created.

    You can check the ALERT file to see whether your incomplete recovery was actually a complete recovery. If the recovery was a complete recovery, the message in the ALERT file is as follows:

```
RESETLOGS after complete recovery through change scn
```

If the recovery was incomplete, the following message is recorded:

```
RESETLOGS after incomplete recovery UNTIL CHANGE scn
```

12. After opening the database using the **RESETLOGS** option, perform a normal shutdown and a full database backup. If you do not do this, any changes made after the recovery and before the next full backup are unrecoverable. If you did not reset the logs, the database is still recoverable.

## Time-Based Recovery

Like cancel-based recovery, time-based recovery allows the DBA to recover to a desired point. This situation is most likely to occur when archive logfiles or redo logfiles that are needed for recovery are lost or damaged and cannot be restored. In this situation, you would apply all logs until a point in time specified by the **UNTIL TIME** clause of the **RECOVER** command. Follow these steps to execute a time-based recovery:

1. If the database is still open, shut down the database using the **SHUTDOWN** command with the **ABORT** option.

2. Make a full backup of the database, including all datafiles, a control file, and the parameter files in case an error is made during the recovery.

3. Correct the problem that caused the media failure. If the problem cannot be corrected, the datafiles must be restored to an alternate location. If this is the case, you must use the **ALTER TABLESPACE RENAME DATAFILE** command to change the location of the datafile in the control file.

4. If the current control files do not match the physical structure of the database at the time you want to recover to, restore a backup of the control file that matches the database's physical file structure at the point in time you want to recover to. Replace all current control files of the database with the one you want to use for recovery. If you do not have a backup copy of the control file, you can create a new one.

5. Restore backups of all datafiles. Make sure that the backups were taken before the point in time you want to recover to. Any datafiles added after the point in time you are recovering to should not be restored. They will not be used in the recovery and will need to be re-created after recovery is complete. Any data in the datafiles created after the point of recovery will be lost.

   Make sure that read-only tablespaces are offline before you start recovery so that recovery does not try to update the datafile headers.

6. Start Server Manager and connect to Oracle as SYS or INTERNAL.

7. Start the instance and mount the database using the **STARTUP** command with the **MOUNT** option.

8. If you restored files to an alternate location, change the location now in the control file by using the **ALTER TABLESPACE RENAME DATAFILE** command.

9. Make sure that all the datafiles in the database are online. You can check the status of datafiles by querying the **V$DATAFILE** view. If any datafiles are offline, use the **ALTER DATABASE** command with the **DATAFILE ONLINE** option.

10. Use the **RECOVER DATABASE UNTIL TIME 'YYYY-MM-DD:HH24:MI:SS'** command to start time-based recovery.

Oracle will now start the roll forward by applying the archived redo logfiles and the online redo logfile. If **AUTORECOVERY** is set to **ON** in Server Manager, applying the logfiles is automatic. If it is not set to **ON**, you will be prompted for each logfile. If you used a backup control file, you must enter the names of the online redo logfiles.

11. Oracle will automatically stop recovery when the time specified in the **RECOVER** command has been reached. Oracle will respond with a message that recovery was successful.

12. Use the **ALTER DATABASE OPEN** command with the **RESETLOGS** or **NORESETLOGS** option. You should use the **RESETLOGS** option if you used a backup of the control file in recovery or if the recovery was incomplete. Use the **NORESETLOGS** option if the recovery was complete. If you are using a standby database and must reset the logs, the standby database will need to be re-created.

You can check the alert file to see whether your incomplete recovery was actually a complete recovery. If the recovery was a complete recovery, the message in the alert file is as follows:

```
RESETLOGS after complete recovery through change scn
```

If the recovery was incomplete, the following message is recorded:

```
RESETLOGS after incomplete recovery UNTIL CHANGE scn
```

13. After opening the database using the **RESETLOGS** option, perform a normal shutdown and a full database backup. If you do not do this, any changes made after the recovery and before the next full backup are unrecoverable. If you did not reset the logs, the database is still recoverable.

## Change-Based Recovery

Like cancel-based recovery, change-based recovery allows the DBA to recover to a desired point. This situation is most likely to occur when archive logfiles or redo logfiles that are needed for recovery are lost or damaged and cannot be restored. In this situation, you would apply all logs until a point in time specified by the **UNTIL CHANGE** clause of the **RECOVER** command. The **UNTIL CHANGE** clause uses the SCN as its parameter. To determine the SCN needed for recovery, you can query the **V$LOG_HISTORY** view. The following query is an example:

```
Select * from v$log_history;

THREAD#  SEQUENCE#       TIME      LOW_CHANGE# HIGH_CHANGE#
-------- --------------  --------- ----------- ------------
ARCHIVE_NAME
------------------------------------------------------------

    1  47213 06/26/98  12:47:55    116098950    116098954
/u01/app/oracle/admin/HIU1/arch/log_47213.arc

    1  47212 06/26/98  12:47:33    116098947    116098949
/u01/app/oracle/admin/HIU1/arch/log_47212.arc
```

The **LOW_CHANGE#** column represents the SCN at the beginning of the logfile, and the **HIGH_CHANGE#** represents the SCN at the end of the logfile.

Follow these steps to execute a time-based recovery:

1. If the database is still open, shut down the database using the **SHUTDOWN** command with the **ABORT** option.

2. Make a full backup of the database, including all datafiles, a control file, and the parameter files in case an error is made during the recovery.

3. Correct the problem that caused the media failure. If the problem cannot be corrected, the datafiles must be restored to an alternate location. If this is the case, the **ALTER TABLESPACE RENAME DATAFILE** command must be used to change the location of the datafile in the control file.

4. If the current control files do not match the physical structure of the database at the time you want to recover to, restore a backup of the control file that matches the database's physical file structure at the point in time you want to recover to. Replace all current control files of the

database with the one you want to use for recovery. If you do not have a backup copy of the control file, you can create a new one.

5. Restore backups of all datafiles. Make sure that the backups were taken before the point in time you want to recover to. Any datafiles added after the point in time you are recovering to should not be restored. They will not be used in the recovery and will need to be re-created after recovery is complete. Any data in the datafiles created after the point of recovery will be lost.

   Make sure that read-only tablespaces are offline before you start recovery so that recovery does not try to update the datafile headers.

6. Start Server Manager and connect to Oracle as SYS or INTERNAL.

7. Start the instance and mount the database using the **STARTUP** command with the **MOUNT** option.

8. If you restored files to an alternate location, change the location now in the control file by using the **ALTER TABLESPACE RENAME DATAFILE** command.

9. Make sure that all the datafiles in the database are online. You can check the status of datafiles by querying the **V$DATAFILE** view. If any datafiles are offline, use the **ALTER DATABASE** command with the **DATAFILE ONLINE** option.

10. Use the **RECOVER DATABASE UNTIL CHANGE** *SCN* command to start time-based recovery. The SCN should be used without quotation marks.

    Oracle will now start the roll forward by applying the archived redo logfiles and the online redo logfile. If **AUTORECOVERY** is set to **ON** in Server Manager, applying the logfiles is automatic. If it is not set to **ON**, you will be prompted for each logfile. If you used a backup control file, you must enter the names of the online redo logfiles.

11. Oracle will automatically stop recovery when the SCN specified in the **RECOVER** command has been reached. Oracle will respond with a message that recovery was successful.

12. Use the **ALTER DATABASE OPEN** command with the **RESETLOGS** or **NORESETLOGS** option. You should use the **RESETLOGS** option if you used a backup of the control file in recovery or if the recovery was incomplete. Use the **NORESETLOGS** option if the recovery was complete. If you are using a standby database and must reset the logs, the standby database will need to be re-created.

You can check the ALERT file to see whether your incomplete recovery was actually a complete recovery. If the recovery was a complete recovery, the message in the ALERT file is as follows:

```
RESETLOGS after complete recovery through change scn
```

If the recovery was incomplete, the following message is recorded:

```
RESETLOGS after incomplete recovery UNTIL CHANGE scn
```

13. After opening the database using the **RESETLOGS** option, perform a normal shutdown and a full database backup. If you do not do this, any changes made after the recovery and before the next full backup are unrecoverable. If you did not reset the logs, the database is still recoverable.

# Parallel Recovery

Parallel recovery can be accomplished in two ways. The first way is to use several Server Manager sessions to perform the recovery. For example, if you have three tablespaces to recover, you can recover each tablespace in a different session simultaneously. Although this might be better than performing a single process recovery, all processes must still read all the logfiles used in recovery. The second way is to use the **PARALLEL** option of the **RECOVER** command. This works just like Oracle's parallel query option. From one Server Manager process, Oracle reads the redo logfile and dispatches redo information to multiple recovery processes that will then apply the changes to the datafiles. The number of recovery processes is determined by the degree specified in the **RECOVER** command.

As with parallel query, parallel recovery benefits most when the datafiles being recovered are on many different disks. Because recovery is very disk-intensive, no more than two recovery processes per disk should be used.

# Distributed Recovery

If a complete recovery is performed on one database of a distributed system, no other action is required on any other databases. If an incomplete recovery is performed on one database of a distributed system, a coordinated time-based and change-based recovery should be performed on all databases that have dependencies to the database that needed recovery.

Coordinating SCNs among the nodes of a distributed system allows global distributed read consistency at both the statement and the transaction level. If necessary, global distributed time-based recovery can also be completed by following these steps:

1. Use time-based recovery on the database that had the failure.

2. After recovering the database, open it using the **RESETLOGS** option. Look in the ALERT file for the RESETLOGS message.

   If the message is "RESETLOGS after complete recovery through change *scn*," you have performed a complete recovery. Do not recover any of the other databases.

   If the reset message is "RESETLOGS after incomplete recovery UNTIL CHANGE *scn*," you have performed an incomplete recovery. Record the SCN from the message.

3. Recover all other databases in the distributed database system using change-based recovery and specifying the SCN from Step 2.

# Things To Remember About Recovery

You can use the **V$RECOVER_FILE** view to determine which file to recover and then the **V$DATAFILE** view to find the name associated with the file number. You can use the following query:

```
SELECT file#, online, error FROM v$recover_file;

FILE#  ONLINE       ERROR
- - - - - - - - - - - - - - - - - - - - - - - - - - - - - - - - - - - - - - - -
0034   OFFLINE      OFFLINE NORMAL
0035   ONLINE       FILE NOT FOUND
0036   ONLINE
```

If a backup control file is being used, the **V$RECOVER** view will not contain the correct information. If media failure occurs to any datafile of the **SYSTEM** tablespace, the database will shut down. The last backup of the damaged system datafiles must be restored before recovery can continue.

If no backup of a datafile is available, you can use the **ALTER DATABASE CREATE DATAFILE** *old datafile name* **AS** *new datafile name*. This will create an empty file that matches the one that is damaged. Now you can perform media recovery. Oracle will request all logfiles since the new empty tablespace was created. This method of recovery cannot be used on the first file of the **SYSTEM** tablespace.

# Practice Questions

## Question 1

> Your database has grown very large, and your last media recovery required an unacceptable amount of time. What can you do to reduce the recovery time?
>
> ○ a. Recover more often
>
> ○ b. Recover using the parallel capability
>
> ○ c. Nothing; it takes a long time to recover large databases

The correct answer is b. Parallel recovery can reduce the amount of time it takes to recover a database. Answer a is incorrect because you would not recover unless it was necessary. Answer c is incorrect because there are ways to speed up the recovery of large databases.

## Question 2

> Which statement is true if you are running the database in **NOARCHIVELOG** mode?
>
> ○ a. Each datafile should be backed up on its own schedule
>
> ○ b. You must perform a complete recovery
>
> ○ c. You must back up the entire set of database datafiles, and control files during each backup
>
> ○ d. Export cannot be used

The correct answer is c. A complete backup must be performed every time when the database is in **NOARCHIVELOG** mode. Answer a can only be done in **ARCHIVELOG** mode. Complete recovery can be done with the database in **ARCHIVELOG** mode as well as **NOARCHIVELOG** mode. Export is a logical backup and is not affected by running the database in **NOARCHIVELOG** mode.

# Question 3

> You would like to be able to restore a tablespace while the database is open and in use. In which mode must the database be running?
>
> ○ a. Mount exclusive mode
> ○ b. **NOARCHIVELOG** mode
> ○ c. Restricted mode
> ○ d. **ARCHIVELOG** mode

The correct answer is d. The database must be in **ARCHIVELOG** mode to perform an online recovery. Answers a and c will not allow users to access the system during recovery. Answer b would require the database to be shutdown and restored from operating system backups.

# Question 4

> Which part of the database is accessible to users while a full database recovery is being performed?
>
> ○ a. Undamaged datafiles
> ○ b. Tables not being recovered
> ○ c. None; the database is not accessible during this kind of recovery
> ○ d. Tablespaces that were not damaged

The correct answer is c. During a full database recovery, the entire database is being recovered and is unavailable for use.

# Question 5

> Which recovery is an example of a complete recovery?
>
> ○ a. Control file recovery
> ○ b. Change-based recovery
> ○ c. Cancel-based recovery
> ○ d. Time-based recovery
> ○ e. Datafile recovery

The correct answer is e. Although it is possible for an incomplete recovery to end up as a complete recovery, only the datafile recovery is listed as a complete recovery option.

## Question 6

> Some, but not all, of the datafiles of the **DATA** tablespace have been damaged, and the database is in **ARCHIVELOG** mode. Which type of recovery should you use?
>
> ○ a. Database recovery
>
> ○ b. Export recovery
>
> ○ c. Datafile recovery
>
> ○ d. Tablespace recovery

The correct answer is c. Datafile recovery would be faster than recovering the entire tablespace.

## Question 7

> How many parallel recovery processes are considered sufficient to perform parallel recovery?
>
> ○ a. Five per disk drive
>
> ○ b. Four per datafile
>
> ○ c. Two per tablespace
>
> ○ d. One or two per disk drive

The correct answer is d. Recovery is a very disk-intensive operation. In most cases, adding more than two processes per drive will not improve performance.

## Question 8

> Which action must you take before recovering a tablespace?
>
> ○ a. Take the tablespace offline
>
> ○ b. Shut down the database
>
> ○ c. Delete all datafiles belonging to the tablespace
>
> ○ d. Take all tablespaces offline

The correct answer is a. A tablespace must be offline for recovery. The key word in this question is "must." The other answers may need to be done depending on the circumstances, but only answer a must be done to recover a tablespace.

## Question 9

> What is a disadvantage of running a database in **NOARCHIVELOG** mode?
>
> ○  a. Recovery is simple
>
> ○  b. Lost data must be reentered manually
>
> ○  c. Recovery time is fast

The correct answer is b. A database running in **NOARCHVIELOG** mode cannot perform a point-in-time recovery.

## Question 10

> In which state must the database be when issuing the following command?
>
> ALTER DATABASE RENAME FILE ...
>
> ○  a. Open
>
> ○  b. Mount
>
> ○  c. Mount exclusive
>
> ○  d. Restricted

The correct answer is b. The database must be started with the **MOUNT** option. The key word is "must." The database could be mounted exclusive, but it is not mandatory.

## Question 11

Your database requires recovery, and you need to shut down the
database. If the **SHUTDOWN** command does not work, what will
you most likely need to do?

- ○ a. **SHUTDOWN IMMEDIATE**
- ○ b. **SHUTDOWN NORMAL**
- ○ c. **SHUTDOWN ABORT**
- ○ d. **SHUTDOWN FORCE**

The correct answer is c. When a database requires recovery and a **SHUT-DOWN NORMAL** will not shut down the database, a **SHUTDOWN ABORT** will most likely be required. A **SHUTDOWN IMMEDIATE** may work, but because recovery is required, a **SHUTDOWN ABORT** is the more likely course of action.

## Question 12

What is the first step you should take to recover a damaged
datafile?

- ○ a. Restore the most recent backup of the file
- ○ b. Take the datafile offline
- ○ c. Dismount the database

The correct answer is b. Answer a is done after the datafile is taken offline. Answer c would only be done if the database must be shut down to recover.

## Question 13

You have a disk failure and must restore a datafile to a new location. Which command must be issued to do this?

- O  a. **ALTER TABLESPACE MOVE DATAFILE**
- O  b. **ALTER DATABASE BACKUP CONTROLFILE TO TRACE**
- O  c. **ALTER DATABASE RENAME FILE**
- O  d. **ALTER DATAFILE MOVE**

The correct answer is c. The file must be renamed and recorded in the control file using the **ALTER DATABASE RENAME FILE** command. This does not move the file at the operating system level. You must still use an operating system utility to restore the file to the new location.

# Need To Know More?

 Backup and recovery are covered in the *Oracle Server Concepts Book* and the *Server Administrator's Guide*.

 Loney, Kevin: *DBA Handbook, 7.3 Edition*. Oracle Press, 1996. ISBN 0-07882-289-0.

 Velpuri, Rama: *Oracle Backup and Recovery Handbook*. Oracle Press, 1995. ISBN 0-07882-106-1.

# Troubleshooting Backups

**14**

## Terms you'll need to understand:

√  Alert log

√  BACKGROUND_DUMP_DEST

√  V$RECOVERY_STATUS

√  DBVERIFY

√  LOG_BLOCK_CHECKSUM

√  V$RECOVERY_FILE_STATUS

## Techniques you'll need to master:

√  Querying the status of recovery

√  Verifying the integrity of datafiles

√  Finding errors in logfiles

The Oracle database automates most of the backup and recovery procedures, but it is important to understand where to look if you experience problems with the recovery process.

# Alert Log File

The alert log (alert_<SID>.log) contains informational, warning, and error messages related to Oracle's core processes and the system global area (SGA). Additionally, the alert log contains a history of any physical changes that have been made to the database, such as the addition or a change in status of datafiles, redo logs, or rollback segments. Information concerning checkpoints can also be recorded in the alert log by using optional initialization parameters. The initialization parameter **BACKGROUND_DUMP_DEST** controls where the alert log as well as where background process trace files are put.

The alert log is the only location where errors are reported. These errors include a corrupted member of a mirrored redo log or the filling of the archive log destination (archiver stuck). Other informational messages that are useful for tuning are also reported in the alert log. These messages signal excessive archive waits for a checkpoint or waits that occur while redo logs are writing to archive. Oracle recommends that the log be checked at least once a day. Some database administrators (DBAs) run an active "tail -f" session in Unix for each database being monitored (on a Windows 95 or X-Window monitor) to know at a glance whether anything odd is happening. If you are experiencing database problems, look at the alert log first for clues about what is occurring. An Oracle alert file looks like the following:

```
Starting up ORACLE RDBMS Version: 7.3.2.3.0.
System parameters with non-default values:
   _trace_files_public      = TRUE
   processes                = 1000
   timed_statistics         = TRUE
   shared_pool_size         = 9000000
   control_files            = /u02/oradata/HIP1/control01.ctl,
   /u03/oradata/HIP1/control02.ctl, /u03/oradata/HIP1/control03.ctl
   compatible               = 7.3.2.3
   log_archive_start        = TRUE
   log_archive_dest         = /u01/app/oracle/admin/HIP1/arch/log
   log_archive_format       = _%s.arc
   log_buffer               = 163840
   log_checkpoint_interval  = 999999999
   db_files                 = 50
   checkpoint_process       = TRUE
   log_checkpoints_to_alert = TRUE
```

```
rollback_segments          = r01, r02, r03, r04
sequence_cache_entries     = 30
sequence_cache_hash_buckets= 23
remote_os_authent          = TRUE
remote_os_roles            = TRUE
remote_login_passwordfile= EXCLUSIVE
global_names               = TRUE
mts_service                = HIP1
mts_servers                = 0
mts_max_servers            = 0
mts_max_dispatchers        = 0
audit_trail                = NONE
sort_area_size             = 131072
sort_area_retained_size    = 131072
sort_direct_writes         = AUTO
db_name                    = HIP1
open_cursors               = 600
ifile                   = /u01/app/oracle/admin/HIP1/pfile/
                          configHIP1.ora
v733_plans_enabled         = TRUE
job_queue_processes        = 2
hash_join_enabled          = FALSE
background_dump_dest        = /u01/logs/oracle/HIP1/bdump
user_dump_dest             = /u01/logs/oracle/HIP1/udump
core_dump_dest             = /u01/logs/oracle/HIP1/cdump
use_async_io               = TRUE
PMON started
DBWR started
ARCH started
LGWR started
CKPT started
RECO started
SNP0 started
SNP1 started
Thu Sep  4 06:39:28 1997
alter database  mount exclusive
Thu Sep  4 06:39:29 1997
Successful mount of redo thread 1.
Thu Sep  4 06:39:29 1997
Completed: alter database  mount exclusive
Thu Sep  4 06:39:29 1997
alter database open
Thu Sep  4 06:39:31 1997
Thread 1 opened at log sequence 852
  Current log# 3 seq# 852 mem# 0: /u02/oradata/HIP1/redo03a.log
  Current log# 3 seq# 852 mem# 1: /u03/oradata/HIP1/redo03b.log
```

```
Successful open of redo thread 1.
Thu Sep  4 06:39:31 1997
SMON: enabling cache recovery
Thu Sep  4 06:39:33 1997
Completed: alter database open
Thu Sep  4 06:39:33 1997
SMON: enabling tx recovery
Thu Sep  4 09:00:10 1997
Beginning database checkpoint by background
Thu Sep  4 09:00:10 1997
Thread 1 advanced to log sequence 853
  Current log# 1 seq# 853 mem# 0: /u02/oradata/HIP1/redo01a.log
  Current log# 1 seq# 853 mem# 1: /u03/oradata/HIP1/redo01b.log
Thu Sep  4 09:00:18 1997
Completed database checkpoint by background
Thu Sep  4 11:55:39 1997
Beginning database checkpoint by background
Thu Sep  4 11:55:39 1997
Thread 1 advanced to log sequence 854
  Current log# 2 seq# 854 mem# 0: /u02/oradata/HIP1/redo02a.log
  Current log# 2 seq# 854 mem# 1: /u03/oradata/HIP1/redo02b.log
Thu Sep  4 11:55:45 1997
Completed database checkpoint by background
Thu Sep  4 12:25:37 1997
Beginning database checkpoint by background
Thu Sep  4 12:25:37 1997
Thread 1 advanced to log sequence 864
  Current log# 3 seq# 855 mem# 0: /u02/oradata/HIP1/redo03a.log
  Current log# 3 seq# 855 mem# 1: /u03/oradata/HIP1/redo03b.log
Thu Sep  4 14:45:24 1997
Completed database checkpoint by background
Thu Sep  4 16:14:24 1997
Beginning database checkpoint by background
Thu Sep  4 16:14:24 1997
Thread 1 advanced to log sequence 865
  Current log# 1 seq# 856 mem# 0: /u02/oradata/HIP1/redo01a.log
  Current log# 1 seq# 856 mem# 1: /u03/oradata/HIP1/redo01b.log
Thu Sep  4 16:14:32 1997
Completed database checkpoint by background
Fri Sep  5 01:04:05 1997
Shutting down instance (immediate)
License high water mark = 39
Fri Sep  5 01:04:05 1997
ALTER DATABASE CLOSE NORMAL
Fri Sep  5 01:04:05 1997
SMON: disabling tx recovery
SMON: disabling cache recovery
```

```
Fri Sep  5 01:04:06 1997
Thread 1 closed at log sequence 856
  Current log# 1 seq# 856 mem# 0: /u02/oradata/HIP1/redo01a.log
  Current log# 1 seq# 856 mem# 1: /u03/oradata/HIP1/redo01b.log
Fri Sep  5 01:04:06 1997
Completed: ALTER DATABASE CLOSE NORMAL
Fri Sep  5 01:04:06 1997
ALTER DATABASE DISMOUNT
Completed: ALTER DATABASE DISMOUNT
```

# Online Redo Logfile Corruption

If you suspect that the database is having problems writing redo logfiles, you can configure Oracle to use checksums to verify blocks in the redo logfiles. Setting the **LOG_BLOCK_CHECKSUM** initialization parameter to **TRUE** will enable redo log block checking. The default value of **LOG_BLOCK_CHECKSUM** is **FALSE**. When redo log block checking is enabled, Oracle computes a checksum for each redo log block written to the current log and writes that checksum in the header of the block. Oracle uses the checksum to detect corruption in a redo log block. Oracle will try to verify the redo log block when it writes the block to an archive logfile and when the block is read from an archived log during recovery.

If a redo log block is corrupted while trying to write the archive, Oracle will try to read the block from another member in the group. If all members have a corrupted block, archiving will stop.

Setting **LOG_BLOCK_CHECKSUM** to **TRUE** will cause more I/O and CPU usage. The system should be monitored closely while this parameter is set.

# DBVERIFY

DBVERIFY is a command-line utility that performs a physical data structure integrity check on database files. It can be used on backup files and online files. You can use DBVERIFY to verify that backed-up datafiles are valid before they are used to restore a database.

The name and location of DBVERIFY depends on your operating system; on AIX, Sun, and Sequent, it is dbv. See your Oracle documentation for using DBVERIFY on your system.

The following list defines the parameters used with the DBVERIFY utility:

➤ **FILE** The name of the database file to verify

➤ **START** The block at which DBVERIFY will start; the default is to start at the beginning of the file

➤ **END** The last block address to verify; the default is to verify to the end of the file

➤ **BLOCKSIZE** The Oracle block size; the default is 2K

➤ **LOGFILE** The logfile for screen output

➤ **FEEDBACK** Causes DBVERIFY to display a single period (.) for every *n* number of pages verified; the default is no feedback

➤ **HELP** Lists onscreen help

➤ **PARFILE** Specifies the name of the parameter file to use

The following example shows how to get online help:

```
collip@hqba14 $ dbv help=y

DBVERIFY: Release 7.3.2.1.0 - Production on Tue Jun 30 23:48:12
1998

Copyright (c) Oracle Corporation 1979, 1994.  All rights reserved.

Keyword    Description        (Default)
------------------------------------------------
FILE       File to Verify     (NONE)
START      Start Block        (First Block of File)
END        End Block          (Last Block of File)
BLOCKSIZE  Logical Block Size (2048)
LOGFILE    Output Log         (NONE)
FEEDBACK   Display Progress   (0)
```

The following is sample output of the DBVERIFY utility:

```
collip@hqba14 $ dbv tools01.dbf blocksize=4096

DBVERIFY: Release 7.3.2.1.0 - Production on Tue Jun 30 23:48:40
1998

Copyright (c) Oracle Corporation 1979, 1994.  All rights reserved.

DBVERIFY - Verification starting : FILE = tools01.dbf

DBVERIFY - Verification complete

Total Pages Examined      : 9984
Total Pages Processed (Data) : 2218
Total Pages Failing   (Data) : 0
```

```
Total Pages Processed (Index): 738
Total Pages Failing    (Index): 0
Total Pages Empty             : 6540
Total Pages Marked Corrupt    : 0
Total Pages Influx            : 0
```

# V$ Recovery Views

Four recovery views will help you during recovery. These views can be queried even when the database is mounted but not open. They provide information to aid the DBA in determining the type of recovery needed for the database and what files need recovery.

Table 14.1 shows **V$RECOVER_LOG, V$RECOVER_FILE, V$RECOVERY_FILE_STATUS**, and **V$RECOVERY_STATUS** views.

| Table 14.1 | The V$ recovery views. | |
|---|---|---|
| **Column** | **Type** | **Description** |
| **V$RECOVERY_LOG** | | |
| THREAD# | NUMBER | Archive log thread number |
| SEQUENCE# | NUMBER | Archive log sequence number |
| TIME | DATE | Time of lowest SCN |
| ARCHIVE_NAME | VARCHAR2(257) | Name of archived logfile |
| **V$RECOVER_FILE** | | |
| FILE# | NUMBER | File ID number |
| ONLINE | VARCHAR2(7) | Online/offline status |
| ERROR | VARCHAR2(18) | Reason for recovery |
| CHANGE# | NUMBER | Starting recovery SCN |
| TIME | DATE | Time of the starting SCN |
| **V$RECOVERY_FILE_STATUS** | | |
| FILENUM | NUMBER | Number of the file being recovered |
| FILENAME | VARCHAR2(257) | Datafile name being recovered |
| STATUS | VARCHAR2(13) | Status of recovery |

*(continued)*

| Table 14.1 | The V$ recovery views *(continued)*. | |
|---|---|---|
| **Column** | **Type** | **Description** |
| **V$RECOVERY_STATUS** | | |
| RECOVERY_CHECKPOINT | DATE | The current point in time of recovery |
| THREAD | NUMBER | The redo thread number being processed |
| SEQUENCE_NEEDED | NUMBER | The sequence number of the log needed |
| SCN_NEEDED | VARCHAR2(16) | Low SCN of log needed |
| TIME_NEEDED | DATE | Time the log was created |
| PREVIOUS_LOG_NAME | VARCHAR2(257) | File name of log |
| PREVIOUS_LOG_STATUS | VARCHAR2(13) | Status of previously applied log |
| REASON | VARCHAR2(13) | Reason recovery has stopped |

After using the **ALTER DATABASE RECOVER** command, you can view all the files that have been considered for recovery in the **V$RECOVERY_FILE_STATUS** view. The status of each file is in the **V$RECOVERY_STATUS** view.

The **V$RECOVER_FILE** view can be used to determine which files to recover. This view lists all files that need to be recovered and the error that is causing recovery. The **V$RECOVER_FILE** cannot be used for this purpose if the control file that is used for recovery is from a backup or was re-created for recovery.

Use the following query to display the file IDs of datafiles that need recovery:

```
SELECT file#, online, error FROM v$recover_file;

FILE#    ONLINE     ERROR
------------------------------------
0064     ONLINE

0022     ONLINE     FILE NOT FOUND

0018     OFFLINE    OFFLINE NORMAL
```

Use the **V$DATAFILE** view to cross-reference the file number to the file name.

# Practice Questions

## Question 1

> Which view can be queried to find out the status of recovery?
>
> ○  a. **V$DATAFILE**
>
> ○  b. **V$RECOVERY_FILE_STATUS**
>
> ○  c. **V$RECOVERY_LOG**

The correct answer is b. The status of recovery is in the **STATUS** field of the V$RECOVERY_FILE_STATUS view. The status will be **IN RECOVERY, CURRENT**, or **NOT RECOVERED**.

## Question 2

> Which utility can be used to verify the blocks of an Oracle datafile that is online?
>
> ○  a. Oracle Enterprise Backup Utility (EBU)
>
> ○  b. DBVERIFY
>
> ○  c. Import
>
> ○  d. Server Manager

The correct answer is b. The DBVERIFY utility can be used to verify files that are both online and offline.

## Question 3

> You have set the **LOG_BLOCK_CHECKSUM** to **TRUE**. What happens when an I/O error reading occurs from all members of a redo log group?
>
> ○  a. A new redo log is written
>
> ○  b. The ARCH process hangs
>
> ○  c. The ARCH process skips the bad redo blocks and continues
>
> ○  d. The database goes into automatic recovery

The correct answer is b. If the checksum fails, the redo log cannot be archived.

## Question 4

---

> What happens when an invalid checksum is detected on one redo
> log member?
>
> ○ a. A new redo log is written
>
> ○ b. The ARCH process hangs
>
> ○ c. The database goes into automatic recovery
>
> ○ d. An attempt is made to archive another member of the
> redo log group

The correct answer is d. If attempts to archive all members of the redo log
group fail, the ARCH process will hang. Failing to write an archive does not
put the database in an automatic recovery. Online redo logs can only be rewritten if they have been archived.

## Question 5

---

> Which utility checks the structural integrity of data blocks?
>
> ○ a. Oracle Enterprise Backup Utility (EBU)
>
> ○ b. DBVERIFY
>
> ○ c. Import
>
> ○ d. Server Manager

The correct answer is b. EBU is used to schedule operating system backups.
Import uses an export file as its source, so it cannot check data blocks for
errors. There are no Server Manager options to validate the integrity of data
blocks.

## Question 6

---

> Which file will show the last time an instance was started?
>
> ○ a. config.ora
>
> ○ b. init.ora
>
> ○ c. startup.trc
>
> ○ d. alert.log

The correct answer is d. The alert logfile keeps a historical log of all startups,
shutdowns, errors, and structural changes made to the database.

## Question 7

> Where is the first place a DBA should look if an Oracle instance is having problems?
>
> ○  a. pmon.trc
>
> ○  b. smon.trc
>
> ○  c. sga.trc
>
> ○  d. alert.log

The answer is d. The alert lo file is always the best place to start when you are troubleshooting the database.

## Question 8

> You suspect that the DBWR process is getting errors. Where should you look?
>
> ○  a. **BACKGROUND_DUMP_DEST**
>
> ○  b. **USER_DUMP_DEST**
>
> ○  c. **LOG_ARCHIVE _DEST**
>
> ○  d. **CORE_DUMP_DEST**

The correct answer is a. **BACKGROUND_DUMP_DEST** is where all background process trace files go.

# Need To Know More?

 Backup and recovery are covered in the *Oracle Server Concepts Book* and the *Server Administrator's Guide.*

 Loney, Kevin: *DBA Handbook, 7.3 Edition.* Oracle Press, 1996. ISBN 0-07882-289-0.

 Velpuri, Rama: *Oracle Backup and Recovery Handbook.* Oracle Press, 1995. ISBN 0-07882-106-1.

# Sample Test: Backup And Recovery

The sample test that follows covers material likely to appear on Test 3 of the Oracle Certified Database Administrator track, "Oracle7.3: Backup and Recovery Workshop." This sample test contains 60 questions. You should be able to complete the test in 90 minutes. The answers to this sample test can be found in the next chapter. For test-taking strategy, helpful pointers, and other exam preliminaries, refer to Chapter 9.

# Sample Test: Backup And Recovery

## Question 1

Which command do you issue to put your database in **ARCHIVELOG** mode?

- ○ a. **ALTER DATABASE**
- ○ b. **ALTER SYSTEM**
- ○ c. **ALTER ALL TABLESPACES**
- ○ d. **ALTER ALL DATAFILES**

## Question 2

What should you do first after you have put your database in **ARCHIVELOG** mode?

- ○ a. Nothing special needs to be done after changing **ARCHIVELOG** mode
- ○ b. Export the database
- ○ c. Run DBVERIFY on all datafiles
- ○ d. Shut down the database and perform a full backup

## Question 3

You want to perform an offline full database backup. Which shutdown method should you use if there are active connections to the database?

- ○ a. **SHUTDOWN ABORT**
- ○ b. **SHUTDOWN NORMAL**
- ○ c. **SHUTDOWN IMMEDIATE**
- ○ d. **SHUTDOWN FORCE**

# Question 4

Which type of recovery should you perform if you want to recover to a specific archived redo logfile?

○ a. Change-based recovery

○ b. Cancel-based recovery

○ c. Time-based recovery

○ d. Import-based recovery

# Question 5

Which Oracle database role has the privileges necessary to do a full database export or import?

○ a. ORACLE

○ b. CONNECT

○ c. DBA

○ d. RESOURCE

# Question 6

What is retrieved when you execute the following SQL command?

```
SELECT file_name FROM dba_data_files;
```

○ a. A listing of archive logfiles

○ b. A listing of online redo logfiles

○ c. A listing of datafiles

○ d. A listing of control files

○ e. A listing of tablespaces

# Question 7

Which background process is active when the database is in **ARCHIVELOG** mode?

○ a. PMON

○ b. ARCH

○ c. CKPT

○ d. LGWR

○ e. DBWR

# Question 8

You are running your database in **ARCHIVELOG** mode and suffer a media failure. Which recovery method should you use to recover to the point of failure?

○ a. Import recovery

○ b. Change-based recovery

○ c. Cancel-based recovery

○ d. Datafile recovery

# Question 9

What happens when the following command is issued in Server Manager?

```
ARCHIVE LOG LIST
```

○ a. The database does a log switch and displays the next log sequence

○ b. The database changes into **ARCHIVELOG** mode and displays the next log sequence

○ c. Current information about archiving is displayed

# Question 10

You perform an offline operating system backup. Which type of backup is this?

○  a. Physical backup

○  b. Logical backup

○  c. **ARCHIVELOG** mode backup

# Question 11

Which command can be used to create script for creating a new control file?

○  a. **ALTER CONTROL FILE**

○  b. **ALTER DATABASE**

○  c. **ALTER SYSTEM**

○  d. **ALTER INSTANCE**

# Question 12

What must you have to roll forward all transactions to the point of failure after a disk drive failure?

○  a. A backup of the control file

○  b. All archived redo logfiles

○  c. The current init.ora file

○  d. A backup of all datafiles

○  e. A copy of the last export

# Question 13

What should be your first step when planning a backup?

○  a. Put the database in **ARCHIVELOG** mode

○  b. Shut down the database

○  c. Make a list of all files that need to be included in the backup

○  d. List the current **ARCHIVE LOG** information

## Question 14

What is a standby database used for?

- O a. To serve the same purpose as a parallel server instance
- O b. To provide a read-only copy of the database
- O c. To replace the primary database when it fails
- O d. To restore the primary database when it fails

## Question 15

How can you protect your control file from media failure?

- O a. Execute the **ALTER DATABASE BACKUP CONTROLFILE TO TRACE** command
- O b. Make multiple copies of the control file and put them in the same directory
- O c. Put multiple copies on multiple disks
- O d. Load the control file into the system global area (SGA)

## Question 16

Which initialization parameter will make the database verify redo logfiles before they are archived?

- O a. **LOG_CHECKPOINT_TO_TRACE**
- O b. **LOG_BLOCK_CHECKSUM**
- O c. **LOG_ARCHIVE_CHECK**
- O d. **LOG_ARCHIVE_DEST**

## Question 17

Which export option should you use if users are accessing the database during export?

- O a. **DIRECT=Y**
- O b. **IGNORE=Y**
- O c. **CONSISTENT=Y**
- O d. **CONSTRAINTS=Y**

# Question 18

How will your backup strategy affect recoverability?

O  a. It determines whether incomplete or complete recovery can be performed

O  b. It will not affect recoverability

O  c. It will help determine the need for more tape drives

O  d. It will help you get management support

# Question 19

Which functions does the database administrator (DBA) do during recovery? [Check all correct answers]

☐  a. Rollback

☐  b. Apply archived redo logfiles

☐  c. Roll forward

☐  d. Restore database backup

# Question 20

Which Oracle process performs automatic instance recovery?

O  a. LGWR

O  b. DBWR

O  c. PMON

O  d. ARCH

O  e. SMON

## Question 21

You have just altered a tablespace to be read-only. In which file will the structure change be identified and used by the database?

○ a. Alert file

○ b. Trace file

○ c. Control file

○ d. Redo logfile

○ e. Rollback file

## Question 22

Which Oracle background process cleans up failed user processes?

○ a. SMON

○ b. LGWR

○ c. DBWR

○ d. PMON

## Question 23

One of the Oracle background processes is getting errors. Where are the errors recorded?

○ a. **BACKGROUND_DUMP_DEST**

○ b. **USER_DUMP_DEST**

○ c. **LOG_ARCHIVE_DEST**

○ d. **CORE_DUMP_DEST**

## Question 24

What would you use to recover a media failure to the point of failure?

○ a. An export file

○ b. An operating system backup

○ c. An operating system backup with archive logs

# Question 25

You have a read-only tablespace that was made read-write for changes. The tablespace was lost because of media failure. To which point can you recover this tablespace?

○ a. To the time the tablespace was made read-only

○ b. To the point of failure

○ c. None; this tablespace is unrecoverable

# Question 26

You administer an Oracle7 database that supports Internet banking. Which backup strategy should you use in this situation?

○ a. Back up less often so that transactions are not interrupted

○ b. Back up often because of the rapid changes made to the database

○ c. Back up every transaction

○ d. Backups are impractical on this kind of system

# Question 27

You are the DBA for a data warehouse that is updated monthly. Which backup strategy should you use?

○ a. Back up daily

○ b. Back up weekly

○ c. Back up after updates are made

○ d. Back up before updates are made

# Question 28

For a read-only tablespace, in which state should the datafiles be during backup?

○ a. Offline

○ b. Online

○ c. Either offline or online

○ d. Neither; the database should be shut down

## Question 29

You want to archive the next online redo logfile group manually. Which command should you use?

○ a. **ALTER SYSTEM ARCHIVE LOG NEXT**

○ b. **ALTER SYSTEM SWITCH LOGFILE**

○ c. **ALTER DATABASE CHANGE LOG**

○ d. **ALTER DATABASE SWITCH LOGFILE**

## Question 30

When a user reboots a computer without disconnecting from the database, which kind of failure occurs?

○ a. Database failure

○ b. Instance failure

○ c. Media failure

○ d. User process failure

○ e. Statement failure

## Question 31

Which file does the DBA look in when an instance has a problem?

○ a. Configuration file

○ b. Trace file

○ c. Alert file

○ d. SGA file

# Question 32

Which type of recovery does deferred transaction recovery in Oracle7.3 speed up?

○  a. Transaction processing

○  b. Instance recovery

○  c. DBWR processing

○  d. Checkpointing

# Question 33

Which utility can you use to verify online datafiles as well as backed-up datafiles?

○  a. Enterprise Backup Utility (EBU)

○  b. Server Manager

○  c. Import

○  d. DBVERIFY

# Question 34

The memory on the computer holding the SGA has failed. Which type of failure is this?

○  a. Media failure

○  b. User process failure

○  c. Instance failure

○  d. Statement failure

# Question 35

Which file shows the last time the database was started?

○  a. alert.log

○  b. smon.trc

○  c. config.ora

○  d. init.ora

## Question 36

You are the administrator of a distributed database. What special considerations do you need to make in terms of backup and recovery?

○ a. None; there are no special consideration for distributed databases

○ b. Make sure that each database has its own backup and recovery plan

○ c. Coordinate the backup and recovery plan between all databases

## Question 37

Which type of export will back up objects updated since the last export of any type?

○ a. Cumulative

○ b. Incremental

○ c. Complete

## Question 38

In which mode must a tablespace be to perform an online backup?

○ a. **MOUNT EXCLUSIVE**

○ b. **NOMOUNT**

○ c. **RESTRICTED**

○ d. **BACKUP**

## Question 39

How should you start the database if you want to restore individual datafiles?

○ a. **STARTUP MOUNT**

○ b. **STARTUP NOMOUNT**

○ c. **STARTUP MOUNT EXCLUSIVE**

# Question 40

The system administrator has deleted a database file by mistake. Which type of failure is this?

○ a. User error

○ b. Media failure

○ c. Statement failure

○ d. Instance failure

○ e. User process failure

# Question 41

In Server Manager, you use the **RECOVER DATABASE** command. How does this affect the use of the database?

○ a. Any datafiles not being recovered are available for use

○ b. Any tablespaces not being recovered are available for use

○ c. Only read-only tablespaces are accessible

○ d. Tablespaces can be used as they are recovered

○ e. No part of the database is available to users until the recovery is finished

# Question 42

When performing online backups, which kind of backup is performed?

○ a. Instance-level backup

○ b. Table-level backup

○ c. Tablespace-level backup

○ d. Database-level backup

## Question 43

When performing datafile recovery, to what time will the datafile be recovered?

○ a. The current time

○ b. The point of failure

○ c. A future point in time

## Question 44

Which Oracle background process is active only in **ARCHIVELOG** mode?

○ a. SMON

○ b. ARCH

○ c. RECO

○ d. CKPT

## Question 45

Which files must be synchronized for recovery? [Check all correct answers]

❑ a. Redo logfiles

❑ b. Trace files

❑ c. Export files

❑ d. Control files

❑ e. Datafiles

❑ f. Rollback files

## Question 46

After reviewing the alert.log file, you have determined that the SMON process has failed. What do you need to do to recover the instance?

○ a. Restart the SMON process

○ b. Reload the SGA

○ c. Restart the instance

○ d. Reboot the server

## Question 47

The PMON process has failed. Which type of failure is this?

○ a. Media failure

○ b. User error

○ c. User process failure

○ d. Instance failure

○ e. Statement failure

## Question 48

You are running the database in **ARCHIVELOG** mode. What are your complete recovery options? [Check all correct answers]

❐ a. Change-based recovery

❐ b. Datafile recovery

❐ c. Full database recovery

❐ d. Cancel-based recovery

❐ e. Time-based recovery

❐ f. Tablespace recovery

❐ g. Export/import recovery

## Question 49

You add a datafile to a database that has a standby database. What other actions must you take for the standby database?

○ a. Re-create the standby control file

○ b. Nothing; the datafile will be added to the standby database automatically

○ c. Add the datafile to the standby database

## Question 50

Which objects can you recover using the **PARALLEL** clause? [Check all correct answers]

❑ a. Database

❑ b. Datafiles

❑ c. Tablespaces

❑ d. Tables

❑ e. Control file

❑ f. Redo file

❑ g. Rollback segments

## Question 51

In which mode must the database be to operate on a 24x7 basis?

○ a. **ARCHIVELOG** mode

○ b. **NOARCHIVELOG** mode

○ c. **STANDBY** mode

○ d. **NOSTANDBY** mode

# Question 52

Which database file holds all the synchronization information?

- ○ a. Export file
- ○ b. Datafiles
- ○ c. Redo files
- ○ d. Rollback
- ○ e. Control file

# Question 53

While processing an **UPDATE** to a table, a user gets a "failed to allocate an extent" error. Which type of failure is this?

- ○ a. Statement failure
- ○ b. User process failure
- ○ c. Instance failure
- ○ d. Media failure

# Question 54

A user deleted all the rows of a table by mistake. You have determined that the table can be recovered from the last export taken. Which export option should you use to avoid "object already exists" errors?

- ○ a. **DIRECT=Y**
- ○ b. **INDEXES=N**
- ○ c. **CONSISTENT=Y**
- ○ d. **IGNORE=Y**

## Question 55

One of the datafiles of a tablespace has been damaged because of media failure. Which type of recovery should you perform?

○ a. Import recovery

○ b. Database recovery

○ c. Table recovery

○ d. Datafile recovery

○ e. Tablespace recovery

## Question 56

As a new DBA, you are handed the disaster recovery plan from the last DBA. What should you do?

○ a. Nothing; assume that the other DBA did a good job

○ b. Ask the information systems manager whether the plan was tested

○ c. Test the plan to make sure that you can recover using it

○ d. Make sure that all the documentation is in order

## Question 57

You are recovering an Oracle7.3 database. When are uncommitted transactions rolled back?

○ a. Before the roll forward is done

○ b. After the roll forward is done

○ c. As soon as the database starts

○ d. When a request for the data is made

## Question 58

By default, in which mode does an Oracle database operate?

○ a. **ARCHIVELOG** mode with automatic archiving

○ b. **ARCHIVELOG** with manual archiving

○ c. **NOARCHIVELOG** mode

# Question 59

In which state must the database be to issue the following command?

```
ALTER DATABASE RENAME FILE
```

- ○ a. **MOUNT EXCLUSIVE**
- ○ b. **NOMOUNT**
- ○ c. **MOUNT**

# Question 60

The control file is lost because of media failure, and you must restore it to a new location. Which steps must you perform before opening the database? [Check all correct answers]

- ☐ a. Edit the configuration file with the new location
- ☐ b. Use the **RENAME DATAFILE** command to change the control file location
- ☐ c. Restore the control file to the new location
- ☐ d. Use the **ALTER DATABASE RENAME CONTROL FILE** command

# Answer Key To Backup And Recovery Sample Test

**16**

| | | |
|---|---|---|
| 1. a | 21. c | 41. e |
| 2. d | 22. d | 42. c |
| 3. c | 23. a | 43. b |
| 4. b | 24. c | 44. b |
| 5. c | 25. a | 45. a, d, e |
| 6. c | 26. b | 46. c |
| 7. b | 27. c | 47. d |
| 8. d | 28. c | 48. b, c, f |
| 9. c | 29. a | 49. c |
| 10. a | 30. d | 50. a, b, c |
| 11. b | 31. c | 51. a |
| 12. b | 32. b | 52. e |
| 13. c | 33. d | 53. a |
| 14. c | 34. c | 54. d |
| 15. c | 35. a | 55. d |
| 16. b | 36. c | 56. c |
| 17. c | 37. b | 57. d |
| 18. a | 38. d | 58. c |
| 19. b, d | 39. a | 59. c |
| 20. e | 40. b | 60. a, c |

This is the answer key to the sample test presented in Chapter 15.

## Question 1

The correct answer is a. Remember that the instance must be started with the **MOUNT** option. Do not open the database until after you have changed archiving modes. The **ALTER SYSTEM** command is used to alter characteristics of the Oracle background processes that make up the instance and not the database. Answers c and d are not valid commands.

## Question 2

The correct answer is d. A cold backup is recommended but not mandatory. A hot backup can serve as a recovery starting point as well. Just remember that until a complete hot or cold backup is performed, you are in an unrecoverable state.

## Question 3

The correct answer is c. A **SHUTDOWN IMMEDIATE** will not allow new connections to the database and will end all transactions. All uncommitted transactions are rolled back. **SHUTDOWN IMMEDIATE** does not require recovery when the database is restarted. Answer a is incorrect because **SHUTDOWN ABORT** requires a recovery when the database is restarted. Answer b is incorrect because **SHUTDOWN NORMAL** will wait for all users to disconnect from the database before it shuts down and does not allow you to start the backup.

## Question 4

The correct answer is b. Cancel-based recovery is accomplished by using the **RECOVER DATABASE UNTIL CANCEL** statement and then when entering "CANCEL" instead of an archive logfile name to cancel the recovery when appropriate. Answer a is incorrect because a change-based recovery is based on the SCN, not the redo logfile. Answer c is incorrect because time-based recovery recovers to a point in time, not to a specific redo logfile. Answer d is incorrect because recovery through Import does not use archived redo logfiles at all.

## Question 5

The correct answer is c. DBA is granted the EXPORT_FULL_DATABASE and IMPORT_FULL_DATABASE roles by default. Answers a is not a valid role. Answers b and d are roles but are incorrect because they are not granted the correct privileges to export the entire database.

## Question 6

The correct answer is c. Only datafiles are listed in the **DBA_DATA_FILES** view.

## Question 7

The correct answer is b. ARCH is the archiver process.

## Question 8

The correct answer is d. Datafile recovery is a complete recovery. Answer a is incorrect because Import can recover the database only to the time of the last export. Answers b and c are incorrect because, although cancel-based recovery and change-based recovery can recover to the point of failure, they are considered incomplete recoveries. This is explained further in the *Oracle Server Administrator's Guide*.

## Question 9

The correct answer is c. This command makes no changes to the database. It only lists information about archiving.

## Question 10

The correct answer is a. Operating system backups are physical backups, and exports are logical backups. Therefore, answer b is incorrect. Answer c is incorrect because there is no **ARCHIVELOG** mode backup.

## Question 11

The correct answer is b. **ALTER DATABASE BACKUP CONTROL FILE TO TRACE** writes SQL statements to a database trace file. The SQL commands in the trace file can be used to start up the database, re-create the control file, and recover and open the database. You can copy the commands from the trace file into a script file, edit the commands as necessary, and use the script to recover the database.

## Question 12

The correct answer is b. Without all the archive logfiles needed for recovery, a complete recovery is not possible.

## Question 13

The correct answer is c. A backup will not be valid for recovery unless all needed files are part of the backup, regardless of whether you are in ARCHIVELOG mode.

## Question 14

The correct answer is c. The standby database is in a constant state of recovery, applying the archive logs from the primary database. When the primary database fails, the standby database completes recovery and becomes the new primary database. A standby database cannot be used for queries while it is in standby mode.

## Question 15

The correct answer is c. You can specify multiple locations for the control file in the configuration file, and Oracle will place a copy in each location and keep them all in sync.

## Question 16

The correct answer is b. This will cause the archiver to verify that all blocks are written. The LOG_CHECKPOINT_TO_TRACE parameter puts a message in the alert file every time the database does a checkpoint. Answer c is invalid and LOG_ARCHIVE_DEST is the location where archive log files are written.

## Question 17

The correct answer is c. This will make sure that each table is backed up in a consistent state. It does not guarantee consistency between tables. All the other answers are valid export parameters but do not affect consistency.

## Question 18

The correct answer is a. Answers b, c, and d do not affect recoverability.

## Question 19

The correct answers are b and d. The roll forward and the rollback are performed automatically by the database.

## Question 20

The correct answer is e. SMON, the system monitor process, performs instance recovery.

## Question 21

The correct answer is c. The control file is where all structural changes made to the database are recorded. Answers a and b are incorrect because alert and trace files are logfiles and are never read by the database. Answer d is incorrect because the redo logfile holds redo information. Answer e is incorrect because there is no such thing as a rollback file.

## Question 22

The answer is d. PMON is the process monitor.

## Question 23

The correct answer is a. BACKGROUND_DUMP_DEST is a parameter set in the Oracle configuration files. This is where all background process trace files will go. Answer b is incorrect because USER_DUMP_DEST is where user process trace files will go. Answer c is incorrect because LOG_ ARCHIVE_DEST is where archive logfiles will go. Answer d is incorrect because CORE_DUMP_DEST is where core dump files will go.

## Question 24

The correct answer is c. The only way to recover to the point of failure is to be in ARCHIVELOG mode, restore the last backup, and apply archive logfiles. Answers a and b will only recover the database to the point in time when the backup was taken.

## Question 25

The correct answer is a. Because no backups were made after the tablespace was made read-write, the only option is to restore to the backup made when the tablespace was made read-only.

## Question 26

The correct answer is b. Answer a is incorrect because backing up less often would incur longer recovery times in case of a failure. Answer c is incorrect because backing up after every transaction is unrealistic. Answer d is incorrect because backups are practical and should be done frequently.

## Question 27

The correct answer is c. Because the data changes only once a month, the backup schedule should match.

## Question 28

The correct answer is c. Datafiles can be backed up while they are offline or online.

## Question 29

The correct answer is a. Answer b is incorrect because this command will simply switch to the next redo logfile and might not cause an archive. Answers c and d are incorrect because these are not valid commands.

## Question 30

The correct answer is d. This is an abnormal termination of a user process.

## Question 31

The correct answer is c. The alert file is a historical view of what has happened to the database and records all background process errors and structural changes made to the database.

## Question 32

The correct answer is b. Transaction recovery is done after an instance is started.

## Question 33

The correct answer is d. DBVERIFY is used to verify online datafiles as well as backed-up datafiles.

## Question 34

The correct answer is c. This would cause the background processes to fail, causing the instance to crash.

## Question 35

The correct answer is a. The alert.log file shows every startup and shutdown for the database.

## Question 36

The correct answer is c. In some cases, the recovery of a distributed node must be coordinated with other nodes in the distributed system.

## Question 37

The correct answer is b. Answer a is incorrect because a cumulative export will export all objects that have changed since the last cumulative export. Answer c is incorrect because a complete export will export all objects every time.

## Question 38

The correct answer is d. You must use the **ALTER TABLESPACE BEGIN BACKUP** command to put the tablespace in backup mode.

## Question 39

The correct answer is a. Answer b is incorrect because you cannot do recovery if the database is not mounted. The **EXCLUSIVE** option simply means that the database can be used by only one instance.

## Question 40

The correct answer is b. The physical loss of files, for any reason, is a media failure.

## Question 41

The correct answer is e. During tablespace or datafile recovery, the parts of the database not being recovered can be available. The **RECOVER DATABASE** command puts the entire database into recovery whether it needs it or not, making it unavailable to users.

## Question 42

The correct answer is c. Online backups are done at the tablespace level by issuing the **ALTER TABLESAPCE BEGIN BACKUP** command.

## Question 43

The correct answer is b. Normally, a datafile recovery is a complete recovery and would be recovered to the point of failure.

## Question 44

The correct answer is b. ARCH is the archive process.

## Question 45

The correct answers are a, d, and e. Answer b is incorrect because trace files are not used in recovery. Answer f is incorrect because there are no such things as rollback files. Answer c is incorrect because export files do not require synchronization.

## Question 46

The correct answer is c. Instance recovery is automatic when the instance is restarted.

## Question 47

The correct answer is d. An instance failure occurs whenever a background process fails.

## Question 48

The correct answers are b, c, and f. Answers a, d, and e are incorrect because these are incomplete options. Answer g is incorrect because export/import is a logical backup and recovery.

## Question 49

The answer is c. You must manually add datafiles to the standby database.

## Question 50

The correct answers are a, b, and c. Answer d is incorrect because tables can be restored only from an export file. Answers e, f, and g are incorrect because these are not composed of datafiles and cannot be recovered using the **PARALLEL** clause.

## Question 51

The correct answer is a. Only a database in **ARCHIVELOG** mode can be recovered to the point of failure.

## Question 52

The correct answer is e. The control file holds the synchronization information.

## Question 53

The correct answer is a. A statement failure occurs whenever a SQL statement fails. Oracle handles these automatically.

## Question 54

The correct answer is d. The **IGNORE=Y** option tells Import to ignore "object already exists" errors. Because the table was not dropped, this option is needed.

## Question 55

The correct answer is d. Because only one datafile is damaged, there is no need to recover the whole tablespace. Simply recover the bad datafile.

## Question 56

The correct answer is c. Always test recovery plans to make sure that they work. After all, if they do not work, your job is on the line.

## Question 57

The correct answer is d. This was an enhancement in Oracle7.3 that speeded up recovery considerably.

## Question 58

The correct answer is c. An Oracle database, by default, operates in the **NOARCHIVELOG** mode.

## Question 59

The correct answer is c. The database must be in the **MOUNT** state to issue the mentioned command.

## Question 60

The correct answers are a and c. Answers b and d are incorrect because these are not Oracle commands.

# Glossary

**ACCEPT**—A SQL*Plus command that enables a SQL program to prompt a user for a variable at runtime and accept an input.

**alert log**—Used to record database level errors and alerts. All database-structure-affecting commands are logged, as are some optional events, such as redo log switches. Alternatively known as the alert_<SID>.log, where the SID corresponds to the SID of the database.

**ALTER**—A Data Definition Language (DDL) command that is used to change database objects.

**analysis**—The step in the system development process where the users' needs are gathered and analyzed to produce documentation used to design a program system.

**ANALYZE**—A DDL command that causes the database to gather or drop statistics on tables, clusters, or indexes.

**application error**—An error that occurs whenever an application issues an improper command to the database, resulting in an error condition or undesired effect on the database.

**archive log**—An archive copy of the redo log. The archive log is used to recover to an earlier point in time or to roll forward from a backup to the present time.

**ARCHIVELOG mode**—A database can be in either **ARCHIVELOG** or **NOARCHIVELOG** mode. In **ARCHIVELOG** mode, the database copies filled redo logs to an archive destination, thus allowing for full recovery to point of failure or to a previous point in time.

**attribute**—A detail concerning a thing of significance (entity). For example, a *PERSON* entity may have the attributes of name, address, and birth date.

**audit trail**—In Oracle, a defined set of actions that are specified to be audited using system audit tools. For example, you can audit connects to the database.

**AUTOTRACE**—A SQL*Plus command that causes all SQL statements to be traced.

**BACKGROUND_DUMP_DEST**—An option that is placed in the initialization file (init<SID>.ora) and specifies the location where the trace files for all background processes and the alert_<SID>.log are placed.

**backup**—The process of taking a physical or logical copy of the database in order to allow archival or for disaster recovery purposes. Alternatively, a mode into which the tablespaces in a database can be placed to allow online backups to be performed.

**buffer**—In Oracle, a memory area used to hold data, redo, or rollback information. Usually the buffers are specified using the **DB_BLOCK_BUFFERS**, **DB_BLOCK_SIZE**, and **LOG_BUFFER** initialization parameters.

**cache**—A memory area that is self-managing and is used to hold information about objects, locks, and latches. The caches are usually contained in the shared pool area of the system global area (SGA) and are preallocated as far as size, based on internal algorithms that control how the shared pool memory is allocated.

**cardinality**—A term used in relational analysis to show how two objects relate; it tells how many. For example, "A person may have zero or one nose" shows a cardinality of zero or one. "A person may have zero, one, or many children" shows a cardinality of zero to many. And, "A person has one or many cells" shows a cardinality of one or many. In reference to indexes, cardinality shows how many rows in the indexed table relate back to the index value. A low cardinality index, such as a person's sex (M or F) should be placed in a bitmapped index if it must be indexed, whereas a high cardinality value, such as a person's social security number or employee ID, should be placed in a standard B-tree index.

**careful reading**—Reading for content and without distraction. Avoiding surface reading by consciously participating in the reading through outlining, underlining, and highlighting.

**chaining**—The process in which a database entry is split between two (or more) database blocks. Chaining usually happens with either **VARCHAR2** or **NUMBER** fields that grow too large to fit inside the available freespace in a block due to **UPDATE** activity.

**checkbox**—Part of a GUI interface that allows a mouse click to be registered visually as a checkmark or other mark indicating a selection from a list of values or answers.

**checkpoint**—A process where the DBWR or optional CHKP process writes SCN and transaction information into all data file headers to synchronize the database.

**cluster**—A database structure made up of one or more tables that jointly store key values in the same physical database blocks. Clusters allow for rapid retrieval of clustered data but may cause problems to tables that undergo frequent **INSERT** or **UPDATE** activity.

**column**—Part of a table's row. A column will have been mapped from an attribute in an entity. Columns have datatypes, and may have constraints mapped against them.

**COMMIT**—A Data Manipulation Language (DML) command. A **COMMIT** marks a transaction as completed successfully and causes data to be written first to the redo logs and, once DBWR writes, to the disk. A **COMMIT** isn't complete until it receives word from the disk subsystem that the redo log write is complete. Committed data cannot be rolled back using the **ROLLBACK** command, and must be removed using more DML commands.

**complete media recovery**—The process involving use of archive logs, redo logs, and rollback segments allowing an Oracle database to be completely restored to the time of a media failure.

**CONNECT**—This is a Server Manager (SVRMGRL), SQL*Worksheet, or SQL*Plus command that enables a user to connect to the database or to a remote database.

**contention**—When two or more processes compete for the same resource, such as a table, a latch, or memory. Contention results in database wait events and slow performance.

**control file**—The Oracle file that contains information on all database files and maintains System Change Number (SCN) records for each. The control file must be present and current for the database to start up properly. Control files may be mirrored; mirrored copies are automatically updated by Oracle as needed. The control file provides for maintenance of system concurrency and consistency by providing a means of synchronizing all database files.

**conventional path load**—The most used form of SQL*Loader database load. A conventional path load uses DML statements to load data from flat operating system files into Oracle tables.

**CREATE**—A DDL command that allows creation of database objects.

**data dictionary**—A collection of C structs, tables, and views that contain all of the database metadata (information about the database's data). The data dictionary is used to store information used by all database processes to find out about database data structures.

**database buffer cache**—This cache is defined by the **DB_BLOCK_SIZE** and **DB_BLOCK_BUFFERS** initialization parameters. All data that enters or leaves the database passes through the database buffer cache.

**DBMS_APPLICATION_INFO**—This is an Oracle-supplied stored PL/ SQL package of procedures and functions that allows for tracking of application status and performance through application coded calls to the package contents that results in data being sent to the **V$SESSION** dynamic performance view.

**DBVERIFY**—This utility is an Oracle-supplied database verification tool. DBVERIFY is used to check the internal consistency of Oracle database data files.

**DDL (Data Definition Language)**—A SQL statement used to create or manipulate database structures is classified as DDL. Examples are **CREATE**, **ALTER**, and **DROP** commands.

**deadlock**—A deadlock occurs when a process is holding an exclusive lock on a resource, such as a table, that is required by another process. The process that detects the deadlock is rolled back to resolve the deadlock automatically. Deadlocks usually result from improperly specified application coded explicit locking.

**DELETE**—A DML command used to remove data by rows (generally speaking) from the database tables.

**DESCRIBE**—A SQL*Plus or Server Manager command that is used to retrieve information on database structure. Any stored object (except triggers) can be described.

**dictionary cache**—The dictionary cache is an internal component of the shared pool section of the SGA. The dictionary cache is used to track data dictionary items such as latches, tables, indexes, and so on. The dictionary cache is automatically sized based on internal algorithms taking into account the values of various initialization parameters and rationing them to the size of the shared pool.

**direct path load**—In SQL*Loader, this disables all triggers, constraints, and indexes and loads data directly into the table by prebuilding and then inserting database blocks. It does not use DML commands. There are conventional and direct path loads in SQL*Loader.

**discarded records**—A record that SQL*Loader rejects for loading based on internal rules for data validation and conversion.

**disk sort**—This occurs when the size of a sort request exceeds the **SORT_AREA_SIZE** specified memory size. Generally disk sorts take orders of magnitude longer than the equivalent memory sort and should be avoided if possible.

**DISTINCT SELECT**—A **DISTINCT SELECT** is a **SELECT** that uses either the **DISTINCT** or **UNIQUE** operator to force no duplicate entries to be returned by a **SELECT**. All **DISTINCT SELECT** operations result in sorts and should be avoided if possible.

**DROP**—A DDL command used to remove database objects.

**DSS (decision support system)**—A general type of database. Usually DSS systems use a number of large **SELECT** operations and perform multiple full table scans.

**dynamic SQL**—SQL used to build SQL. Essentially, queries are issued against data dictionary tables using embedded literal strings to build a set of commands. Usually, dynamic SQL is used to automate a long series of virtually identical commands against similar types of database objects. An example would be creating a script to disable or enable all triggers for a set of database tables using the **DBA_TRIGGERS** table and a single SQL statement.

**entity**—In relational modeling, a thing of significance. Examples of entities are *PERSON*, *CAR*, and *EXPENSE*. Entities are singular in nature and are mapped to tables. Tables contain entities.

**equijoin**—A join between two or more tables using equality comparisons.

**ERD (entity relationship diagram)**—A pictorial representation using a standard symbology and methodology (such as Chen or Yourdon) of a relational database.

**exhibit**—In the realm of the OCP exams, extra information that is usually required to solve the question posed. Always look at any provided exhibits.

**EXPLAIN PLAN**—The Explain Plan facility is incorporated into the SQL*Plus engine and in the TKPROF utility. In SQL*Plus, explain plans are generated either automatically if **AUTOTRACE** with the **EXPLAIN** option is set to **ON**, or manually by means of the **EXPLAIN PLAN** command. Explain plans show the method Oracle will use to execute a specified SQL (usually **SELECT**) command. The **EXPLAIN PLAN** function doesn't execute the specified query, but provides the execution plan for review and tuning.

**foreign key**—A value or set of values mapped from a primary or parent table into a dependent or child table used to enforce referential integrity. A foreign key, generally speaking, must be either **NULL** or exist as a primary key in a parent table.

**freelist**—A segment header structure that allows for tracking of blocks that are updatable or can be inserted into. To be on a freelist, a block must have more than or equal to the percentage of freespace as specified by **PCTFREE**.

**full database export**—The export utility **exp** allows for the creation of a logical database copy. A full export is one where all users' (schemas') grants, constraints, and other database items are logically copied into an export-formatted file. The export also allows for table- and schema- (user-) level logical copies and for incremental and cumulative exports as well.

**function**—One of several structures. An implicit function is one that is provided as a part of the SQL language. An explicit function is one that is created by the user using PL/SQL. A function must return a value and must be named. As a part of the SQL standard, a function cannot change a database's or package's state, but can only act on external variables and values.

**GET**—A SQL*Plus command that loads SQL or PL/SQL commands from an external operating system file into the SQL*Plus command buffer.

**get**—A successful acquisition of a database resource.

**high water mark**—Oracle keeps track of the highest level a database table is utilized, which becomes the high water mark for that table. A table can only reclaim empty space between currently filled blocks and the high water mark through a rebuild or truncation process. To accurately get a reading on how much space is actually used in a table, you must count the blocks used (by parsing and counting the block IDs from the **ROWID**s) and not simply perform a count of used extents because used extents are counted up to the high water mark.

**hint**—An explicitly stated "suggestion" to the Oracle optimizer embedded into a SQL statement as a comment.

**hit ratio**—A calculated ratio of the number of times an attempt to obtain a resource was successful against the total number of times the resource was requested.

**hybrid system**—A database that combines one or more generic types of database such as a DSS (decision support system) and an OLTP (online transaction processing) system.

**incomplete media recovery**—This happens when one or more of the files required for a media recovery are damaged or not available. The loss of the online redo log or rollback segment, or loss of all copies of the control file result in the requirement for an incomplete media recovery.

**index**—A structure that enhances data retrieval by providing rapid access to frequently queried column values. Indexes can be either B-tree structured or bitmapped. The two general types of index are unique and nonunique. A unique index forces all values entered into its source column to be unique. A nonunique index allows for repetitive and null values to be entered into its source column. Generally speaking, a column with high cardinality should be indexed using a B-tree type index (standard, default type of index), whereas low cardinality values should be indexed using a bitmapped index.

**INITIAL**—A storage parameter that sets the size in bytes (no suffix), kilobytes (K suffix), or megabytes (M suffix) of the **INITIAL** extent allocated to a table, index, rollback segment, or cluster.

**INITRANS**—A storage parameter that reserves space in the block header for the transaction records associated with a table's blocks.

**INSERT**—A DML command that enables users to place new records into a table.

**instance failure**—Occurs when one or more of the Oracle base instance processes (DBWR, SMON, PMON, LGWR, and so on) fail, causing the instance to crash (shut down abnormally). Almost all instance failures are recovered automatically by Oracle upon instance restart.

**latch**—A low-level locking mechanism usually used to protect internal database resources, such as memory.

**library cache**—An alternative name for the shared pool.

**lock**—A high-level construct used to protect hard system resources, such as tables, clusters, stored objects, or indexes.

**lock-tree**—A simple diagram showing which locks are waiting for other locks.

**LOG_BLOCK_CHECKSUM**—An initialization parameter that forces the checking of the block checksums as a precaution against database corruption. If any corruption is found, it usually generates an alert log message, a trace file, a core dump, and an instance crash.

**logical backup**—Files generated by the Export facility of Oracle that contain DDL and DML commands used to rebuild all or part of the database. The operative word in this explanation is *rebuild*. The logical copy of the database can only be recovered by use of the Import facility, which is also provided by Oracle.

**MAXEXTENTS**—Sets the maximum number of extents an object can grow into. The **MAXEXTENTS** value can be altered up to the maximum number of extents allowed based on block size.

**MAXTRANS**—A companion to the **INITRANS** storage parameter. **MAXTRANS** sets the maximum number of transactions that can access a block concurrently.

**media failure**—Occurs when one or more of the physical disks in your facility fail (mechanically or electronically). A media failure always requires a database recovery if it involves active database files. Also known as a disk failure.

**memory sort**—A sort performed in the user's allocated sort area in the computer's memory. If possible, you should strive for all sorts to be done as memory sorts because they are orders of magnitude faster than disk sorts. If a sort is smaller than the specified **SORT_AREA_SIZE** parameter in the initialization file, the sort is done in memory.

**migration**—*See* chaining.

**mirroring**—A simple form of RAID where one disk or set of disks is either made by software or hardware to exactly mirror an original or active set. Usually mirroring is accomplished by simultaneous writes to both disk sets. Mirroring protects against media failure.

**miss**—Occurs when a database resource is requested but is not made available within a specified time period.

**multiple-choice question formats**—A question format where the question is posed and two or more answers are given. The test-taker must choose the proper answer or answers from the ones listed.

**multithreaded server (MTS)**—In Oracle, the process that allows multiplexing of database connections. In Oracle, the MTS system consists of a listener process, one or more dispatcher processes, and multiple server processes. This multiplexing of database connections allows more users than would normally be serviced to use the database and is especially useful on systems short on physical memory.

**NEXT**—Storage parameter that specifies the size in bytes (no suffix), kilobytes (K suffix), or megabytes (M suffix) of the **NEXT** extent allocated to a table, index, rollback segment, or cluster. The **NEXT** parameter is used with the **PCTINCREASE** parameter to determine the size of all extents after the **INITIAL** and **NEXT** extents.

**object auditing**—The specification of auditing options that pertains to database objects rather than database operations.

**OLTP (online transaction processing)**—These systems usually have multiple small, simultaneous transactions involving **SELECT, INSERT, UPDATE,** and **DELETE** operations. An example of an OLTP system would be an order-entry system.

**Optimal Flexible Architecture (OFA)**—A standard, authored by internal Oracle Corporation experts, that tells how to optimally configure an Oracle database.

**optimizer**—The section of the database engine that decides the best methods to use to resolve queries against the database. In Oracle, there are two possible optimizers—the rule- and the cost-based optimizers. Generally, rule-based optimizers are easier to tune for because they are easily predictable if you know their rule context. Cost-based optimizers are harder to tune for because the optimization methodology may change based on database table and index statistics.

**ORAPWD**—A generalized term for the Oracle Password Manager that creates and is used to maintain the external password file. The external password file is used to tell the Oracle Enterprise Manager and Server Manager who is authorized to perform DBA functions against a specific database.

**ORDER BY SELECT**—A **SELECT** statement that uses the **ORDER BY** clause to override any implicit ordering a query would perform. An **ORDER BY SELECT** always performs a sort operation and thus should be avoided if possible.

**OSDBA**—A role that is assigned to users who are authorized to create and maintain Oracle databases. If a user is given the OSDBA role, he or she is also given an entry in the external password file.

**OSOPER**—A role that is assigned to users who are authorized to maintain Oracle databases. If a user is given the OSOPER role, he or she is also given an entry in the external password file.

**outside join**—A type of join where data not meeting the join criteria (that is, the join value is **NULL**) is also returned by the query. An outside join is signified by using the plus sign inside parentheses (+) to indicate the outside join value beside the join column for the table deficient in data.

**package**—A stored PL/SQL construct made of related procedures, functions, exceptions, and other PL/SQL constructs. Packages are called into memory when any package object is referenced. Packages are created or dropped as a unit.

**parallel recovery**—When using Oracle Parallel Server, parallel recovery allows for more than one instance in a parallel database to perform recovery operations simultaneously against the shared database.

**parallelism**—The number of explicitly configured parallel query slaves that will be assigned against a specific database object. Parallelism is also referred to as **DEGREE**. A query that uses parallelism will generally outperform a non-parallel query if the proper resources are available.

**PCTFREE**—Used in an Oracle block to determine the amount of space reserved for future updates. Too low of a **PCTFREE** can result in row chaining for frequently updated tables and too high a value requires more storage space.

**PCTINCREASE**—Determines what percentage each subsequent extent after **INITIAL** and **NEXT** grows over the previously allocated extent.

**PCTUSED**—Determines when a block is placed back on the free block list. Once used space in a block drops below **PCTUSED**, the block can be used for subsequent new row insertion.

**performance pack**—An optional software package that may be purchased from Oracle to allow for monitoring and tuning of the Oracle database.

**PGA (process global area)**—Represents the memory area allocated to each process that accesses an Oracle database.

**physical backup**—A backup that is performed through operating system backup commands or routines and consist of full copies of the actual database files. Using only physical backups, you can recover to the time of the backup. Using physical backups and archive logs, you can recover to point of failure. Physical backups are either hot backups taken with the database in backup mode but still active, or cold backups taken with the database shutdown.

**primary key**—In a relational database, the unique identifier for a table. A primary key must be unique and not null. A primary key can be either natural (derived from a column or columns in the database) or artificial (drawn from a sequence).

**private**—Refers to either rollback segments or procedures and functions. A private rollback segment (the ones generally recommended for use) must be specifically brought online either through manual commands or through use of the **ROLLBACK_SEGMENTS** initialization file parameter. For procedures and functions, a private procedure or function is one addressable only from within a master package or procedure that is usually fully contained within the structure of the calling package or procedure.

**privilege auditing**—Auditing of what privileges are granted and by and to whom.

**procedures**—Stored PL/SQL objects that may, but aren't required to, return a value. Procedures are allowed to change a database or package state. Procedures can be placed into packages.

**process failure**—What occurs when a user process terminates improperly. Oracle will automatically roll back a process's transactions and reclaim its memory if it detects a failed process.

**process of elimination**—The process by which incorrect answers are eliminated by logic, intuition, knowledge, and luck.

**production**—The final stage of the system development cycle. The production stage corresponds to normal maintenance and backup and recovery operations against a developed system.

**profiles**—Sets of resource allocations that can be assigned to a user. These resources are used to limit idle time, connect time, memory, and CPU usage.

**PROMPT**—A SQL*Plus command used to pass a string out of a SQL script to the executing user. The **PROMPT** command can be used with the **ACCEPT** command to prompt for values needed by the script.

**public**—Refers to either rollback segments or procedures and functions. A public rollback segment (the ones generally not recommended for use) are brought online automatically based on a ratio of the initialization parameters **TRANSACTIONS/TRANSACTIONS_PER_ROLLBACK_SEGMENT**. For procedures and functions, a public procedure or function is one addressable from outside of a master package or procedure.

**radio button**—A feature of a GUI interface that can be activated by a mouse click to cause specific operations (such as the display of an exhibit) to occur. Usually they look like buttons and are labeled as to functionality.

**RAID (Redundant Array of Inexpensive Disks)**—RAID is usually specified by a level: 0 through 5 or a combination, such as 0/1 (striped and shadowed [or mirrored]). Usually you will only see RAID 0, RAID 1, RAID 0/1, and RAID 5.

**raw devices**— n Unix, this is used when you want to bypass the internal Unix buffering systems. Generally, raw devices, or file systems, will perform faster than a standard or "cooked" Unix file system. Raw file systems must be used if you utilize Oracle Parallel Server on most Unix boxes.

**read-only tablespaces**—A tablespace that has been altered into read-only mode. No redo or rollback is generated against a read-only tablespace, because, as the name implies, you cannot insert, update, or delete data from a read-only structure. Read-only tablespaces are backed up when they are placed in read-only state and then never (as long as the tablespace isn't placed back into normal mode) backed up again.

**RECOVER**—A command used in Server Manager to explicitly perform database recovery operations.

**redo**—Placed inside of redo logs. Redo information is any information that allows transactions to be redone in the event of a failure. The opposite of redo is undo or rollback data, which allows uncommitted transactions to be undone or rolled back.

**redo allocation latch**—Small transactions are copied into the redo logs using this. On single-CPU systems, the redo allocation latch may be the only way to copy transaction data into the redo logs.

**redo copy latch**—Large transactions are copied on these into the redo logs. Generally, redo copy latches are used on multiple-CPU systems.

**redo log buffer**—A memory structure inside the SGA that buffers writes to the redo logs. The redo log buffer is sized as a product of the **LOG_ARCHIVE_BUFFERS** and **LOG_ARCHIVE_BUFFER_SIZE** initialization file parameters.

**redo logs**—External database files that store information on all database-changing transactions. Redo logs are combined in groups of at least one redo log each, and each database must have at least two groups assigned to be able to start up. Usually there are two redo logs per group and, if **ARCHIVELOG** mode is set, a minimum of three groups assigned to the instance.

**referential integrity**—The process by which a relational database maintains record relationships between parent and child tables via primary key and foreign key values.

**rejected records**—In SQL*Loader, records that don't meet load criteria for the table being loaded either due to value, datatype, or other restrictions.

**relationship**—A named association between two things of significance. For example, if you say that a wheeled vehicle has one or many wheels, *has* is the relationship, or an employee works for one or more employer, *works for* is the relationship.

**report.txt**—Generated by the utlestat.sql script. The report.txt file is a collection of "delta" or difference reports based on data previously stored by use of the utlbstat.sql script. The utlbstat.sql and utlestat.sql scripts are located in the $ORACLE_HOME/rdbms/admin directory and the report.txt file is usually generated there as well.

**resources**—The database and system resources that are controlled by use of a profile.

**restore**—The process by which database files are brought back from an archive location or backup site.

**roll-forward operation**—Accomplished automatically by an Oracle database during recovery operations. In a roll-forward operation, the transactions stored in the redo logs, and sometimes the archived redo logs, are applied to the database in order. Once a roll forward is accomplished, the rollback segments are used to remove any uncommitted transactions in a rollback operation.

**ROLLBACK**—A DML command used to undo database changes that have not been committed. This is also used to describe the operation performed after a roll forward during recovery of a database. A rollback during recovery consists of removing uncommitted transaction changes from the database.

**rollback segment**—A database object that contains records used to undo database transactions. Whenever a parameter in the database refers to **UNDO**, it is actually referring to rollback segments.

**row-level lock**—A row-level lock is the lowest level of locking utilized by the Oracle database. Row-level locking is usually implicit in nature and allows the maximum flexibility in locking options.

**SAVE**—A SQL*Plus command used to store command buffer contents in an external operating system file.

**SCN (System Change Number)**—A number assigned to a specific transaction. The SCN is used to track a transaction throughout its life, even once it has been transferred to the archive log. The most current SCNs that apply to the system datafiles are tracked in the datafile headers and in the control files.

**SELECT**—A DML command used to retrieve values from the database.

**SEP (sort extent pool)**—An area of the SGA that tracks all available sort extents for the temporary tablespaces. The SEP is not initialized until the first sort operation requiring disk space is initialized.

**Server Manager line mode**—The Server Manager has a GUI mode and a line mode. In line mode, all commands are entered at the command line.

**SET**—A SQL*Plus command used to change the values of SQL*Plus environment parameters, such as line width and page length.

**SGA (system global area)**—Consists of the database buffers, shared pool, and queue areas that are globally accessible by all database processes. The SGA is used to speed Oracle processing by providing for caching of data and structure information in memory.

**shared pool**—A section of the SGA that contains the data dictionary cache, shared SQL area, and, in some cases, the response queues.

**SHOW**—A SQL*Plus command that is used to show the value of a variable set with the **SET** command.

**SHUTDOWN**—A Server Manager command used to shut down the database. **SHUTDOWN** has three modes: **NORMAL, IMMEDIATE,** and **ABORT. NORMAL** prohibits new connections, waits for all users to log off, and then shuts down. **IMMEDIATE** prohibits new connections, backs out uncommitted transactions, and then logs users off and shuts down. **ABORT** shuts down right now and not gracefully.

**Sleeps**—Occur when a latch or lock on a system resource is requested and the resource is not available. The process making the request "sleeps" until the resource is available or a timeout happens, whichever comes first.

**sort direct writes**—Define that writes to a sort segment bypass the SGA buffer pool and instead are routed directly though a set of sort direct write buffers held by each process. Sort direct writes should not be used unless the system has sufficient disk and memory resources.

**spin**—One CPU cycle. The default wait time for latches or locks is defined by the initialization variable **SPIN_COUNT** on many platforms. You can reduce the number of misses by increasing the **SPIN_COUNT** setting, but performance may degrade.

**SPOOL**—A SQL*Plus command that is used to send SQL*Plus output to either a printer or a file.

**SQL buffer**—A memory area used to store the last SQL command. The SQL buffer can store only the last command executed, unless it is loaded with the **GET** command. A SQL*Plus command such as **SET, DESCRIBE,** or **SPOOL** is not placed in the SQL buffer.

**SQL Trace**—Allows user and system processes to create trace files that can then be studied later to determine what SQL statements need tuning.

**standby database**—A duplicate database that is maintained in **RECOVERY** mode. An automatic process copies the archived redo logs from the active database to the standby database and applies them, thus keeping the databases in sync.

**STARTUP**—A Server Manager command used to start up the database. A database can be started in one of several modes: **MOUNT, NOMOUNT, OPEN, EXCLUSIVE,** and **PARALLEL.**

**statement auditing**—Audits statement actions such as inserts, updates, and deletes.

**statement failure**—This occurs if a transaction statement is improperly terminated either due to an error or a manual action. A statement failure results in an automatic rollback of the statement's actions if required.

**STORAGE**—The **STORAGE** clause is what Oracle uses to determine current and future settings for an object's extents. If a storage clause isn't specified, the object's storage characteristics are taken from the tablespace default **STORAGE** clause.

**strategy**—In this step of the system development cycle (usually paired with the analysis step), the overall methodology for the rest of the development effort is mapped out.

**striping**—The process where either disks, tablespaces, or tables are deliberately fragmented and placed across several disks to improve performance or allow for larger files. In disk striping, the process is usually automatically done by a disk management system such as VERITAS and is invisible to the casual user.

**SYSDBA**—*See* OSDBA.

**SYSOPER**—*See* OSOPER.

**table**—The structure used to store data in an Oracle database. Entities map to tables in relational databases.

**table mode export**—An export that makes only a logical copy of one or more tables and their related objects such as triggers, constraints, indexes, and grants.

**table-level lock**—An explicitly defined lock because Oracle doesn't practice lock escalation (only lock conversion). A table-level lock locks an entire table and will result in dead locks is not used properly.

**temporary tablespace**—A tablespace that is used for temporary (sort) segments only. A permanent tablespace can contain either permanent or temporary segments, whereas a tablespace that has been designated by either the **CREATE TABLESPACE** or **ALTER TABLESPACE** command as a temporary tablespace can contain only temporary segments. A user can be assigned either a temporary or permanent tablespace as his or her designated temporary (sort) tablespace.

**TIMED_STATISTICS**—The initialization file parameter that tells the Oracle kernel to record time-based statistics.

**TKPROF**—The TKPROF utility converts the normal, difficult to read format of a process trace file into human readable format. The TKPROF utility is used for tuning Oracle applications.

**transaction-level lock**—A DML lock. It is always implicitly created.

**transition**—In this step of the system development cycle, user testing is performed and support of the application moves from development to production personnel.

**TRUNCATE**—A DDL statement used to remove all rows from a table. Because it is a DDL statement, it cannot be rolled back.

**UGA (user global area)**—Used to store user-specific variables and stacks.

**UID (unique identifier)**—Uniquely identifies a row in a table and usually maps to the natural primary key value. Each entity must have a unique identifier to qualify as a relational table.

**Undo**—*See* rollback segments.

**UPDATE**—A DML command that allows data inside tables to be changed.

**user error**—An error in the database caused by a user, such as an accidental erasure or an insertion or update to a table or to the database structure itself. User errors are usually the most difficult to recover from.

**user mode export**—A user mode export is an export that provides a logical copy of the objects owned by a single user. This is also known as a schema export.

**utlbstat.sql**—The script that creates a set of tables and loads them with statistics garnered from the V$ series of dynamic performance views. The utlbstat.sql script is usually located in the $ORACLE_HOME/rdbms/admin directoryu (or its equivalent). Short for "utility begin statistics."

**utlestat.sql**—The script that reads the current values for the statistics gathered by the utlbstat.sql script and then generates the report.txt file based on the differences between the two sets of statistics. The utlestat.sql script drops all tables created by the utlbstat.sql script after the report.txt file is generated. If a shutdown occurs before the utlestat.sql script is run, both of the scripts must be run in order to generate a proper report.txt file. If you see negative results for statistics in the utlestat.sql report.txt file, this indicates a shutdown happened between the time the utlbstat.sql and utlestat.sql scripts were run. Short for "utility end statistics."

**V$RECOVERY_FILE_STATUS**—This dynamic performance view is used to show the status of datafile recovery.

**V$RECOVERY_STATUS**—This dynamic performance view is used to show the status of database recovery.

**variable**—A user- or process-defined storage area used to hold a value that will probably be different each time a script or procedure is executed.

**view**—A preset select against one or more tables that is stored in the database and has no physical representation. A view is also known as a virtual table.

# Index

Bold page numbers indicate sample exam questions

STANDBY parameter (RECOVER
command), 294
Standby databases, 262, **269**, 282-283,
**332, 342, 350, 354**
activating, 282
creating, 281-282
START parameter (DBVERIFY
utility), 319
STARTUP MOUNT option, **338, 353**
Statement failure, 256, 292, **343, 355**
Statement ID, 51
STATISTICS option, ANALYZE
command and, 18
STATISTICS parameter (Export
utility), 276
Striping
by hand, 93, **118, 218, 233, 239, 250**
with operating system, 91-92
RAID 0 configuration, 92
RAID 0 + 1 configuration, 92
RAID 1 configuration, 92
RAID 3 configuration, 92
RAID 5 configuration, 92
tables, 91-93
Swapping, 32, **45**
Sylvan Prometric Testing Center, 2
Symmetric multiprocessor computer.
*See* SMP (symmetric multiprocessor)
computers.
System design, performance tuning, 32
System global area.
*See* SGA (system global area).
SYSTEM rollback segment, 160
SYSTEM tablespace, 36, 90

# T

Table export mode, 273
Table extent allocation, striping by
hand, 93
Table-level locks.
*See* TM (table-level) locks.
Tables
clustering, 107-108
striping, 91-93
striping by hand, **218, 233, 239, 250**
TABLES parameter (Export utility), 276
TABLESPACE parameter (RECOVER
command), 294-295
Tablespace-level backups, 284, **339, 341,
353, 354**

Tablespace storage default, striping by
hand, 93
Tablespaces
backup mode, **335, 338, 351, 353**
backups in read-write mode, **285**
DATA, 91
INDEX, 91
RBS, 90
recovery and, **311**
ROLLBACK, 90
striping by hand, **118**
SYSTEM, 90
TEMPORARY, 90
USERS, 90
"tail -f" sessions, 316
TEMPORARY tablespace, 90
Temporary tablespaces, **208**
default storage clause, 201
sorts and, 201-202
Testing. *See also* Practice tests.
budgeting time for, 7
exhibits, 5, 212
marking questions for later review, 5
memorization, 214-215
multiple answer questions, 4, 212
multiple-choice format, 3
non-standardized nature of, 212
preparation for, 215
question inversion, 213
question review strategies, 6-7
questions, 212
software overview, 5-6
terminology problems, 214
time limits for, 3
unanswered test questions, 5
Time limits for testing, 3
Time-based recovery, 302-303
Time-based statistics, 22
TIMED_STATISTICS parameter, 17, 56,
**236, 254**
TKPROF utility, **79**
EXPLAIN option, **82**
INSERT option, **82**
RECORD option, **82**
SORT option, **82**
SQL Trace formatting, 56-62
SYS option, **82**
TM (table locks), 184, **191, 194, 218, 226,
239, 245**
tnsnames.ora file, 41
Trace files, 30-31
Transaction recovery, **337, 352**

# W

WHERE clause
  cluster keys and, 107
WILLING_TO_WAIT requests, **219, 239**
WWW (World Wide Web)
  "404 File Not Found" error message, 10
  Oracle's education and certification site,
    8-9, 215
  RevealNet, Inc. Web site, 11
  Self Test Software Web site, 11, 215

# X

X (exclusive) locks, 186-187
X$ tables, 16
X$KCBRBH table, **232, 250**
  COUNT column, 146, 148, **233, 250**
  INDX column, 146, 148

# Learn More Faster

In addition, you are sure to find relevant tips, techniques, and topics faster as well.

**CORIOLIS**
**Technology Press™**

Blue, Black, and Gold books. Novice, intermediate, advanced. Easy-to-identify classifications for an innovative new concept in technology publishing.

A completely new series. Each title written to address the specific needs of the system developer, user, or engineer— at the level of his or her concern.

**ACQUIRE MORE KNOWLEDGE**

When you are learning a new technology, Blue Books are the complete, hands-on tutorials you'll want to reach for first. Their highly-interactive, project-based, "learn-by-doing" approach helps ensure that you will learn more at a much faster rate than you can with other tutorials.

**USE YOUR KNOWLEDGE**

Black Books are indispensable problem-solving guides. Their unique format, which provides very thorough, in-depth, highly technical overviews followed by highly practical "immediate solutions," will help you quickly

complete any task: large or small, simple or complex.

**EXPAND YOUR KNOWLEDGE**

Gold Books are the professional-level guides you'll turn to when you want to expand your horizons. Their highly conceptual but practical approach will teach you how to think in new ways and push your skills to a new level.

Blue, Black, and Gold. They're comprehensive, illustrated, and easy to understand. Experience the difference. Look for these and other soon-to-be-released titles from Coriolis. Of course!

*Available at Bookstores and Computer Stores Nationwide*

Telephone 800.410.0192 • International callers 602.483.0192
**www.coriolis.com**

# CERTIFICATION INSIDER PRESS

## The Road to Certification Success

Pass It!

IIS 4

Learn It!
Intermediate

Do It!
Advanced

WORD 97

ON SITE
Microsoft
PROXY
SERVER 2

| SERIES | MAIN FEATURES | DETAILS | CONTENT FOCUS | AUDIENCE |
|---|---|---|---|---|
| **EXAM PREP** <br> EXCEL 97 <br> Learn It! | Comprehensive and interactive study guide designed to teach technology or an application with an exam perspective. <br><br> Project-based approach with hands-on activities and in-depth reviews. **Takes readers beyond an exam's objectives.** <br><br> Innovative CD-ROM learning system integrated with each book. Provides custom practice exams that really work and prepare readers for exam success! | Technical (MCSE, MCSD, etc.): <br> 7 3/8" x 9 1/4" <br> 600 to 800 pages <br> CD-ROM <br> $44.99 to $59.99 (U.S.) <br> $62.99 to $84.99 (CAN) <br><br> Applications (MSOUS): <br> Full color <br> 8.5" x 11" <br> 300 to 400 pages <br> CD-ROM <br> $29.99 (U.S.) • $41.99 (CAN) | Technical certification programs: <br> *MCSE, MCSD, A+, Oracle, Java* <br><br> User-level certification programs: <br> *MSOUS (Word, Excel, Access, etc.)* | Certification candidates and professionals wishing to brush up on their skills: <br><br> Networking professionals, programmers, developers, office workers, and application users |
| **EXAM CRAM** <br> NT Server 4 <br> Pass It! | Main focus: **Helps readers quickly pass an exam and get a high score.** <br><br> Includes cram sheets, study tips, shortcuts, exam warnings, study alerts, and end of chapter practice exams. <br><br> Perfect complement to the *Exam Prep*. <br><br> *100% focused on an exam—no fluff!* | 6" x 9" lay flat binding <br> 300 to 450 pages <br> $26.99 to $29.99 (U.S.) <br> $37.99 to $41.99 (CAN) <br><br> MSOUS titles include disk with practice files and solutions. | All major certification programs: <br> *MCSE, MCSD, MSOUS (Word, Excel, etc.), A+, Oracle, Java* | Certification candidates: <br> Networking professionals, programmers, developers, office workers, and application users |
| **ON SITE** <br> Microsoft EXCHANGE SERVER 5.5 <br> Do It! | The ultimate on-the-job solution finder: **Real working knowledge for on-site use by practicing professionals.** <br><br> Provides practical information on planning, configuration, deployment, and troubleshooting network technologies. <br><br> Includes valuable decision making and troubleshooting tools (decision trees, checklists, tips, and problem assessment charts). | 7 3/8" x 9 1/4" <br> 400 to 600 pages <br> CD-ROM <br> $39.99 (U.S.) <br> $55.99 (CAN) <br><br> CD-ROM features network troubleshooting tools, deployment resources, and configuration utilities. | Networking and client/server products and technologies: <br> *MS Exchange Server, Proxy Server, IIS, SQL Server* | Networking professionals, IT managers, system administrators, consultants, system engineers, and other professionals |